The Least of These

The Least of These

Selected Readings in Christian History

edited by

ERIC R. SEVERSON

Cascade Books
A division of *Wipf & Stock Publishers*
199 West 8th Avenue, Suite 3 • Eugene OR 97401

THE LEAST OF THESE
Selected Readings in Christian History

ISBN 13: 978-1-55635-106-8

Cataloging-in-Publication data

The least of these : selected readings in Christian history / edited by Eric R. Severson

xviii + 264 p.; 23 cm.

Includes bibliographic references

ISBN 13: 978-1-55635-106-8 (alk. paper)

1. Church history. I. Title. II. Severson, Eric R.

BR145.3 L25 2007

Manufactured in the U.S.A.

Contents

General Introduction

This volume is a simple tool intended to provide primary readings for students exploring the range of Christian history and theology. You will find here writings from twenty-eight Christian authors composed from the close of the New Testament era into the eighteenth century. Many good collections of primary texts are currently available in the field of Christian history, but they are typically organized in a different manner. Most anthologies gather famous or representative excerpts written by each author. This method is helpful, allowing the reader to quickly access the material that has had a profound impact on the development of Christian theology. Despite the ongoing value of this approach and the collections it produces, a number of difficulties arise for students attempting to engage these authors. This anthology has been created to address these problems.

The readings collected here are each selected for their specific engagement of Matthew 25:31–46, the famous Parable of the Sheep and Goats. I have culled the vast collection of classical Christian readings in the public domain to discover how this text has been approached and appropriated by key Christian thinkers and figures. The resulting cross-section of readings is highly eclectic in some respects, gathered from sermons, letters, exhortations, tracts, and commentaries. At the same time there is a consistent focus in each of the readings centered around the issues that arise from Jesus' remarkable parable concerning "the least of these." The operative question of this book is "how does this important Christian thinker interpret this parable." Along the way we discover that this passage has been used with remarkable range. It has been used to illustrate human dependence on grace, the imperative that Christians be compassionate, the need for good works, the characteristics of heaven and hell, free will and predestination, and much more.

One might suppose that we might miss out on important issues by reading obscure sermons and exegetical works. Instead, I think the reader will discover that the theological commitments of Tertullian, Augustine, Thomas, Luther, Calvin, Wesley, and company are wonderfully illustrated in their appropriation of Matthew 25:31–46. In fact, one can see in Augustine's sermon a deeply pastoral concern that is perhaps less apparent in his *Confessions* or anti-Pelagian work. In other cases these passages reveal how theology has been shaped by the historical pressures of heresy, disease, war, and political conflict. These passages are raw; they appear, for the most part, in the context of ministerial concerns and pastoral anxieties. Hopefully what is lost in reading less celebrated theological passages is more than compensated by these discoveries. One can hardly miss the remarkable manner with which these authors manage to infuse their sermons and commentaries with the theological agendas for which they are famous.

There is another advantage to reading primary texts in this manner, though perhaps an uncomfortable one. Doctrinally motivated anthologies deftly sidestep some of the embarrassing ways that preachers and teachers have manipulated Scripture to provide support for slavery, the patriarchal mistreatment of women, and their own political or financial benefit. Perhaps the best way to avoid repeating these shameful moves in human history is to realize and read the subtle and devious ways that the Bible has been enlisted to support oppression. One of the more powerful articulations of Jesus' parable comes from George Whitefield, who writes, "were we to judge by the practice of Christians, one should be tempted to think there were no such verses in the Bible."[1] Later in the same sermon Whitefield uses an illustration from slavery to reinforce his point, underscoring the sad irony of his slave ownership and political support of slavery in Georgia and early American history. It seems important that we not edit our way around this sad and ironic juxtaposition of faithful preaching and ethical tragedy. It also seems mandatory that students learning theology be aware of how this discipline can both unite and divide, heal and wound.

---

1. George Whitefield, *Selected Sermons of George Whitefield* (Bellingham, WA: Logos Research Systems Incorporated), public domain.

We also discover along the way that the concerns of the ancients occasionally sound remarkably contemporary. Clement shows concern that exotic pets are well-fed while humans go hungry. Gregory of Nazianzus preaches his sermon on Matthew 25 with a wounded indignation after his congregation refused to turn out to hear him preach on Easter Sunday. In the sermon from Luther included here, he reveals the maturity of his animosity toward Rome and his gentle concern for the fragile and young "Lutheran" church. The goal in selecting these readings is to show that theology happens in the raw and contextualized stories in which we live. In these readings you will find theology embedded in the sermonic. Theological doctrine cannot and perhaps should not be extricated from these settings.

This volume is also intended to serve as a gentle reminder about the importance of careful hermeneutics and the great dangers that arise when people assume that a passage of Scripture serves their intended purpose. We ought to be at least mildly suspicious when Matthew 25:31–46 is cited alternately as evidence for both free will and the lack thereof. Careful exegesis requires a watchful eye on our tendency to find in texts exactly what we expect to find. Good hermeneutics requires a profound openness to the text and to the freedom of its past, present, and future meanings.

This text is designed to be used alongside a secondary source in Christian history. The reading questions primarily ask students to connect their knowledge of these authors to the language and imagery used in these sermons, letters, and commentaries. Ideally, this will stimulate some academic curiosity that will enhance class preparation and discussion.

I have relied rather heavily on Sherman W. Gray's fine book *The Least of My Brothers: Matthew 25:31–46, A History of Interpretation.*[2] Gray's work is absolutely critical to this book; it is by his research that I was directed to more than half of the excerpts included in this volume. He explores in *The Least of My Brothers* the question of the identity of "the least of these," a question which occurs frequently in my "reading questions" below.

2. Sherman W. Gray, *The Least of My Brothers: Matthew 25:31–46, A History of Interpretation* (Atlanta, GA: Scholars Press, 1989).

Students who are just beginning to read Christian historical texts are often intimidated by the use of Old English words like "thee," "thou," "ye," and "thine." In situations where I could comfortably alter translations from Greek and Latin I have updated the language of the original translations. It seems exceedingly unlikely that the original authors and (mostly) nineteenth-century translators would want the English renderings to sound inaccessible to contemporary readers. In cases where the original language was English, or in the case of the poetic prayer of St. Francis of Assisi, such language has not been altered. In many cases enough changes have been made to consider these excerpts new translations, but each remains deeply dependent on the work on the referenced translator. These original translations are cited for each reading, many of them available online through The Christian Classics Ethereal Library: www.ccel.org.

This volume was originally developed for students at Eastern Nazarene College in Quincy, Massachusetts. I am grateful for steady and helpful input and support on this project from these students and my colleagues at Eastern Nazarene.

Note to Instructors

Behind this text is a theory of theological pedagogy. My contention is that theology is learned and taught best at the raw level of sermons, personal correspondence, and scriptural interpretation. This has not been a dominant model for teaching theology. Most collections of primary readings aim to deliver to the student the most refined, paradigmatic, or concise excerpt from the works of Origen, Augustine, Thomas, and company. These readings, as technically appropriate as they may be, often divorce the theologian from the exegetical, historical, and political contexts in which their theology was forged. By focusing primary readings on sermons and exegetical texts we find a very different, albeit less direct, approach to reading theology. If theology is a process of hammering out treatises which are the most logically defensible, this collection may be barking up the wrong tree. I am contending here that theology originates and must continue to dwell in the raw experiences of worshipping communities. If this is the case, then reading a sermon from Augustine may help us understand his theology even better than a classic passage from *City of God* or *Confessions*. As bishop and pastor, Augustine's sermonic theology lives in the daily disputes and tribulations of the congregations under his care. Sermons are theology for the masses, and we ought to expect that Christianity's best minds found creative ways to bring such important theology to the people entrusted to their care.

Students should also be able to see the way this portion of Scripture has been a pivotal source of comfort and encouragement over the ages. You may find important opportunities to show students how to critique the way that exegesis has occasionally been stretched very thin to bring Matthew 25 into contextual relevance. There also should be ample opportunities in this collection to point out when careful exegesis has allowed this text to speak in a less restricted manner.

There are also ways that this method becomes particularly important in an introductory class on Christian history. New students to the field of Christian theology need to see that exploring Christian history is not merely an academic exercise. They need to see that theology is relevant, that it "preaches." My assumption is that you will utilize a secondary text alongside this collection which provides a broad summary of Augustine's thought. Here you will find a sample of Augustine in action. I think you will discover Augustine does not bypass the opportunity to reveal many of his distinctive theological contributions in his sermon on this passage of Scripture.

There are several other compelling reasons to organize primary readings in the manner offered here. Theologians have in recent decades become increasingly suspicious of the biases which seem to control our attention when we determine to read classical Christian literature. By using a thematic cross-section of Christian literature we are intentionally avoiding the impulse to read Augustine where he is most provocative or perhaps most vulnerable. We are, instead, reading him as he might have wished newcomers to encounter his thought, by "listening" to him preach.

In the same vein, this method also has the advantages of looking past some of the ways that we tend to bias our own readings. Those who oppose Calvin often make use of a logic that supposes that followers of Calvin have little reason to be concerned about good works; no reason to show concern for "the least of these." But in the excerpt from Calvin's commentary we discover an important elevation of "good works," even as Calvin insists that the good works are the rich product of a grace we could never choose for ourselves. Calvin's exegetical work is rich in pastoral application, revealing a remarkable vision for the real-life tensions that come from elevating both grace and righteousness. Perhaps through this text Christians can see past some of the grand theological differences that are so often hyperbolically emphasized in our reading selections.

It is also true that the challenges of postmodernism have called into question some of the methodologies by which theologians once determined where they ought to turn to best understand the Christian fathers and mothers. It is often popular to collect readings around topics like "atonement," "incarnation," "Trinity," "Christology," etc. Such collections remain valuable, but we are now increasingly aware that these may be unfair ways to take up Origin, Tertullian, and the Cappadocians. Reading excerpts selected in such a manner forces dynamic thought into models and modes which are quite foreign to the original compositions.

By reading selections that make use of Matthew 25 we have not avoided all of these pitfalls; indeed, some of these problems seem intractable. Without reading the whole of Augustine's corpus, emphasizing the right portions and ignoring the right portions (whichever they may be) we cannot hope to give him anything close to a fair reading. But with this one sermon we at least admit outright that we are selecting this passage without any controlling topical ambition. We can now read Augustine well aware that his corpus is too broad to be easily distilled. We read Augustine with humility and openness to the way this text may subvert our generalizations and force new considerations of what might rightly be considered "Augustinian" theology. It should also be admitted that in many cases there were an abundance of alternatives for primary readings dealing with the Matthew 25 parable, which required a (potentially biased) editorial choice regarding which readings should be included.

It is also the case that the systematic categories which once seemed like logical tools for straining through the endless volumes of Christian historical writings no longer carry the same thunderous weight. Liberation theologians have challenged us to construct theology with a keen eye for the plight of the oppressed. Feminist theologians have made obvious the patriarchal tendencies of Christian theology. One might claim, justifiably, that our "collections" of primary texts reinforce our biases. In reality, this critique continues to operate against this collection as well, for there is admitted bias in the selection of this particular passage of Scripture. Still, for better or worse, it is the exegesis of Scripture that remains the undeniable center of Christian theology. Liberationists, feminists, postmodern thinkers, modern thinkers, Roman Catholics, Eastern Orthodox, and Southern Baptists still congregate around what is roughly the same body of sacred writings. So I believe that the future of theology, like the past, will be about what we do with the Bible and the theological implications of biblical claims. It is Scripture that is the key vocabulary for Christian theology. So perhaps we discover more than we might think by reading about the ways our Christian leaders have approached Jesus' parable.

Finally, theology has its origins in the liturgy of the church. The earliest Trinitarian statements occur within the contexts of baptism and prayer. Christology does not develop first as a logical conundrum but as the mystery of the Eucharist. Theology in recent centuries has developed an unhealthy prejudice against the sermonic. By turning to the sermons, letters, and commentaries we are intentionally reversing this trend and elevating the sermons of Augustine, Leo the Great, Martin Luther, Jonathan Edwards, and others. Perhaps with such a methodology we may regain some of our taste for theology which is richly imbedded in the realm of the liturgical.

Note to Students

There are generally two different kinds of academic sources when it comes to theology and Christian history, primary and secondary. Primary sources are the actual original writings of theologians who have struggled to articulate their understanding of God, sin, salvation, grace, etc. Secondary sources are written to enhance our understanding of these original thinkers. Sometimes this is absolutely critical. You might quickly become discouraged if you tried to read the works of Origen or Tertullian cover to cover. Secondary sources summarize and categorize and create a larger picture of Christian theology into which each of the primary sources may fit. Still, it remains essential that you read primary sources so that you will see the way these thinkers fit, or fail to fit, with the generalizations and simplifications you see in your secondary readings.

This is often a difficult challenge for students because primary readings are generally more difficult to read and understand than secondary texts. Since most of them were written many centuries ago the style and illustrations seem foreign and outdated. These obstacles have made the reading of primary texts a difficult task for most introductory students in Christian theology. This book is an attempt to overcome some of these obstacles.

Each of the primary readings that have been bundled into this collection pertains to the parable Jesus told in Matthew 25:31–46, the Parable of the Sheep and the Goats. This parable has been interpreted a number of different ways across history, and it has been used to make a wide variety of points about the nature of the church, how Christians should act, who Christians ought to love, what eternity may be like, and many others. You will find that many of the interpreters in this volume disagree with one another about what this passage means. For the most part, their disagreements are a part of the healthy way in which Christians show their passion for Scripture and how hard they fight to ensure that it is read carefully. Since this passage is a parable it invites listeners into a dynamic relationship with this story. By telling a story Jesus makes it clear that part of the job of discovering his meaning belongs to us. Jesus employed stories like this one to communicate to his followers in a way that only narrative can.

Part of the beauty of this parable is the way it defies any single concrete interpretation. The "sheep" in the story are surprised to discover they have been faithful. The "goats" in the story are surprised to discover they have been unfaithful. Their faithfulness, or lack thereof, was not produced by any body of knowledge but by a lifestyle that drove them to comfort, welcome, and care for "the least of these." This means we should not expect this parable to ever allow itself to be put to rest. "The least of these" are always, at least potentially, a group of people in whom we are surprised to discover that Christ is present. So with every reading this story invokes a fresh understanding. This may well have been part of what Jesus had in mind when he taught with parables.

Perhaps you can see why this passage is a good one to look at from so many different angles in Christian history. Pope Leo the Great, embroiled in some of the most important doctrinal battles in early Christian history, was quick to equate "the least of these" to people under the influence of heretical teachings. Luther, many centuries later, believed that "the least of these" were people who had been mistreated by the Roman Catholic Church. Each of these excerpts will attempt to draw you into the time period and setting into which this parable spoke. The readings each begin with a short introduction, a brief *secondary* source to orient the primary reading that follows. There are also questions to assist your engagement with the texts and their authors.

Bear in mind that these are, for the most part, small slivers of much larger works. These snippets of theology are not always the most representative, articulate, or coherent theology developed by the authors. The payoff for reading a collection organized in this fashion is the raw manner with which it presents Christian life. Christianity does not occur between the pages of dusty volumes but on the streets and slums of life, where widows mourn, the sick cry out, and the hungry moan. This is the *real* setting for Christian theology; it is fitting that your journey into Christian theology should begin here.

Matthew 25:31–46

When the Son of Man comes in his glory, and all the angels with him, then he will sit on the throne of his glory. ³²All the nations will be gathered before him, and he will separate people one from another as a shepherd separates the sheep from the goats, ³³and he will put the sheep at his right hand and the goats at the left.

³⁴"Then the king will say to those at his right hand, "Come, you that are blessed by my Father, inherit the kingdom prepared for you from the foundation of the world; ³⁵for I was hungry and you gave me food, I was thirsty and you gave me something to drink, I was a stranger and you welcomed me,³⁶I was naked and you gave me clothing, I was sick and you took care of me, I was in prison and you visited me." ³⁷Then the righteous will answer him, "Lord, when was it that we saw you hungry and gave you food, or thirsty and gave you something to drink? ³⁸And when was it that we saw you a stranger and welcomed you, or naked and gave you clothing? ³⁹And when was it that we saw you sick or in prison and visited you?" ⁴⁰And the king will answer them, "Truly I tell you, just as you did it to one of the least of these who are members of my family, you did it to me."

⁴¹Then he will say to those at his left hand, "You that are accursed, depart from me into the eternal fire prepared for the devil and his angels; ⁴²for I was hungry and you gave me no food, I was thirsty and you gave me nothing to drink, ⁴³I was a stranger and you did not welcome me, naked and you did not give me clothing, sick and in prison and you did not visit me." ⁴⁴Then they also will answer, "Lord, when was it that we saw you hungry or thirsty or a stranger or naked or sick or in prison, and did not take care of you?" ⁴⁵Then he will answer them, "Truly I tell you, just as you did not do it to one of the least of

these, you did not do it to me." [46]And these will go away into eternal punishment, but the righteous into eternal life.

For Further Reading

Borsch, Frederick Houk. *Many Things in Parables: Extravagant Stories of New Community.* 1988. Reprinted, Eugene, OR: Wipf & Stock, 2002.

Crossan, John Dominic. *In Parables: The Challenge of the Historical Jesus.* 1973. Reprinted, Sonoma, CA: Polebridge, 1992.

France, Richard Thomas. "On Being Ready (Matthew 25:1–46)." In *The Challenge of Jesus' Parables,* edited by Richard N. Longenecker, 177–95. McMaster New Testament Studies. Grand Rapids: Eerdmans, 2000.

Hedrick, Charles W. *Parables as Poetic Fictions: The Creative Voice of Jesus.* 1994. Reprinted, Eugene, OR: Wipf & Stock, 2005.

Scott, Bernard Brandon. *Hear Then the Parable: A Commentary on the Parables of Jesus.* Minneapolis: Fortress, 1989.

2

Irenaeus

Irenaeus (130–202) is one of the earliest Christian theologians. He was probably ethnically Greek, born into a Christian family in Smyrna in Asia Minor. In 177, as an adult living in Lyons (modern-day France) Irenaeus went on a pilgrimage to Rome. While he was gone his bishop, Pothinus, was killed in persecutions ordered by emperor Marcus Aurelius. Irenaeus became the second bishop of Lyons when he returned from Rome, and had a remarkable and significant career as a pastor and theologian until his death, probably in another persecution, in 202.

Theologically, Irenaeus remains an indispensable part of the formation of Christianity. He was important in the compilation of the New Testament; it was Irenaeus who first suggested that the books of Matthew, Mark, Luke, and John be elevated above other circulating gospels as divinely inspired. His five-book series, Against Heresies, *from which the following reading was taken, is a perfect example of the early Christian theological struggle against Gnosticism.*

. . .

Against Heresies, Book 4, Chapter 18: Concerning sacrifices and oblations, and those who truly offer them[1]

1. The oblation of the Church, therefore, which the Lord gave instructions to be offered throughout all the world, is accounted with God a pure sacrifice, and is acceptable to Him; not that He stands in need of a sacrifice from us, but that he who offers is himself glorified in what he does offer, if his gift be accepted. For by the gift both honor and affection are shown forth towards the King; and the Lord, wishing us to offer it in all simplicity and innocence, did express Himself thus: "Therefore, when you offer your gift upon the altar, and you remember that your brother has ought against you, leave your gift before the altar, and go your way; first be reconciled to your brother, and then return and offer your gift."[2] We are bound, therefore, to offer to God the first-fruits of His creation, as Moses also says, "You will not appear in the presence of the Lord your God empty";[3] so that man, being accounted as grateful, by those things in which he has shown his gratitude, may receive that honor which flows from Him.

2. And the class of oblations in general has not been set aside; for there were both oblations there [among the Jews], and there are oblations here [among the Christians]. Sacrifices there were among the people; sacrifices there are, too, in the Church: but the species alone has been changed, inasmuch as the offering is now made, not by slaves, but by freemen. For the Lord is [ever] one and the same; but the character of a servile oblation is peculiar [to itself], as is also that of freemen, in order that, by the very oblations, the indication of liberty may be set forth. For with Him there is nothing purposeless, nor without signification, nor without design. And for this reason they (the Jews) had indeed the tithes of their goods consecrated to Him, but those who have received liberty set aside all their possessions for the Lord's purposes, bestowing joyfully and freely not the less valuable

1. From *The Apostolic Fathers with Justin Martyr and Irenaeus* (Grand Rapids, MI: Christian Classics Ethereal Library). Text edited and translated by Alexander Roberts and James Donaldson and first published in Edinburgh, 1867. A number of modernizing changes have been made to this translation.

2. Matthew 5:23–24.

3. Deuteronomy 16:16.

portions of their property, since they have the hope of better things [hereafter]; as that poor widow acted who cast all her living into the treasury of God.[4]

3. For at the beginning God had respect to the gifts of Abel, because he offered with single-mindedness and righteousness; but He had no respect unto the offering of Cain, because his heart was divided with envy and malice, which he cherished against his brother, as God says when reproving his hidden [thoughts], "Though you offer rightly, yet, if you do not divide rightly, have you not sinned? Be at rest";[5] since God is not appeased by sacrifice. For if any one will endeavor to offer a sacrifice merely to outward appearance, unexceptionably, in due order, and according to appointment, while in his soul he does not assign to his neighbor that fellowship with him which is right and proper, nor is under the fear of God;—he who thus cherishes secret sin does not deceive God by that sacrifice which is offered correctly as to outward appearance; nor will such an oblation profit him anything, but [only] the giving up of that evil which has been conceived within him, so that sin may not the more, by means of the hypocritical action, render him the destroyer of himself.[6] Wherefore did the Lord also declare: "Woe to you, scribes and Pharisees, hypocrites, for you are like whitewashed tombs. For the sepulcher appears beautiful outside, but within it is full of dead men's bones, and all uncleanness; even so you also outwardly appear righteous unto men, but within you are full of wickedness and hypocrisy."[7] For while they were thought to offer correctly so far as outward appearance went, they had in themselves jealousy like to Cain; therefore they slew the Just One, slighting the counsel of the Word, as did also Cain. For [God] said to him, "Be at rest"; but he did not assent. Now what else is it to "be at rest" than to forego purposed violence? And saying similar things to these men, He declares: "You blind Pharisee, cleanse that which is within the cup, that the outside

4. Luke 21:4.

5. Genesis 4:7, Septuagint.

6. The Latin text is: "ne per assimulatam operationem, magis autem peccatum, ipsum sibi homicidam faciat hominem."

7. Matthew 23:27–28.

may be clean also."[8] And they did not listen to Him. For Jeremiah says, "Behold, neither your eyes nor your heart are good; but [they are turned] to your covetousness, and to shed innocent blood, and for injustice, and for man-slaying, that you may do it."[9] And again Isaiah said, "You have taken counsel, but not of Me; and made covenants, [but] not by My Spirit."[10] In order, therefore, that their inner wish and thought, being brought to light, may show that God is without blame, and works no evil—that God who reveals what is hidden [in the heart], but who works not evil—when Cain was by no means at rest . . . Thus did He in like manner speak to Pilate: "You would have no power at all against Me, unless it were given to you from above";[11] God always giving up the righteous one [in this life to suffering], that he, having been tested by what he suffered and endured, may [at last] be accepted; but that the evildoer, being judged by the actions he has performed, may be rejected. Sacrifices, therefore, do not sanctify a man, for God stands in no need of sacrifice; but it is the conscience of the offerer that sanctifies the sacrifice when it is pure, and thus moves God to accept [the offering] as from a friend. "But the sinner," says He, "who kills a calf [in sacrifice] to Me, is as if he slew a dog."[12]

4. Inasmuch, then, as the Church offers with single-mindedness, her gift is justly reckoned a pure sacrifice with God. As Paul also says to the Philippians, "I am full, having received from Epaphroditus the things that were sent from you, the odour of a sweet smell, a sacrifice acceptable, pleasing to God."[13] For it behoves us to make an oblation to God, and in all things to be found grateful to God our Maker, in a pure mind, and in faith without hypocrisy, in well-grounded hope, in fervent love, offering the first-fruits of His own created things. And the Church alone offers this pure oblation to the Creator, offering to Him, with giving of thanks, [the things taken] from His creation . . . For some, by maintaining that the Father is different from the Creator,

8. Matthew 23:26.
9. Jeremiah 22:17.
10. Isaiah 30:1.
11. John 19:11.
12. Isaiah 66:3.
13. Philippians 4:18.

do, when they offer to Him what belongs to this creation of ours, set Him forth as being covetous of another's property, and desirous of what is not His own. Those, again, who maintain that the things around us originated from apostasy, ignorance, and passion, do, while offering unto Him the fruits of ignorance, passion, and apostasy, sin against their Father, rather subjecting Him to insult than giving Him thanks. But how can they be consistent with themselves, [when they say] that the bread over which thanks have been given is the body of their Lord, and the cup His blood, if they do not call Himself the Son of the Creator of the world, that is, His Word, through whom the wood fructifies, and the fountains gush forth, and the earth gives "first the blade, then the ear, then the full corn in the ear."[14]

5. Then, again, how can they say that the flesh, which is nourished with the body of the Lord and with His blood, goes to corruption, and does not partake of life? Let them, therefore, either alter their opinion, or cease from offering the things just mentioned. But our opinion is in accordance with the Eucharist, and the Eucharist in turn establishes our opinion. For we offer to Him His own, announcing consistently the fellowship and union of the flesh and Spirit. For as the bread, which is produced from the earth, when it receives the invocation of God, is no longer common bread, but the Eucharist, consisting of two realities, earthly and heavenly; so also our bodies, when they receive the Eucharist, are no longer corruptible, having the hope of the resurrection to eternity.

6. Now we make offering to Him, not as though He stood in need of it, but rendering thanks for His gift, and thus sanctifying what has been created. For even as God does not need our possessions, so do we need to offer something to God; as Solomon says: "He who is kind to the poor lends to the Lord."[15] For God, who stands in need of nothing, takes our good works to Himself for this purpose, that He may grant us a recompense of His own good things, as our Lord says: "Come, you blessed of My Father, receive the kingdom prepared for you. For I was hungry, and you gave Me to eat: I was thirsty, and you gave Me drink: I was a stranger, and you took Me in: naked, and

14. Mark 4:28.
15. Proverbs 19:17.

you clothed Me; sick, and you visited Me; in prison, and you came to Me."[16] As, therefore, He does not stand in need of these [services], yet does desire that we should render them for our own benefit, lest we be unfruitful; so did the Word give to the people that very precept as to the making of oblations, although He stood in no need of them, that they might learn to serve God: thus is it, therefore, also His will that we, too, should offer a gift at the altar, frequently and without intermission. The altar, then, is in heaven (for towards that place are our prayers and oblations directed); the temple likewise [is there], as John says in the Apocalypse, "And the temple of God was opened:"[17] the tabernacle also: "For, behold," He says, "the tabernacle of God, in which He will dwell with men."

Reading Questions

1. What might we learn about Irenaeus' understanding of sin from his discussion of Cain and Abel?

2. Without naming his opponent, Irenaeus is clearly battling heresy in this reading. List the characteristics of the heresy he has in mind.

3. What is at stake in these heresies? Why does Irenaeus care?

4. He writes, "sacrifices, therefore, do not sanctify a man." How does this saying relate to his use of "the least of these" passage near the end of this reading?

5. Describe Irenaeus' understanding of the Eucharistic sacrament. Do you agree with his statements about the nature of the bread and the wine? Why or why not?

6. Does Irenaeus believe that Jesus needs us to bring him a cup of cold water, visit him in prison, etc.?

16. Matthew 25:34ff.
17. Revelation 11:19.

For Further Reading

Clark, Mary T. "Irenaeus." In *Encyclopedia of Early Christianity,* edited by Everett Ferguson, 471–73. New York: Garland, 1990.

Donovan, Mary Ann. *One Right Reading? A Guide to Irenaeus.* Collegeville, MN: Liturgical, 1997.

Farkasfalvy, D. "Theology of Scripture in St. Irenaeus." *Revue Bénédictine* 78 (1968) 319–33.

Ferguson, Thomas C. K. "The Rule of Truth and Irenaean Rhetoric in Book 1 of *Against Heresies.*" *Vigiliae Christianae* 55 (2001) 356–75.

Grant, Robert M. *Irenaeus of Lyon.* Early Church Fathers. London: Routledge, 1997.

Osborn, Eric. *Irenaeus of Lyon.* Cambridge: Cambridge University Press, 2001.

Stanton, Graham N. "Jesus Traditions and Gospels in Justin Martyr and Irenaeus." In *The Biblical Canons,* edited by J.-M. Auwers and H. J. de Jonge, 353–70. Bibliotheca Ephemeridum Theologicarum Lovaniensium 163. Leuven: Peeters, 2003.

Vallée, Gérard. *A Study of Anti-gnostic Polemics: Irenaeus, Hippolytus, and Epiphanius.* Studies in Christianity and Judaism 1. Waterloo, ON: Wilfred Laurier University Press, 1981.

3

Clement of Alexandria

Clement (ca. 150–ca. 216) became an important leader in Alexandria, Egypt, in the second century. He was probably born in Athens to a family with some money and influence. His knowledge of Greek philosophers and poets is abundantly evident in his writings. Clement traveled widely before settling in Egypt and connecting with the Christian school there. He soon became the head of this institution and was a teacher of Origin, an important early Christian theologian and biblical scholar. Clement produced three main writings that are designed to bring non-Christians to faith, nurture new Christians, and show the way for mature Christians to advance to perfection. The excerpts below are from the second and third works.

Clement's theology is intensely practical, forged in the concrete setting in which Christianity is actually lived. Salvation, according to Clement, is intimately bound up with a proper knowledge of Jesus Christ, the great Physician. In the entertaining passage below, Clement is deeply concerned with the stark contrast between the ways that rich people are living their lives and the calling of the Christian gospel. Clement is deeply concerned with ethics, and this concern is obvious in what follows.

. . .

The Instructor, Book 3, Chapter 4:
With Whom We are to Associate[1]

But really I have unwittingly deviated in spirit from the order, to which I must now revert, and must find fault with having large numbers of domestic [servants]. For, avoiding working with their own hands and serving themselves, men have recourse to servants, purchasing a great crowd of fine cooks, and of people to lay out the table, and of others to divide the meat skillfully into pieces. And the staff of servants is separated into many divisions; some labor for their gluttony, carvers and seasoners, and the compounders and makers of sweetmeats, and honey-cakes, and custards; others are occupied with their too numerous clothes; others guard the gold, like griffins; others keep the silver, and wipe the cups, and make ready what is needed to furnish the festive table; others rub down the horses; and a crowd of cup-bearers exert themselves in their service, and herds of beautiful boys, like cattle, from whom they milk away their beauty. And male and female assistants at the washroom are employed by the ladies—some for the mirrors, some for the head-dresses, others for the combs. Many are eunuchs; and these panders serve without suspicion those that wish to be free to enjoy their pleasures, because of the belief that they are unable to indulge in lust. But a true eunuch is not one who is unable, but one who is unwilling, to indulge in pleasure. The Word, testifying by the prophet Samuel to the Jews, who had transgressed when the people asked for a king, promised not a loving lord, but threatened to give them a self-willed and voluptuous tyrant, "who will," He says, "take your daughters to be perfumers, and cooks, and bakers,"[2] ruling by the law of war, not desiring a peaceful administration . . . .

But those who impose on the women spend the day with them, telling them silly amatory stories, and wearing out body and soul with their false acts and words. "Do not follow the crowd," it is said, "nor

---

1. From *The Ante-Nicene Fathers*, Volume II, *Fathers of the Second Century* (Grand Rapids: Christian Classics Ethereal Library). Text edited and translated by Alexander Roberts and James Donaldson and first published in Edinburgh, 1867. A number of modernizing changes have been made to this translation.

2. 1 Samuel 8:13.

give yourself to a multitude";[3] for wisdom shows itself among few, but disorder in a multitude. But it is not for grounds of propriety, on account of not wishing to be seen, that they purchase bearers, for it were commendable if out of such feelings they put themselves under a covering; but it is out of luxuriousness that they are carried on their domestics' shoulders, and desire to make a show.

So, opening the curtain, and looking keenly round on all that direct their eyes towards them, they show their manners; and often bending forth from within, disgrace this superficial propriety by their dangerous restlessness. "Look not round," it is said, "in the streets of the city, and wander not in its lonely places."[4] For that is, in truth, a lonely place, though there be a crowd of the licentious in it, where no wise man is present.

And these women are carried about over the temples, sacrificing and practicing divination day by day, spending their time with fortune-tellers, and begging priests, and disreputable old women; and they keep up old wives' whisperings over their cups, learning charms and incantations from soothsayers, to the ruin of the nuptial bonds. And some men they keep; by others they are kept; and others are promised them by the diviners. They know not that they are cheating themselves, and giving up themselves as a vessel of pleasure to those that wish to indulge in wantonness; and exchanging their purity for the foulest outrage. They think what is the most shameful ruin is a great stroke of business. And there are many ministers to this meretricious licentiousness, insinuating themselves, one from one quarter, another from another. For the licentious rush readily into uncleanness, like swine rushing to that part of the hold of the ship which is depressed. Whence the Scripture most strenuously exhorts, "Introduce not every one into your house, for the snares of the crafty are many."[5] And in another place, "Let just men be your guests, and in the fear of the Lord refrain from your boast."[6] Away with fornication. "For know this well," says the apostle, "that no fornicator, or unclean person, or covetous

3. Exodus 23:2.
4. Sirach 9:7.
5. Sirach 11:29.
6. Sirach 9:16.

man, who is an idolater, has any inheritance in the kingdom of Christ and of God."[7]

Crowds of abominable creatures flow in, of unbridled tongue, filthy in body, filthy in language; men enough for lewd offices, ministers of adultery, giggling and whispering, and shamelessly making through their noses sounds of lewdness and fornication to provoke lust, endeavoring to please by lewd words and attitudes, inciting to laughter, the precursor of fornication. And sometimes, when inflamed by any provocation, either these fornicators, or those that follow the rabble of abominable creatures to destruction, make a sound in their nose like a frog, as if they had got anger dwelling in their nostrils. But those who are more refined than these keep Indian birds and Median pea-fowls, and recline with peak-headed creatures;[8] playing with satyrs, delighting in monsters. They laugh when they hear Thersites; and these women, purchasing Thersiteses highly valued, pride themselves not in their husbands, but in those wretches which are a burden on the earth, and overlook the chaste widow, who is of far higher value than a Melitæan pup, and look askance at a just old man, who is lovelier in my estimation than a monster purchased for money. And though maintaining parrots and curlews, they do not receive the orphan child;[9] but they expose children that are born at home, and take up the young of birds, and prefer irrational to rational creatures; although they ought to undertake the maintenance of old people with a character for sobriety, who are fairer in my mind than apes, and capable of uttering something better than nightingales; and to set before them that saying, "He that pities the poor lends to the Lord";[10] and this, "Inasmuch as you have done it unto the least of these My brethren, you have done it to Me."[11] But these, on the other hand, prefer ignorance to

---

7. Ephesians 5:5.

8. A reference to Homer; Clement is making clear his disgust for the concern that the rich make over their exotic pets. He is also putting on display his knowledge of Greek literature.

9. A remarkably relevant reference, considering the enormous expense allocated to pets in the contemporary world.

10. Proverbs 19:17.

11. Matthew 25:40.

wisdom, turning their wealth into stone, that is, into pearls and Indian emeralds. And they squander and throw away their wealth on fading dyes, and bought slaves; like crammed fowls scraping the dung of life. "Poverty," it is said, "humbles a man."[12] By poverty is meant that lowliness by which the rich are poor, having nothing to give away.

The Stromata (Miscellanies): Chapter XVI.—How We Are to Explain the Passages of Scripture which Ascribe to God Human Affections

Here again arise the cavillers, who say that joy and pain are passions of the soul: for they define joy as a rational elevation and exultation, as rejoicing on account of what is good; and pity as pain for one who suffers undeservedly; and that such affections are moods and passions of the soul. But we, as would appear, do not cease in such matters to understand the Scriptures carnally; and starting from our own affections, interpret the will of the impassible Deity similarly to our perturbations; and as we are capable of hearing; so, supposing the same to be the case with the Omnipotent, err impiously. For the Divine Being cannot be declared as it exists: but as we who are fettered in the flesh were able to listen, so the prophets spake to us; the Lord savingly accommodating Himself to the weakness of men.

Since, then, it is the will of God that he, who is obedient to the commands and repents of his sins should be saved, and we rejoice on account of our salvation, the Lord, speaking by the prophets, appropriated our joy to Himself; as speaking lovingly in the Gospel He says, "I was hungry, and you gave Me food, I was thirsty, and you gave Me drink. For inasmuch as you did it to one of the least of these, you did it to Me."[13]

As, then, He is nourished, though not personally, by the nourishing of one whom He wishes nourished; so He rejoices, without suffering change, by reason of him who has repented being in joy, as He wished. And since God pities richly, being good, and giving commands

12. Proverbs 10:4.
13. Matthew 25:35, 40.

by the law and the prophets, and more nearly still by the appearance of his Son, saving and pitying, as was said, those who have found mercy; and properly the greater pities the less; and a man cannot be greater than man, being by nature man; but God in everything is greater than man; if, then, the greater pities the less, it is God alone that will pity us. For a man is made to communicate by righteousness, and bestows what he received from God, in consequence of his natural benevolence and relation, and the commands which he obeys. But God has no natural relation to us, as the authors of the heresies will have it; neither on the supposition of His having made us of nothing, nor on that of having formed us from matter; since the former did not exist at all, and the latter is totally distinct from God unless we dare to say that we are a part of Him, and of the same essence as God. And I know not how one, who knows God, can bear to hear this when he looks to our life, and sees in what evils we are involved. For thus it would turn out, which it were impiety to utter, that God sinned in [certain] portions, if the portions are parts of the whole and complementary of the whole; and if not complementary, neither can they be parts. But God being by nature rich in pity, in consequence of His own goodness, cares for us, though neither portions of Himself, nor by nature His children. And this is the greatest proof of the goodness of God: that such being our relation to Him, and being by nature wholly estranged, He nevertheless cares for us. For the affection in animals to their progeny is natural, and the friendship of kindred minds is the result of intimacy. But the mercy of God is rich toward us, who are in no respect related to Him; I say either in our essence or nature, or in the peculiar energy of our essence, but only in our being the work of His will. And him who willingly, with discipline and teaching, accepts the knowledge of the truth, He calls to adoption, which is the greatest advancement of all. "Transgressions catch a man; and in the cords of his own sins each one is bound."[14] And God is without blame. And in reality, "blessed is the man who always fears [the Lord] through piety."[15]

14. Proverbs 5:22.
15. Proverbs 28:14.

Reading Questions

1. Clement is an animated and almost comedic author. List five of the contrasts he draws between the gospel of Christ and the lives of heathens.

2. In the passage above, Clement leaves clues about his understanding of sin. What is the character of "sin" for Clement?

3. Who are "the least of these" in the first passage?

4. What is the theological issue that concerns Clement in the second passage?

5. What are the implications of Clement's accusations on people with riches? Is he advocating poverty?

6. Consider Clement's attitude toward the elderly. How might his comments challenge Christians today?

For Further Reading

Behr, John. *Asceticism and Anthropology in Irenaeus and Clement.* Oxford Early Christian Studies. Oxford: Oxford University Press, 2000.

Hägg, Henny Fiska. *Clement of Alexandria and the Beginning of Christian Apophaticism.* Oxford: Oxford University Press, 2006.

Karavites, Peter. *Evil, Freedom, and the Road to Perfection in Clement of Alexandria.* Supplements to Vigiliae Christianae 43. Leiden: Brill, 1999.

Osborn, Eric. "Clement of Alexandria." In *Encyclopedia of Philosophy,* edited by Paul Edwards, 1:122–23. New York: Macmillan, 1967.

———. *Clement of Alexandria.* Cambridge: Cambridge University Press, 2005.

Wagner, Walter H. "Clement of Alexandria." In *Encyclopedia of Early Christianity,* edited by Everett Ferguson, 214–16. New York: Garland, 1990.

4

Justin Martyr

✳

The works of Justin (100–166) are among the very first Christian writings after the last books of the New Testament were written. Justin was a passionate writer who sometimes appears to get tangled in his own logic; but he played an important role in the early Christological controversies. When Justin quotes Matthew 25:31–46 in the dialogue below he appears to be most interested in displaying the majesty, power, and divinity of Jesus Christ. This is a very different use of this parable than the passage from Clement above; it is therefore a good illustration of the many ways that this parable has been utilized. Also at stake for Justin are such important questions as: Is Christ equal to the Father? Does Christ have independence from the Father?

The New Testament provides important hints about the way we should understand the nature of Jesus Christ. It took many centuries to work out the theological details about the divinity and humanity of Jesus. Justin writes here in the style of Plato, using dialogue as a manner of developing philosophy. His Dialogue with Trypho *is among the first post-biblical attempts to reconcile the relationship between Jesus and Hebrew messianic prophesies. The first section below is included to illustrate the nature of this dialogue. Justin is embroiled in a conversation with a man name Trypho who stubbornly refuses to admit the possibility that Jesus can be considered divine. The reference to Matthew 25 occurs in the second section below (Chapter 76).*

· · ·

Dialogue with Trypho, Chapter 68: Justin complains of the obstinacy of Trypho and answers his objections[1]

And Trypho said, "You endeavor to prove an incredible and well-nigh impossible thing; [namely], that God endured to be born and become man."

"If I undertook," said I, "to prove this by doctrines or arguments of man, you would not bear with me. But if I quote frequently Scriptures, and so many of them, referring to this point, and ask you to comprehend them, you are hard-hearted in the recognition of the mind and will of God. But if you wish to remain for ever so, I would not be injured at all; and for ever retaining the same [opinions] which I had before I met with you, I will leave you."

And Trypho said, "Look, my friend, you made yourself master of these [truths] with much labor and toil. And we accordingly must diligently scrutinize all that we meet with, in order to give our assent to those things which the Scriptures compel us [to believe]."

Then I said to this, "I do not ask you not to strive earnestly by all means, in making an investigation of the matters inquired into; but [I ask you], when you have nothing to say, not to contradict those things which you said you had admitted."

And Trypho said, "So we will endeavor to do."

I continued again: "In addition to the questions I have just now put to you, I wish to put more: for by means of these questions I will strive to bring the discourse to a speedy termination."

And Trypho said, "Ask the questions."

Then I said, "Do you think that any other one is said to be worthy of worship and called Lord and God in the Scriptures, except the Maker of all, and Christ, who by so many Scriptures was proved to you to have become man?"

And Trypho replied, "How can we admit this, when we have instituted so great an inquiry as to whether there is any other than the Father alone?"

---

1. From *The Apostolic Fathers with Justin Martyr and Irenaeus* (Grand Rapids: Christian Classics Ethereal Library). Text edited and translated by Alexander Roberts and James Donaldson and first published in Edinburgh, 1867. A number of modernizing changes have been made to this translation.

Then I again said, "I must ask you this also, that I may know whether or not you are of a different opinion from that which you admitted some time ago."

He replied, "It is not, sir."

Then again I, "Since you certainly admit these things, and since Scripture says, 'Who will declare His generation?' ought you not now to suppose that He is not the seed of a human race?"

And Trypho said, "How then does the Word say to David, that out of his loins God will take to Himself a Son, and will establish His kingdom, and will set Him on the throne of His glory?"

And I said, "Trypho, if the prophecy which Isaiah uttered, 'Behold, the virgin will conceive,' is said not to the house of David, but to another house of the twelve tribes, perhaps the matter would have some difficulty; but since this prophecy refers to the house of David, Isaiah has explained how that which was spoken by God to David in mystery would take place. But perhaps you are not aware of this, my friends, that there were many sayings written obscurely, or parabolically, or mysteriously, and symbolical actions, which the prophets who lived after the persons who said or did them expounded."

"Assuredly," said Trypho.

"If therefore, I will show that this prophecy of Isaiah refers to our Christ, and not to Hezekiah, as you say, will I not in this matter, too, compel you not to believe your teachers, who venture to assert that the explanation which your seventy elders that were with Ptolemy the king of the Egyptians gave, is untrue in certain respects? For some statements in the Scriptures, which appear explicitly to convict them of a foolish and vain opinion, these they venture to assert have not been so written. But other statements, which they fancy they can distort and harmonize with human actions, these, they say, refer not to this Jesus Christ of ours, but to him of whom they are pleased to explain them.[2] Thus, for instance, they have taught you that this Scripture which we are now discussing refers to Hezekiah, in which, as I promised, I will show they are wrong. And since they are compelled, they agree that some Scriptures which we mention to them, and which expressly prove

2. There are some problems or corruptions in the original manuscripts for this sentence.

that Christ was to suffer, to be worshipped, and [to be called] God, and which I have already recited to you, do refer indeed to Christ, but they venture to assert that this man is not Christ. But they admit that He will come to suffer, and to reign, and to be worshipped, and to be God;[3] and this opinion I will in like manner show to be ridiculous and silly. But since I am pressed to answer first to what was said by you in jest, I will make answer to it, and will afterwards give replies to what follows.

Chap. 76: From Other Passages the Same Majesty and Government of Christ are Proved

"For when Daniel speaks of 'one like unto the Son of man' who received the everlasting kingdom, does he not hint at this very thing? For he declares that, in saying 'like unto the Son of man,' He appeared, and was man, but not of human seed. And the same thing he proclaimed in mystery when he speaks of this stone which was cut out without hands. For the expression 'it was cut out without hands' signified that it is not a work of man, but [a work] of the will of the Father and God of all things, who brought Him forth. And when Isaiah says, 'Who will declare His generation?' he meant that His descent could not be declared. Now no one who is a man of men has a descent that cannot be declared. And when Moses says that He will wash His garments in the blood of the grape, does not this signify what I have now often told you is an obscure prediction, namely, that He had blood, but not from men; just as not man, but God, has begotten the blood of the vine? And when Isaiah calls Him the Angel of mighty counsel,[4] did he not foretell Him to be the Teacher of those truths which He did teach when He came[to earth]? For He alone taught openly those mighty counsels which the Father designed both for all those who have been and will be well-pleasing to Him, and also for those who have rebelled against His will, whether men or angels, when He said: 'They

3. Roberts and Donaldson allow that these two phrases could also be translated, "to be worshipped as God."

4. Isaiah 9:6, from the Septuagint.

will come from the east [and from the west[5]], and will sit down with Abraham, and Isaac, and Jacob, in the kingdom of heaven: but the children of the kingdom will be cast out into outer darkness.'[6] And, 'Many will say to Me in that day, Lord, Lord, have we not eaten, and drunk, and prophesied, and cast out demons in Your name? And I will say to them, Depart from Me.'[7]

"Again, in other words, by which He will condemn those who are unworthy of salvation, He said, Depart into outer darkness, which the Father has prepared for Satan and his angels.'[8] And again, in other words, He said, 'I give to you power to tread on serpents, and on scorpions . . . and on all the might of the enemy.'[9] And now we, who believe on our Lord Jesus, who was crucified under Pontius Pilate, when we exorcise all demons and evil spirits, have them subjected to us. For if the prophets declared obscurely that Christ would suffer, and thereafter be Lord of all, yet that [declaration] could not be understood by any man until He Himself persuaded the apostles that such statements were expressly related in the Scriptures. For He exclaimed before His crucifixion: 'The Son of man must suffer many things, and be rejected by the Scribes and Pharisees, and be crucified, and on the third day rise again.'[10] And David predicted that He would be born from the womb before sun and moon,[11] according to the Father's will, and made Him known, being Christ, as God strong and to be worshipped."

---

5. This phrase is not included in every extant copy.

6. Matthew 8:11.

7. Matthew 7:22.

8. Matthew 25:41.

9. Luke 10:19.

10. Luke 9:22.

11. Psalm 110:3 in the Septuagint, compounded with Proverbs 8:27.

Reading Questions

1. What is Trypho's position on the nature of Jesus Christ?

2. Why does Justin think Jesus should be worshipped?

3. On what do Trypho and Justin agree?

4. Why does Justin make use of Jesus' Parable of the Sheep and Goats?

5. Though Justin uses Matthew 25, there is no mention of "the least of these" here. Do you think Justin's interpretation of this parable is consistent with Jesus' intentions? Why?

6. Are you comfortable with the way Justin uses other passages of Scripture?

For Further Reading

Bellinzoni, Arthur J. *The Sayings of Jesus in Justin Martyr.* Supplements to Novum Testamentum 17. Leiden: Brill, 1967.

Chadwick, Henry. *Early Christian Thought and the Classical Tradition: Studies in Justin, Clement, and Origen.* Oxford: Clarendon, 1984.

Goodenough, Erwin R. *The Theology of Justin Martyr.* 1923. Reprinted, Amsterdam: Philo, 1968.

Osborn, Eric. *Justin Martyr.* Beiträge zur historischen Theologie 47. Tübingen: Mohr/Siebeck, 1973.

Shotwell, Willis A. *The Biblical Exegesis of Justin Martyr.* London: SPCK, 1965.

Stylianopoulos, Theodore. "Justin Martyr." In *Encyclopedia of Early Christianity,* edited by Everett Ferguson, 514–16. New York: Garland, 1990.

5

Origen

✻

Origen (ca. 182–ca. 251) was an early Christian intellectual who was both popular and controversial. Born in Alexandria to a Christian family, Origen showed his passion for the Christian faith when he attempted to follow his father into martyrdom in 202. Tricked out of this fate by his mother, Origen went on to become a popular preacher and teacher. He again revealed his passion and commitment to Christianity when, in an effort to avoid even the appearance of impropriety when he was tutoring women, Origen castrated himself! This move, which he later second guessed, caused him some political trouble since self-castration was a capital offense in ancient Rome.

Origen mentions and uses Matthew 25:31–46 a number of times in his rather vast corpus. The following is a selection from his book On First Principles, *in which he takes up a number of questions in systematic theology. This selection is noteworthy in the way it takes up the issue of free will, a question which has continued to nag Christian theologians down to the present. Origen also displays here his supreme comfort and familiarity with biblical texts.*

.   .   .

De Principiis, Book 3, Chapters 5–8[1]

5. Such being the case, to say that we are moved from without, and to put away the blame from ourselves, by declaring that we are like to pieces of wood and stones, which are dragged about by those causes that act upon them from without, is neither true nor in conformity with reason, but is the statement of him who wishes to destroy the conception of free-will. For if we were to ask such an one what was free-will, he would say that it consisted in this, that when purposing to do some thing, no external cause came inciting to the reverse. But to blame, on the other hand, the mere constitution of the body, is absurd; for the disciplinary reason, taking hold of those who are most intemperate and savage (if they will follow her exhortation), effects a transformation, so that the alteration and change for the better is most extensive,—the most licentious men frequently becoming better than those who formerly did not seem to be such by nature; and the most savage men passing into such a state of mildness, that those persons who never at any time were so savage as they were, appear savage in comparison, so great a degree of gentleness having been produced within them. And we see other men, most steady and respectable, driven from their state of respectability and steadiness by evil customs, so as to fall into habits of licentiousness, often beginning their wickedness in middle age, and plunging into disorder after the period of youth has passed, which, so far as its nature is concerned, is unstable. Reason, therefore, demonstrates that external events do not depend on us, but that it is our own business to use them in this way or the opposite, having received reason as a judge and an investigator of the manner in which we ought to meet those events that come from without.

6. And now, to confirm the deductions of reason by the authority of Scripture—viz., that it is our own doing whether we live rightly or not, and that we are not compelled, either by those causes which come to us from without, or, as some think, by the presence of fate—we

1. From *The Ante-Nicene Fathers*, Volume IV, *Fathers of the Third Century* (Grand Rapids: Christian Classics Ethereal Library). Text edited and translated by Alexander Roberts and James Donaldson and first published in Edinburgh, 1885. A number of modernizing changes have been made to this translation.

adduce the testimony of the prophet Micah, in these words: "If it has been announced to you, O man, what is good, or what the Lord requires of you, except that you should do justice, and love mercy, and be ready to walk with the Lord your God."[2] Moses also speaks as follows: "I have placed before your face the way of life and the way of death: choose what is good, and walk in it."[3] Isaiah, moreover, makes this declaration: "If you are willing, and hear me, you will eat the good of the land. But if you are unwilling, and will not hear me, the sword will consume you; for the mouth of the Lord has spoken this."[4] In the Psalm, too, it is written: "If My people had heard Me, if Israel had walked in My ways, I would have humbled her enemies to nothing";[5] by which he shows that it was in the power of the people to hear, and to walk in the ways of God. The Savior also saying, "I say to you, Resist not evil";[6] and, "Whoever is be angry with his brother will be in danger of the judgment";[7] and, "Whosoever looks at a woman to lust after her, has already committed adultery with her in his heart";[8] and in issuing certain other commands,—conveys no other meaning than this, that it is in our own power to observe what is commanded. And therefore we are rightly rendered liable to condemnation if we transgress those commandments which we are able to keep. And hence He Himself also declares: "Every one who hears my words, and does them, I will show to whom he is like: he is like a wise man who built his house upon a rock," etc.[9] So also the declaration: "Whoever hears these things, and does them not, is like a foolish man, who built his house upon the sand," etc. Even the words addressed to those who are on His right hand, "Come unto Me, all you blessed of My Father," etc.; "for I was hungry, and you gave Me to eat; I was thirsty, and

2. Micah 6:8.

3. Deuteronomy 30:15–16, 19.

4. Isaiah 1:19–20.

5. Psalm 81:13–14.

6. Matthew 5:39.

7. Matthew 5:21.

8. Matthew 5:28.

9. Matthew 7:26.

you gave Me drink,"[10] manifestly show that it depended upon themselves, that either these should be deserving of praise for doing what was commanded and receiving what was promised, or those deserving of censure who either heard or received the contrary, and to whom it was said, "Depart, you cursed, into everlasting fire."[11] Let us observe also, that the Apostle Paul addresses us as having power over our own will, and as possessing in ourselves the causes either of our salvation or of our ruin…You will find also innumerable other passages in Holy Scripture, which manifestly show that we possess freedom of will. Otherwise there would be a contrariety in commandments being given us, by observing which we may be saved, or by transgressing which we may be condemned, if the power of keeping them were not implanted in us . . .

7. But, seeing there are found in the sacred Scriptures themselves certain expressions occurring in such a connection, that the opposite of this may appear capable of being understood from them, let us bring them forth before us, and, discussing them according to the rule of piety, let us furnish an explanation of them, in order that from those few passages which we now expound, the solution of those others which resemble them, and by which any power over the will seems to be excluded, may become clear. Those expressions, accordingly, make an impression on very many, which are used by God in speaking of Pharaoh, as when He frequently says, "I will harden Pharaoh's heart."[12] For if he is hardened by God, and commits sin in consequence of being so hardened, the cause of his sin is not himself. And if so, it will appear that Pharaoh does not possess freedom of will; and it will be maintained, as a consequence, that, agreeably to this illustration, neither do others who perish owe the cause of their destruction to the freedom of their own will. That expression, also, in Ezekiel, when he says, "I will take away their stony hearts, and will give them hearts of flesh, that they may walk in My precepts, and keep My ways,"[13] may impress some, inasmuch as it seems to be a gift of God, either to walk

10. Matthew 25:34.
11. Matthew 25:41.
12. Exodus 4:21.
13. Ezekiel 11:19–20.

in His ways or to keep His precepts, if He take away that stony heart which is an obstacle to the keeping of His commandments, and bestow and implant a better and more impressible heart, which is called now a heart of flesh. Consider also the nature of the answer given in the Gospel by our Lord and Savior to those who inquired of Him why He spoke to the multitude in parables. His words are: "That seeing they may not see; and hearing they may hear, and not understand; lest they should be converted, and their sins be forgiven them."[14] The words, moreover, used by the Apostle Paul, that "it is not of he that desires, nor of his effort, but of God who shows mercy";[15] in another passage also, "to will and to do are of God"[16] and again, elsewhere, "Therefore He has mercy upon whom He will, and whom He will He hardens. You will say then to me, Why does He yet find fault? For who will resist His will? O man, who are you that reply against God? Will the thing formed say to him who has formed it, Why have you made me so? Has not the potter power over the clay, of the same lump to make one vessel unto honor, and another to dishonor?"[17]—these and similar declarations seem to have no small influence in preventing very many from believing that every one is to be considered as having freedom over his own will, and in making it appear to be a consequence of the will of God whether a man is either saved or lost.

8. Let us begin, then, with those words which were spoken to Pharaoh, who is said to have been hardened by God, in order that he might not let the people go; and, along with his case, the language of the apostle also will be considered, where he says, "Therefore He has mercy on whom He will, and whom He will He hardens."[18] For it is on these passages chiefly that the heretics rely, asserting that salvation is not in our own power, but that souls are of such a nature as must by all means be either lost or saved; and that in no way can a soul which is of an evil nature become good, or one which is of a virtuous nature be made bad. And hence they maintain that Pharaoh, too, being of a

14. Mark 4:12.

15. Romans 9:16.

16. Philippians 2:13.

17. Romans 9:18.

18. Ibid.

ruined nature, was on that account hardened by God, who hardens those that are of an earthly nature, but has compassion on those who are of a spiritual nature. Let us see, then, what is the meaning of their assertion; and let us, in the first place, request them to tell us whether they maintain that the soul of Pharaoh was of an earthly nature, such as they term lost. They will undoubtedly answer that it was of an earthly nature. If so, then to believe God, or to obey Him, when his nature opposed his so doing, was an impossibility. And if this were his condition by nature, what further need was there for his heart to be hardened, and this not once, but several times, unless indeed because it was possible for him to yield to persuasion? Nor could any one be said to be hardened by another, save him who of himself was not obdurate. And if he were not obdurate of himself, it follows that neither was he of an earthly nature, but such a one as might give way when overpowered by signs and wonders. But he was necessary for God's purpose, in order that, for the saving of the multitude, He might manifest in him His power by his offering resistance to numerous miracles, and struggling against the will of God, and his heart being by this means said to be hardened. Such are our answers, in the first place, to these persons; and by these their assertion may be overturned, according to which they think that Pharaoh was destroyed in consequence of his evil nature. And with regard to the language of the Apostle Paul, we must answer them in a similar way. For who are they whom God hardens, according to your view? Those, namely, whom you term of a ruined nature, and who, I am to suppose, would have done something else had they not been hardened. If, indeed, they come to destruction in consequence of being hardened, they no longer perish naturally, but in virtue of what befalls them. Then, in the next place, upon whom does God show mercy? On those, namely, who are to be saved. And in what respect do those persons stand in need of a second compassion, who are to be saved once by their nature, and so come naturally to blessedness, except that it is shown even from their case, that, because it was possible for them to perish, they therefore obtain mercy, that so they may not perish, but come to salvation, and possess the kingdom of the good. And let this be our answer to those who devise and invent the fable of good or bad natures, i.e., of earthly or spiritual souls, in consequence of which, as they say, each one is either saved or lost . . .

To show more clearly, however, what we mean, let us take the illustration employed by the Apostle Paul in the Epistle to the Hebrews, where he says, "For the earth, which drinks in the rain that comes upon it often, and brings forth herbs for them by whom it is dressed, will receive blessing from God; but that which bears thorns and briers is rejected, and is nigh unto cursing, whose end is to be burned."[19] Now from those words of Paul which we have quoted, it is clearly shown that by one and the same act on the part of God—that, viz., by which He sends rain upon the earth—one portion of the ground, when carefully cultivated, brings forth good fruits; while another, neglected and uncared for, produces thorns and thistles. And if one, speaking as it were in the person of the rain, were to say, "It is I, the rain, that have made the good fruits, and it is I that have caused the thorns and thistles to grow," however hard the statement might appear, it would nevertheless be true; for unless the rain had fallen, neither fruits, nor thorns, nor thistles would have sprung up, whereas by the coming of the rain the earth gave birth to both. Now, although it is due to the beneficial action of the rain that the earth has produced herbs of both kinds, it is not to the rain that the diversity of the herbs is properly to be ascribed; but on those will justly rest the blame for the bad seed, who, although they might have turned up the ground by frequent plowing, and have broken the clods by repeated harrowing, and have extirpated all useless and noxious weeds, and have cleared and prepared the fields for the coming showers by all the labor and toil which cultivation demands, have nevertheless neglected to do this, and who will accordingly reap briers and thorns, the most appropriate fruit of their sloth. And the consequence therefore is, that while the rain falls in kindness and impartiality equally upon the whole earth, yet, by one and the same operation of the rain, that soil which is cultivated yields with a blessing useful fruits to the diligent and careful cultivators, while that which has become hardened through the neglect of the husbandman brings forth only thorns and thistles. Let us therefore view those signs

19. Hebrews 6:7–8.

and miracles which were done by God, as the showers furnished by Him from above; and the purpose and desires of men, as the cultivated and uncultivated soil, which is of one and the same nature indeed, as is every soil compared with another, but not in one and the same state of cultivation. From which it follows that every one's will, if untrained, and fierce, and barbarous, is either hardened by the miracles and wonders of God, growing more savage and thorny than ever, or it becomes more pliant, and yields itself up with the whole mind to obedience, if it be cleared from vice and subjected to training.

Reading Questions

1. There has been a tension within Christianity from its inception regarding grace, free will, and divine power. Discuss Origen's stance on these issues.

2. Why is Pharaoh an interesting test case for Origen?

3. What role does Jesus' Parable of the Sheep and the Goats play in Origen's arguments?

4. Does the identity of "the least of these" matter for Origen here?

5. Origen wrote long before the New Testament canon was established, but he is often considered the most skilled exegetical scholar of the early church. What signs of this skill do you see in this excerpt?

For Further Reading

Daly, Robert J. "Origen." In *Encyclopedia of Early Christianity*, edited by Everett Ferguson, 667–69. New York: Garland, 1990.

Dively Lauro, Elizabeth Ann. *The Souls and Spirit and Scripture within Origen's Exegesis*. Bible in Ancient Christianity 3. Boston: Brill Academic, 2005.

Faye, Eugene de. *Origen and His Work*. Translated by Fred Rothwell. New York: Columbia University Press, 1929.

Hanson, R. P. C. *Allegory and Event: A Study of the Sources and Significance of Origen's Interpretation of Scripture*. Louisville: Westminster John Knox, 2002.

McGuckin, John Anthony. *The Westminster Handbook to Origen*. Louisville: Westminster John Knox, 2004.

Torjesen, Karen Jo. "'Body,' 'Soul,' and 'Spirit' in Origen's Theory of Exegesis." In *The Bible in the Early Church,* edited by Everett Ferguson. Studies in Early Christianity 3. New York: Garland, 1993.

6

Tertullian

A creative theologian and prolific author, Tertullian (ca. 155–230) rattled early Christianity with a daring form of Christian faith. Tertullian lived in Carthage, where he coined the term "Trinity" and preached a form of strict Christian morality. Though he was a defender of orthodox Christianity for most of his life, Tertullian broke with the Church of Rome later in life and joined the charismatic and controversial Montanist movement.

Tertullian makes use of the Matthew 25 passage in a number of different ways in his writings. The two selections below are very different in character, illustrating the flexibility of biblical texts, for better or for worse. In the first reading we find Tertullian appealing to this passage to illustrate the Lordship of Jesus. In the second passage we find Tertullian concerned with building up Christians who are enduring a variety of persecutions. In the first centuries, Christianity developed as an occasionally dangerous religious movement with the Roman Empire. Many of the early leaders of the church, including most of Jesus' disciples, were killed as martyrs for the new faith.

. . .

Adversus Hermogenum, Chapter 11: Hermogenes Makes Great Efforts to Remove Evil from God to Matter. How He Fails to Do This Consistently with His Own Argument.[1]

But, after all, by what proofs does Hermogenes persuade us that Matter is evil? For it will be impossible for him not to call that evil to which he imputes evil. Now we lay down this principle, that what is eternal cannot possibly admit of diminution and subjection, so as to be considered inferior to another co-eternal Being. So that we now affirm that evil is not even compatible with it, since it is incapable of subjection, from the fact that it cannot in any wise be subject to any, because it is eternal. But inasmuch as, on other grounds, it is evident what is eternal as God is the highest good, whereby also He alone is good-as being eternal, and therefore good-as being God, how can evil be inherent in Matter, which (since it is eternal) must needs be believed to be the highest good? Else if that which is eternal prove to be also capable of evil, this (evil) will be able to be also believed of God to His prejudice; so that it is without adequate reason that he has been so anxious to remove evil from God; since evil must be compatible with l an eternal Being, even by being made compatible with Matter, as Hermogenes makes it. But, as the argument now stands, since what is eternal can be deemed evil, the evil must prove to be invincible and insuperable, as being eternal; and in that case it will be in vain that we labor "to put away evil from the midst of us";[2] in that case, moreover, God vainly gives us such a command and precept; nay more, in vain has God appointed any judgment at all, when He means, indeed, to inflict punishment with injustice. But if, on the other hand, there is to be an end of evil, when the chief thereof, the devil, will "go away into the fire which God hath prepared for him and his angels"[3]—having been first

1. From *The Ante-Nicene Fathers:* Volume IV, *Fathers of the Third Century* (Grand Rapids: Christian Classics Ethereal Library). Text edited and translated by Alexander Roberts and James Donaldson and first published in Edinburgh, 1885. A number of modernizing changes have been made to this translation.

2. 1 Corinthians 5:13.

3. Matthew 25:41.

"cast into the bottomless pit";[4] when likewise "the manifestation of the children of God"[5] will have "delivered the creature"[6] from evil, which had been "made subject to vanity";[7] when the cattle restored in the innocence and integrity of their nature will be at peace with the beasts of the field, when also little children will play with serpents;[8] when the Father will have put beneath the feet of His Son His enemies,[9] as being the workers of evil, if in this way an *end* is compatible with evil, it must follow of necessary that a *beginning* is also compatible with it; and Matter will turn out to have a beginning, by virtue of its having also an end. For whatever things are set to the account of evil, have a compatibility with the condition of evil.

Scorpiace[10]

Chapter XI. In the same manner, therefore, we maintain that the other announcements too refer to the condition of martyrdom. "He," says Jesus, "who will value his own life also more than me, is not worthy of me,"[11]—that is, he who will rather live by denying, than die by confessing, me; and "he who finds his life will lose it; but he who loses it for my sake will find it."[12] Therefore indeed he finds it, who, in winning life, denies; but he who thinks that he wins it by denying, will lose it in hell. On the other hand, he who, through confessing, is killed, will lose it for the present, but is also about to find it unto everlasting life. In fine, governors themselves, when they urge men to deny, say, "Save your life"; and, "Do not lose your life." How would Christ

4. Revelation 20:3.

5. Romans 8:19.

6. Romans 8:21.

7. Romans 8:20.

8. Isaiah 11:6.

9. Psalm 110:1.

10. From *The Ante-Nicene Fathers,* Volume IV, *Fathers of the Third Century* (Grand Rapids, MI: Christian Classics Ethereal Library). Text edited and translated by Alexander Roberts and James Donaldson and first published in Edinburgh, 1885. A number of modernizing changes have been made to this translation.

11. Luke 14:26.

12. Matthew 10:39.

speak, but in accordance with the treatment to which the Christian would be subjected? But when He forbids thinking about what answer to make at a judgment-seat,[13] He is preparing His own servants *for what awaited them*, He gives the assurance that the Holy Spirit will answer *by them*; and when He wishes a brother to be visited in prison,[14] He is commanding that those about to confess be the object of solicitude; and He is soothing their sufferings when He asserts that God will avenge His own elect.[15]

In the parable also of the withering of the word[16] after the green blade had sprung up, He is drawing a picture with reference to the burning heat of persecutions. If these announcements are not understood as they are made, without doubt they signify something else than the sound indicates; and there will be one thing in the words, another in their meanings, as is the case with allegories, with parables, with riddles. Whatever wind of reasoning, therefore, these scorpions may catch (in their sails), with whatever subtlety they may attack, there is now one line of defense: an appeal will be made to the facts themselves, whether they occur as the Scriptures represent that they would; since another thing will then be meant in the Scriptures if that very one (which seems to be so) is not found in actual facts. For what is written, must come to pass. Besides, what is written will then come to pass, if something different does not. But, lo! we are both regarded as persons to be hated by all men for the, sake of the name, as it is written; and are delivered up by our nearest of kin also, as it is written; and are brought before magistrates, and examined, and tortured, and make confession, and are ruthlessly killed, as it is written. So the Lord ordained.

If He ordained these events otherwise, why do they not come to pass otherwise than He ordained them, that is, as He ordained them? And yet they do not come to pass otherwise than He ordained. Therefore, as they come to pass, so He ordained; and as He ordained, so they come to pass. For neither would they have been permitted to

13. Matthew 10:19.
14. Matthew 25:36.
15. Luke 28:7.
16. Matthew 8:3.

occur otherwise than He ordained, nor for His part would He have ordained otherwise than He would wish them to occur. Thus these passages of Scripture will not mean ought else than we recognize in actual
facts; or if those events are not yet taking place which are prophesied,
how are those taking place which have not been announced? For these
events which are taking place have not been prophesied, if those which
are prophesied are different, and not these which are taking place. Well
now, seeing the very occurrences are met with in actual life which are
believed to have been expressed with a different meaning in words,
what would happen if they were found to have come to pass in a different manner *than had been revealed*? But this will be the waywardness
of faith, not to believe what has been demonstrated, to assume the
truth of what has not been demonstrated. And to this waywardness
I will offer the following objection also, that if these events, which
occur as is written, will not be the very ones which are prophesied,
those too (which are meant) ought not to occur as is written, that they
themselves also may not, after the example of these *others*, be in danger
of exclusion, since there is one thing in the words and another in the
facts; and there remains that even the events which have been prophesied are not seen when they occur, if they are announced otherwise
than they have to occur. And how will those be believed (to have come
to pass), which will not have been announced as they come to pass?
Thus heretics, by not believing what is announced as it has been shown
to have taken place, believe what has not been even prophesied.

Reading Questions

1. How is Matthew 25 invoked in the first reading above?

2. How is Matthew 25 invoked in the second reading, from Scorpiace?
   Why is this parable utilized here?

3. If you were a Christian afraid that your faith might cost you your
   life, would this passage bring you comfort? Why or why not?

4. Who are "the least of these" in the Scorpiace passage?

5. Does Tertullian believe that God ordains persecution and
   martyrdom?

For Further Reading

Barnes, Timothy David. *Tertullian: A Historical and Literary Study.* Oxford: Clarendon, 1985.

Dunn, Geoffrey D. *Tertullian.* The Early Church Fathers. London: Routledge, 2004.

Osborn, Eric. *Tertullian: First Theologian of the West.* Cambridge: Cambridge University Press, 1997.

Rankin, David. *Tertullian and the Church.* Cambridge: Cambridge University Press, 1995.

Sider, Robert D. "Approaches to Tertullian: A Study of Recent Scholarship." *Second Century* 2 (1982) 228–60.

———. "Tertullian." In *Encyclopedia of Early Christianity,* edited by Everett Ferguson, 883–85. New York: Garland, 1990.

Waszink, J. H. "Tertullian's Principles and Methods of Exegesis." In *The Bible in the Early Church,* edited by Everett Ferguson. Studies in Early Christianity 3. New York: Garland, 1993.

7

St. Athanasius of Alexandria

Athanasius (298–373) appears in Christian history during the critical fourth century when a great number of debates raged over Scripture, theology, and the relationship between Christianity and politics. Athanasius was an important player at the famous Council of Nicea in 325, where he served as an assistant to the aging Bishop Alexander. In 328 he succeeded Alexander as Bishop and proceeded to have an unprecedented influence on the course of Christian history. He was the first to list the twenty-seven books which are a part of today's New Testament. Athanasius was remarkably bold in his dealings with Roman politics, tenacious in argument and inflexible in his opinions. He was bold enough, legend has it, to grab the reigns of Emperor Constantine's horse and refuse to let go until the Emperor conceded a theological point. Historians have largely looked past the fact that his success theologically and politically was partly underwritten by bullying, violence, kidnapping, and other unseemly practices.

Athanasius, from Nicea until the end of his long career as bishop, was in a constant battle with Arius and Arianism. He managed to, at times almost single-handedly, defend Christian orthodoxy against the various forms of Arianism that were quite popular during the fourth century. The following readings all come from History of the Arians, *one of many writings by Athanasius condemning this heresy and challenging the political influences on Christianity. He writes in this history of his own interactions with Arian leaders and his consternation at their resilient ability to influence Constantine despite "repeated condemnations."*

. . .

History of the Arians[1]

1. And not long after they put in execution the designs for the sake of which they had had recourse to these artifices; for they no sooner had formed their plans, but they immediately admitted Arius and his fellows to communion. They set aside the repeated condemnations which had been passed upon them, and again pretended the imperial authority in their behalf. And they were not ashamed to say in their letters, 'since Athanasius suffered, all jealousy has ceased, and let us henceforward receive Arius and his fellows'; adding, in order to frighten their hearers, 'because the Emperor has commanded it.'[2] Moreover, they were not ashamed to add, 'for these men profess orthodox opinions'; not fearing that which is written, 'Woe unto them that call bitter sweet, that put darkness for light';[3] for they are ready to undertake anything in support of their heresy. Now is it not hereby plainly proved to all men, that we both suffered heretofore, and that you now persecute us, not under the authority of an Ecclesiastical sentence, but on the ground of the Emperor's threats, and on account of our piety towards Christ? As also they conspired in like manner against other Bishops, fabricating charges against them also; some of whom fell asleep in the place of their exile, having attained the glory of Christian confession; and others are still banished from their country, and contend still more and more manfully against their heresy, saying, 'Nothing can separate us from the love of Christ?'[4]

2. *Arians sacrifice morality and integrity to party*
And hence also you may discern its character, and be able to condemn it more confidently. The man who is their friend and their associate in impiety, although he is open to ten thousand charges for other enormities which he has committed; although the evidence and proof

---

1. From *Nicene and Post-Nicene Fathers*, Volume IV (Grand Rapids: Christian Classics Ethereal Library). Text translated by Archibald Robertson and edited by Philip Schaff and Henry Wace, first published in Edinburgh, 1891. A number of modernizing changes have been made to this translation.

2. Here Athanasius writes of himself in the third person.

3. Isaiah 5:20.

4. Romans 8:35.

against him are most clear; he is approved of by them, and straight-way becomes the friend of the Emperor, obtaining an introduction by his impiety; and making very many pretences, he acquires confidence before the magistrates to do whatever he desires. But he who exposes their impiety, and honestly advocates the cause of Christ, though he is pure in all things, though he is conscious of no delinquencies, though he meets with no accuser; yet on the false pretences which they have framed against him, is immediately seized and sent into banishment under a sentence of the Emperor, as if he were guilty of the crimes which they wish to charge upon him, or as if, like Naboth, he had insulted the King; while he who advocates the cause of their heresy is sought for and immediately sent to take possession of the other's Church; and henceforth confiscations and insults, and all kinds of cruelty are exercised against those who do not receive him. And what is the strangest of all, the man whom the people desire, and know to be blameless,[5] the Emperor takes away and banishes; but him whom they neither desire, nor know, he sends to them from a distant place with soldiers and letters from himself. And henceforward a strong necessity is laid upon them, either to hate him whom they love; who has been their teacher, and their father in godliness; and to love him whom they do not desire, and to trust their children to one of whose life and conversation and character they are ignorant; or else certainly to suffer punishment, if they disobey the Emperor.

13. *On the Cruelties of Gregory of Alexandria*

After this the wretched Gregory[6] called upon all men to have com-munion with him. But if you did demand of them communion, they were not worthy of stripes: and if you did scourge them as if evil per-sons, why did you ask it of them as if holy? But he had no other end in view, except to fulfill the designs of them that sent him, and to establish the heresy. Wherefore he became in his folly a murderer and an executioner, injurious, crafty, and profane; in one word, an enemy of Christ. He so cruelly persecuted the Bishop's aunt, that even when she died he would not suffer her to be buried. And this would have

5. I Timothy 3:2.
6. Gregory of Alexandria was a Christian leader much influenced by Arianism.

been her lot; she would have been cast away without burial, had not they who attended on the corpse carried her out as one of their own kindred. Thus even in such things he showed his profane temper. And again when the widows and other mendicants had received alms, he commanded what had been given them to be seized, and the vessels in which they carried their oil and wine to be broken, that he might not only show impiety by robbery, but in his deeds dishonor the Lord; from whom very shortly he will hear those words, 'Inasmuch as you have dishonored these, you have dishonored Me.'[7]

52. The Emperor has no right to rule the Church

Wherefore when Diogenes came, and Syrianus laid in wait for us, both he and we and the people demanded to see the Emperor's letters, supposing that, as it is written, 'Let not a falsehood be spoken before the king'; so when a king has made a promise, he will not lie, nor change. If then 'for his brother's sake he complied,' why did he also write those letters upon his death? And if he wrote them for 'his memory's sake,' why did he afterwards behave so very unkindly towards him, and persecute the man, and write what he did, alleging a judgment of Bishops, while in truth he acted only to please himself? Nevertheless his craft has not escaped detection, but we have the proof of it ready at hand. For if a judgment had been passed by Bishops, what concern had the Emperor with it? Or if it was only a threat of the Emperor, what need in that case was there of the so-named Bishops? When was such a thing heard of before from the beginning of the world? When did a judgment of the Church receive its validity from the Emperor? or rather when was his decree ever recognized by the Church? There have been many Councils held heretofore; and many judgments passed by the Church; but the Fathers never sought the consent of the Emperor thereto, nor did the Emperor busy himself with the affairs of the Church. The Apostle Paul had friends among them of Cæsar's household, and in his Epistle to the Philippians he sent salutations from them; but he never took them as his associates in Ecclesiastical judgments.

Now however we have witnessed a novel spectacle, which is a discovery of the Arian heresy. Heretics have assembled together with

7. Matthew 25:45.

the Emperor Constantine, in order that he, alleging the authority of the Bishops, may exercise his power against whomsoever he pleases, and while he persecutes may avoid the name of persecutor; and that they, supported by the Emperor's government, may conspire the ruin of whomsoever they will and these are all such as are not as impious as themselves. One might look upon their proceedings as a comedy which they are performing on the stage, in which the pretended Bishops are actors, and Constantine the performer of their requests, who makes promises to them, as Herod did to the daughter of Herodias, and they dancing before him accomplish through false accusations the banishment and death of the true believers in the Lord.

61–62. *Ill-treatment of the poor*

But the Arians, as being grieved at this, again devised another yet more cruel and unholy deed; cruel in the eyes of all men, but well suited to their antichristian heresy. The Lord commanded that we should remember the poor; He said, 'Sell what you have, and give alms' and again 'I was a hungry, and you gave Me meat; I was thirsty, and you gave Me drink; for inasmuch as you have done it unto one of these little ones, you have done it unto Me.'[8] But these men, as being in truth opposed to Christ, have presumed to act contrary to His will in this respect also. For when the Duke gave up the Churches to the Arians, and the destitute persons and widows were unable to continue any longer in them, the widows sat down in places which the Clergy entrusted with the care of them appointed. And when the Arians saw that the brethren readily ministered unto them and supported them, they persecuted the widows also, beating them on the feet, and accused those who gave to them before the Duke. This was done by means of a certain soldier named Dynamius. And it was well-pleasing to Sebastian, for there is no mercy in the Manichæans; nay, it is considered a hateful thing among them to show mercy to a poor man. Here then was a novel subject of complaint; and a new kind of court now first invented by the Arians. Persons were brought to trial for acts of kindness which they had performed; he who showed mercy was accused, and he who had received a benefit was beaten; and they wished rather that a poor

8. Matthew 25:35, 40.

man should suffer hunger, than that he who was willing to show mercy should give to him. Such sentiments these modern Jews, for such they are, have learned from the Jews of old, who when they saw him who had been blind from his birth recover his sight, and him who had been a long time sick of the palsy made whole, accused the Lord who had bestowed these benefits upon them, and judged them to be transgressors who had experienced His goodness.[9]

Who was not struck with astonishment at these proceedings? Who did not execrate both the heresy, and its defenders? Who failed to perceive that the Arians are indeed more cruel than wild beasts? For they had no prospect of gain from their iniquity, for the sake of which they might have acted in this manner; but they rather increased the hatred of all men against themselves. They thought by treachery and terror to force certain persons into their heresy, so that they might be brought to communicate with them; but the event turned out quite the contrary. The sufferers endured as martyrdom whatever they inflicted upon them, and neither betrayed nor denied the true faith in Christ. And those who were without and witnessed their conduct, and at last even the heathen, when they saw these things, execrated them as antichristian, as cruel executioners; for human nature is prone to pity and sympathize with the poor. But these men have lost even the common sentiments of humanity; and that kindness which they would have desired to meet with at the hands of others, had themselves been sufferers, they would not permit others to receive, but employed against them the severity and authority of the magistrates, and especially of the Duke.

9. John 9; Matthew 9:3.

Reading Questions

1. On what grounds is Arianism critiqued here?

2. What, according to Athanasius, is the character of a healthy relationship between church and state?

3. What can be ascertained from these readings regarding the relationship between Athanasius and Emperor Constantine?

4. Who are "the least of these" for Athanasius? Why are they invoked in this discussion?

For Further Reading

Anatolios, Khaled. *Athanasius.* The Early Church Fathers. London: Routledge, 2004.

Barnes, Timothy D. *Athanasius and Constantius: Theology and Politics in the Constantinian Empire.* Cambridge: Harvard University Press, 1993.

Ernest, James D. *The Bible in Athanasius of Alexandria.* The Bible in Ancient Christianity 2. Boston: Brill Academic, 2004.

Kannengieser, Charles. "Athanasius." In *Encyclopedia of Early Christianity,* edited by Everett Ferguson, 110–12. New York: Garland, 1990.

Molloy, Michael E. *Champion of Truth: The Life of St. Athanasius.* New York: St. Pauls, 2003.

8

Basil the Great

❋

In the fourth century, Christianity began to show clear signs of theological differences that seemed to follow geographical lines. Distinctly different forms of theology developed in the East and the West, and these differences would eventually lead to the schism between the Roman Catholic and the Eastern Orthodox forms of Christianity. The seeds of these differences are already blossoming when we reach Basil the Great (330–379). Basil was born in Caesarea, Cappadocia (modern Turkey), into a family of rich spiritual heritage. During his education he befriended Gregory of Nazianzus, whose reading follows this one. Together with his younger brother, Gregory of Nyssa, the three are considered the "Cappadocian Fathers." Basil was highly influenced to become a priest by his sister, Macrina. Basil became a bishop in 370 and immediately began to battle Arianism and other heresies. He was famous for his preaching, artful in correspondence, and politically effective.

To illustrate these strengths I have chosen two references of Matthew 25 from Basil's many works. The first is an excerpt from his sermon on "Selfish Wealth and Greed," and the second is a letter written at a particularly difficult time in his life. Basil found out in 360 that Dianius, the bishop who had baptized him, was an Arian. Disturbed by this, and troubled by the implications of his baptism by a heretic, Basil withdrew from Caesarea and spent time with his friend Gregory of Nazianzus. The excerpt from this letter is theologically sophisticated, as was the case with most of Basil's writings.

. . .

Homily 6, on Luke 12:18: On Selfish Wealth and Greed[1]

These things are written that we may shun their imitation. Imitate the earth, O man. Bear fruit, as she does, lest you prove inferior to that which is without life. She produces her fruits, not that she may enjoy them, but for your service. You gather for yourself whatever fruit of good works you have done, because the grace of good works returns to the giver. You have given to the poor, and the gift becomes your own, and comes back with increase. Just as grain that has fallen on the earth becomes a gain to the sower, so the loaf thrown to the hungry man renders abundant fruit thereafter. May the end of your labors be the beginning of the heavenly sowing.[2] 'Sow,' it is written, 'to yourselves in righteousness.'[3] Why then are you distressed? Why do you harass yourself in your efforts to shut up your riches in clay and bricks? 'A good name is rather to be chosen than great riches.'[4] If you admire riches because of the honor that comes from them, think how very much more it tends to your honor that you should be called the father of innumerable children than that you should possess innumerable staters [coins] in a purse. Your wealth you will leave behind you here, like it or not. The honor won by your good deeds you will convey with you to the Master. Then all people standing around you in the presence of the universal Judge will hail you as feeder and benefactor, and give you all the names that tell of loving kindness.

Do you not see theatre-goers flinging away their wealth on boxers and buffoons and beast-fighters, fellows whom it is disgusting even to see, for the sake of the honor of a moment, and the cheers and clapping of the crowd? And are you sparing in your expenses, when you are destined to attain glory so great? God will welcome you, angels will laud you, mankind from the very beginning will call you blessed.

1. From *Nicene and Post-Nicene Fathers, Second Series,* Volume III (Grand Rapids: Christian Classics Ethereal Library). Text translated by Blomfield Jackson and edited by Philip Schaff and Henry Wace, first published in Edinburgh, 1894. A number of modernizing changes have been made to this translation.

2. Jackson renders this, "Be the end of thy husbandry the beginning of the heavenly sewing."

3. Hosea 10:12.

4. Proverbs 2:1.

For your stewardship of these corruptible things your reward will be glory everlasting, a crown of righteousness, the heavenly kingdom. You think nothing of all this. Your heart is so fixed on the present that you despise what is waited for in hope. Come then; dispose of your wealth in various directions. Be generous and liberal in your expenditure on the poor. Let it be said of you, 'He has dispersed, he has given to the poor; his righteousness endures forever.'[5] Do not press heavily on necessity and sell for great prices. Do not wait for a famine before you open your barns. 'People curse the one that withholds grain.'[6] Watch not for a time of want for gold's sake—for public scarcity to promote your private profit. Drive not a huckster's bargains out of the troubles of mankind. Make not God's wrathful visitation an opportunity for abundance. Wound not the sores of men smitten by the scourge. You keep your eye on your gold, and will not look at your brother. You know the marks on the money, and can distinguish good coins from fake coins. But you cannot tell who is your brother in the day of distress. . . .

'Ah!'—it is said—'words are all very fine: gold is finer.' I make the same impression as I do when I am preaching to adulterers against their unchaste living. Their mistress is blamed, and the mere mention of her serves but to enkindle their passions. How can I bring before your eyes the poor man's sufferings that you may know out of what small groanings you are accumulating your treasures, and of what high value will seem to you in the day of judgment [when you hear] the famous words, 'Come, you blessed of my Father, inherit the kingdom prepared for you from the foundation of the world: for I was an hungred and you gave me meat: I was thirsty and you gave me drink: . . . I was naked and you clothed me.'[7] What shuddering, what sweat, what darkness will be shed round you, as you hear the words of condemnation!—'Depart from me, you cursed, into outer darkness prepared for the devil and his angels: for I was an hungred and you gave me no meat: I was thirsty and you gave me no drink: . . . I was naked and

5. Psalm 112:9.
6. Proverbs 11:26.
7. Matthew 25:34.

you clothed me not.'[8] I have told you what I have thought profitable. To you now it is clear and plain what are the good things promised for you if you obey. If you disobey, for you the threat is written. I pray that you may change to a better mind and thus escape its peril. In this way your own wealth will be your redemption. Thus you may advance to the heavenly blessings prepared for you by the grave of Him who has called us all into His own kingdom, to Whom be glory and might for ever and ever. Amen.

Letter 8: To the Caesareans. A defense of his withdrawal, and concerning the faith.

He once spoke of Himself as persecuted—"Saul, Saul," He says, "why do you persecute me?"[9] on the occasion when Saul was hurrying to Damascus with a desire to imprison the disciples. Again He calls Himself naked, when any one of his brethren is naked. "I was naked," He says, "and you clothed me";[10] and so when another is in prison He speaks of Himself as imprisoned, for He Himself took away our sins and bare our sicknesses.[11] Now one of our infirmities is not being subject, and He bare this. So all the things which happen to us to our hurt He makes His own, taking upon Him our sufferings in His fellowship with us.

9. But another passage is also seized by those who are fighting against God to the perversion of their hearers: I mean the words "The Son can do nothing of Himself."[12] To me this saying too seems distinctly declaratory of the Son's being of the same nature as the Father. For if every rational creature is able to do anything of himself, and the inclination which each has to the worse and to the better is in his own power, but the Son can do nothing of Himself, then the Son is not a

8. Matthew 25:41.
9. Acts 9:4.
10. Matthew 25:36.
11. Isaiah 53:4; Matthew 8:17.
12. John 5:19.

creature. And if He is not a creature, then He is of one essence and substance with the Father. Again; no creature can do what he likes. But the Son does what He wills in heaven and in earth. Therefore the Son is not a creature. Again; all creatures are either constituted of contraries or receptive of contraries. But the Son is very righteousness, and immaterial. Therefore the Son is not a creature, and if He is not a creature, He is of one essence and substance with the Father.

10. This examination of the passages before us is, so far as my ability goes, sufficient. Now let us turn the discussion on those who attack the Holy Spirit, and cast down every high thing of their intellect that exalts itself against the knowledge of God.[13] You say that the Holy Ghost is a creature. And every creature is a servant of the Creator, for "all are your servants."[14] If then He is a servant, His holiness is acquired; and everything of which the holiness is acquired is receptive of evil; but the Holy Ghost being holy in essence is called "fount of holiness."[15] Therefore the Holy Ghost is not a creature. If He is not a creature, He is of one essence and substance with the Father. How, tell me, can you give the name of servant to Him who through your baptism frees you from your servitude? "The law," it is said, "of the Spirit of life has made me free from the law of sin."[16] But you will never venture to call His nature even variable, so long as you have regard to the nature of the opposing power of the enemy, which, like lightning, is fallen from heaven and fell out of the true life because its holiness was acquired, and its evil counsels were followed by its change. So when it had fallen away from the Unity and had cast from it its angelic dignity, it was named after its character "Devil," its former and blessed condition being extinct and this hostile power being kindled.

Furthermore if he calls the Holy Ghost a creature he describes His nature as limited. How then can the two following passages stand? "The Spirit of the Lord fills the world";[17] and "Where shall I go from

---

13. 2 Corinthians 11:5.
14. Psalm 19:91.
15. Romans 1:4.
16. Romans 8:2.
17. Wisdom of Solomon 1:7.

your Spirit?"[18] But he does not, it would seem, confess Him to be simple in nature; for he describes Him as one in number. And, as I have already said, everything that is one in number is not simple. And if the Holy Spirit is not simple, He consists of essence and sanctification, and is therefore composite. But who is mad enough to describe the Holy Spirit as composite, and not simple, and consubstantial with the Father and the Son?

11. If we ought to advance our argument yet further, and turn our inspection to higher themes, let us contemplate the divine nature of the Holy Spirit from the following point of view. In Scripture we find mention of three creations. The first is the evolution from non-being into being. The second is change from the worse to the better. The third is the resurrection of the dead. In these you will find the Holy Ghost cooperating with the Father and the Son. There is a bringing into existence of the heavens; and what says David? "By the word of the Lord were the heavens made and all the host of them by the breath of His mouth."[19] Again, man is created through baptism, for "if any man be in Christ he is a new creature."[20] And why does the Savior say to the disciples, "Go therefore and teach all nations, baptizing them in the name of the Father and of the Son and of the Holy Ghost"? Here too you see the Holy Ghost present with the Father and the Son. And what would you say also as to the resurrection of the dead when we will have failed and returned to our dust? Dust we are and to dust we will return.[21] And He will send the Holy Ghost and create us and renew the face of the earth.[22] For what the holy Paul calls resurrection David describes as renewal. Let us hear, once more, him who was caught into the third heaven. What does he say? "You are the temple of the Holy Ghost which is in you."[23] Now every temple is a temple of God, and if we are a temple of the Holy Ghost, then the Holy Ghost is God. It is also called Solomon's temple, but this is in the sense of his being its

18. Psalm 139:7.
19. Psalm 33:6, from the Septuagint.
20. 2 Corinthians 5:17.
21. Genesis 3:1.
22. Psalm 53:30.
23. 1 Corinthians 6:19.

builder. And if we are a temple of the Holy Ghost in this sense, then the Holy Ghost is God, for "He that built all things is God."[24]

If we are a temple of one who is worshipped, and who dwells in us, let us confess Him to be God, for you will worship the Lord your God, and Him only will you serve.[25] Supposing them to object to the word "God," let them learn what this word means. God is called "God" either because He placed all things or because He beholds all things. If He is called "God" because He "placed" or "beholds" all things, and the Spirit knows all the things of God, as the Spirit in us knows our things, then the Holy Ghost is God. Again, if the sword of the spirit is the word of God,[26] then the Holy Ghost is God, inasmuch as the sword belongs to Him of whom it is also called the word. Is He named the right hand of the Father? For "the right hand of the Lord brings mighty things to pass";[27] and "your right hand, O Lord, has dashed in pieces the enemy."[28] But the Holy Ghost is the finger of God, as it is said "if I by the finger of God cast out devils,"[29] of which the version in another Gospel is "if I by the Spirit of God cast out devils."[30] So the Holy Ghost is of the same nature as the Father and the Son.

Reading Questions

1. What does Basil mean by "imitate the earth"?

2. Who are "the least of these" in Basil's sermon?

3. What are the incentives Basil gives for doing good deeds? Do you agree with the motivations?

4. In the letter, do you see any signs that Basil is stinging over the heresy of Arianism?

---

24. Hebrews 3:4.
25. Matthew 9:10.
26. Ephesians 6:17.
27. Psalm 118:16, from the Septuagint.
28. Exodus 15:6.
29. Luke 11:20.
30. Matthew 12:28.

5. Why does the Holy Spirit play an important role for him in this discourse (the letter)?

6. How, according to Basil, is the Spirit united with the Father and the Son? How is the Spirit distinct?

For Further Reading

Fedwick, Paul Jonathan, editor. *Basil of Caesarea, Christian, Humanist, Ascetic: A Sixteen-Hundredth Anniversay Symnposium.* 2 vols. Toronto: Pontifical Institute of Mediaeval Studies, 1981.

Gribomont, J. "Basil the Great." In *Encyclopedia of the Early Church,* edited by Angelo Di Berardino, 1:114–15. Translated by Adrian Walford. New York: Oxford University Press, 1992.

Meredith, Anthony. *The Cappadocians.* Crestwood, NY: St. Vladimir's Seminary Press, 1995.

Norris, Frederick W. "Basil of Caesarea." In *Encyclopedia of Early Christianity,* edited by Everett Ferguson, 139–41. New York: Garland, 1990.

Rousseau, Philip. *Basil of Caesarea.* The Transformation of the Classical Heritage 20. Berkeley: University of California Press, 1994.

Sterk, Andrea. *Renouncing the World Yet Leading the Church: The Monk-Bishop in Late Antiquity.* Cambridge: Harvard University Press, 2004.

9

Gregory of Nazianzus

Gregory of Nazianzus (329–389) was deeply influenced by his close friend Basil the Great. A thoughtful and eloquent theologian but less effective than Basil from the pulpit, Gregory was well-suited to help Christianity clear the important heretical hurdles that continued to nag the church in the late fourth century. Ever the wise politician, Basil realized that his friend Gregory could be a very important asset for the church as a leader. So Basil ordained Gregory, who retreated to the wilderness to practice asceticism for a while before returning to Nazianzus to preach and care for congregations there. Gregory was not a terribly successful pastor nor a very effective preacher, but he was perfectly positioned by Basil to have a great influence in the key First Council of Constantinople in 381.

The sermon I have selected to represent Gregory's interpretation of Matthew 25 is from his very first year as a pastor (362). Gregory is puzzled and disturbed that so few people came out to hear him preach his Easter homily. This sermon springs from the wounded heart of a pastor who felt ill-received by his congregation; the empty church on Easter is a small symptom of deep tension between a church and its new priest.

. . .

Oration 3: To Those Who Had Invited Him, and Not Come to Receive Him[1]

I. How slow you are, my friends and brethren, to come to listen to my words, though you were so swift in tyrannizing over me, and tearing me from my Citadel Solitude,[2] which I had embraced in preference to everything else, and as assistant and mother of the divine ascent, and as deifying man,[3] I had especially admired, and had set before me as the guide of my whole life.[4] How is it that, now you have got it, you thus despise what you so greatly desired to obtain, and seem to be better able to desire the absent than to enjoy the present; as though you preferred to *possess* my teaching rather than to *profit* by it? Yes, I may even say this to you: "I became an excess to you before you even tasted of me, or gave me a trial"—which is most strange.

II. And neither did you entertain me as a guest,[5] nor, if I may make a remark of a more compassionate kind, did you allow yourselves to be entertained by me, reverencing this command if nothing else;[6] nor did you take me by the hand, as beginning a new task; nor encourage me in my timidity, nor console me for the violence I had suffered; but—I shrink from saying it, though say it I must—you made my festival no festival, and received me with no happy introduction; and you mingled the solemn festival with sorrow, because it lacked that which most of all would have contributed to its happiness, the presence of you my conquerors, for it would not be true to call you people who love me. So easily is anything despised which is easily conquered,

1. From *Nicene and Post-Nicene Fathers*, Second Series, Volume VII: *Cyril of Jerusalem, Gregory Nazianzen* (Grand Rapids: Christian Classics Ethereal Library). Text translated by Edwin Hamilton Gifford and edited by Philip Schaff and Henry Wace, first published in Edinburgh, 1893. A number of modernizing changes have been made to this translation.

2. He is probably referring to the time of ascetic solitude in the wilderness which immediately preceded his new pastorate.

3. 2 Peter 1:4.

4. Or: "had preferred to every other kind of life."

5. Sherman Gray claims that the Greek formation of this phrase strongly suggestions Matthew 25:45, *The Least of These*, 46.

6. Matthew 25:31–46?

and the proud receives attention, while he who is humble before God is slighted.

III. What do you want? Shall I be judged by you, or shall I be your judge? Shall I pass a verdict, or receive one, for I hope to be acquitted if I be judged, and if I give sentence, to give it against you justly? The charge against you is that you do not answer my love with equal measure, nor do you repay my obedience with honor, nor do you pledge the future to me by your present alacrity—though even if you had, I could hardly have believed it. But each of you has something which he prefers to both the old and the new Pastor, neither reverencing the grey hairs of the one, nor calling out the youthful spirit of the other.

IV. There is a Banquet in the Gospels,[7] and a hospitable Host and friends; and the Banquet is most pleasant, for it is the marriage of His Son. He calls them, but they come not: He is angry, and—I pass over the interval for fear of bad omen—but, to speak gently, He fills the Banquet with others. God forbid that this should be your case; but yet you have treated me (how can I put it gently?) with as much haughtiness or boldness as they who after being called to a feast rise up against it, and insult their host; for you, though you are not of the number of those who are without, or are invited to the marriage, but are yourselves those who invited me, and bound me to the Holy Table, and showed me the glory of the Bridal Chamber, then deserted me (this is the most splendid thing about you)—one to his field, another to his newly bought yoke of oxen, another to his just-married wife, another to some other trifling matter; you were all scattered and dispersed, caring little for the Bride chamber and the Bridegroom.[8]

V. On this account I was filled with despondency and perplexity—for I will not keep silence about what I have suffered—and I was very near withholding the discourse which I was minded to bestow as a Marriage-gift, the most beautiful and precious of all I had; and I very nearly let it loose upon you, whom, now that the violence had once been done to me, I greatly longed for: for I thought I could get from this a splendid theme, and because my love sharpened my

7. Luke 14:16.
8. Matthew 22:10.

tongue—love which is very hot and ready for accusation when it is stirred to jealousy by grief which it conceives from some unexpected neglect. If any of you has been pierced with love's sting, and has felt himself neglected, he knows the feeling, and will pardon one who so suffers, because he himself has been near the same frenzy.

VI. But it is not permitted to me at the present time to say to you anything upbraiding; and God forbid I ever should. And even now perhaps I have reproached you more than in due measure, the Sacred Flock, the praise-worthy nurslings of Christ, the Divine inheritance; by which, O God, You are rich, even you were poor in all other respects. To You, I think, are fitting those words, "The boundary lines have fallen for me in pleasant places, I have a goodly heritage."[9] Nor will I allow that the most populous cities or the broadest flocks have any advantage over us, the little ones of the smallest of all the tribes of Israel, of the least of the thousands of Judah,[10] of the little Bethlehem among cities,[11] where Christ was born and is from the beginning well-known and worshipped; among those whom the Father is exalted, and the Son is held to be equal to Him, and the Holy Ghost Spirit is glorified with Them: we who are of one soul, who mind the same thing, who in nothing injure the Trinity, neither by preferring One Person above another, nor by cutting off any: as those bad umpires and measurers of the Godhead do, who by magnifying One Person more than is fit, diminish and insult the whole.

VII. But do you also, if you bear me any good will—you who are my husbandry, my vineyard, my own bowels, or rather His Who is our common Father, for in Christ he hath begotten you through the Gospels[12]—show to us also some respect. It is only fair, since we have honored you above all else: you are my witnesses, you, and they who have placed in our hands this—shall I say *Authority*, or *Service*? And if to him that loves most is due, how will I measure the love, for which I have made you my debtors by my own love? Rather, show respect for

9. Psalm 16:6.

10. I Samuel 23:23.

11. Micah 5:2.

12. I Corinthians 4:15.

yourselves, and the Image committed to your care,[13] and Him Who committed it, and the Sufferings of Christ, and your hopes in him, holding fast the faith which you have received, and in which you were brought up, by which also you are being saved, and trust to save others (for not many, be well assured, can boast of what you can), and reckoning piety to consist, not in often speaking about God, but in silence for the most part, for the tongue is a dangerous thing to men, if it be not governed by reason. Believe that listening is always less dangerous than talking, just as learning about God is more pleasant than teaching. Leave the more accurate search into these questions to those who are the Stewards of the Word; and for yourselves, worship a little in words, but more by your actions, and rather by keeping the Law than by admiring the Lawgiver; show your love for Him by fleeing from wickedness, pursuing after virtue, living in the Spirit, walking in the Spirit, drawing your knowledge from Him, building upon the foundation of the faith, not wood or hay or stubble,[14] weak materials and easily spent when the fire will try our works or destroy them; but gold, silver, precious stones, which remain and stand.

VIII. So may you act, and so may you honor us, whether present or absent, whether taking your part in our sermons, or preferring to do something else: and may you be the children of God, pure and unblameable blameless, in the midst of a crooked and perverse generation;[15] and may you never be entangled in the snares of the wicked that go round about, or bound with the chain of your sins. May the Word in you never be smothered with cares of this life and so you become unfruitful: but may you walk in the King's Highway, turning aside neither to the right hand nor to the left,[16] but led by the Spirit through the straight gate. Then all our affairs will prosper, both now and at the inquest there, in Christ Jesus our Lord, to whom be the glory for ever. Amen.

13. Genesis 1:27.
14. I Corinthians 3:12.
15. Philippians 2:15.
16. Numbers 21:22; Isaiah 49:3.

Reading Questions

1. Do you see any reasons from this sermon that the laypeople in his church had poor Sunday attendance?

2. Gregory passionately begs his congregation to return his love and he accuses them of leaving him lonely in the Bridal Chamber and chained to the Holy Table. What does this language tell you about Gregory's pastoral heart?

3. What is his marriage-gift? Why was it such a precious gift from Gregory to this church?

4. Ever the theologian, Gregory manages to work in a reference to the Trinity. How does the Trinity relate to his particular ecclesial problem? How are his people failing to be like the Trinity?

5. The reference to Matthew 25 is not found in any single quotation but is strongly and repeatedly suggested in the way Gregory uses the Greek language. Who are "the least of these" in this sermon?

For Further Reading

McGuckin, John C. *St. Gregory of Nazianzus: An Intellectual Biography.* Crestwood, NY: St. Vladimir's Seminary Press, 2001.

Meredith, Anthony. *The Cappadocians.* Crestwood, NY: St. Vladimir's Seminary Press, 1995.

Norris, Frederick W. *Faith Gives Fullness to Reasoning.* Supplements to Vigiliae Christianae 13. Leiden: Brill, 1991.

———. "Gregory of Nazianzus." In *Encyclopedia of Early Christianity,* edited by Everett Ferguson, 397–400. New York: Garland, 1990.

Ruether, Rosemary Radford. *Gregory of Nazianzus: Rhetor and Philosopher.* Oxford: Clarendon, 1969.

Sterk, Andrea. *Renouncing the World Yet Leading the Church: The Monk-Bishop in Late Antiquity.* Cambridge: Harvard University Press, 2004.

Winslow, Donald F. *The Dynamics of Salvation: A Study of Gregory of Nazianzus.* Patristic Monograph Series 7. Cambridge, MA: Philadelphia Patristic Foundation, 1979.

10

John Chrysostom

It is entirely appropriate to study John Chrysostom (347–407) by reading one of his sermons. He was given the name "Chrysostom," which means "golden-tongue," after his death because he was such an influential and extraordinary preacher. It is also particularly suitable that we read a sermon about the poor, since Chrysostom was constantly concerned with the plight of poor people and commoners. He was the son of a highly ranked Roman officer; but since his pagan father died in his infancy, he was raised by his Christian mother. After spending a period as a hermit in the wilderness as a young adult, John returned to society for health reasons and earned a great deal of respect for his insightful expositions on scripture and homiletical skills.

His pastoral success led to his appointment as bishop, which put him in an influential political position. His concern for the poor, popularity with commoners, and distaste for the excesses of high ranking Christians made him unpopular with powerful religious leaders. Chrysostom led a bold career of clergy reform and he defiantly challenged the eastern emperor and his wife until he was eventually exiled. He continues to be particularly highly regarded in the Eastern Orthodox Church, but is revered as a saint by Roman Catholics as well. In a relevant contemporary twist, his remains were stolen by Crusaders in 1204 from Constantinople, the center of Eastern Orthodox Christianity. Eight hundred years later in 2004 Pope John Paul II returned these relics to Constantinople as an act of reconciliation.

. . .

Homily 79 on the Gospel of Matthew, Matthew 25:31–46[1]

Unto this most delightful portion of Scripture . . . let us now listen with all earnestness and compunction, this with which Jesus' discourse ended, even as the last thing, reasonably; for great indeed was his regard for philanthropy and mercy. While in what precedes he had discussed this in a different way, here in some respects he discusses it more clearly, and more earnestly, not dealing with two nor three nor five persons, but the whole world . . . But here Jesus delivers the word more fearfully, and with fuller light. Here he no longer says, "The kingdom is like," but openly shows his meaning, saying, "When the Son of Man comes in his glory." For now is he come in dishonor, now in affronts and reproaches; but then will he sit upon the throne of his glory.

Jesus continually makes mention of glory. Since the cross was near, a thing that seemed to be matter of reproach, for this cause he raises up the hearer; and brings before his sight the judgment seat, and all the world sits around him.

And not in this way only does he make his discourse awful, but also by showing the heavens opened . . . and everything will help to render that day fearful. Then, he says "all nations will be gathered together" that is, the whole [human] race. "And he will separate them one from another, as the shepherd his sheep." For now they are not separated, but all mingled together, but the division then will be made with all exactness. And for a while it is by their place that he divides them, and makes them manifest; afterwards by the names he indicates the dispositions of each, calling the one goats, the other sheep, that he might indicate the unfruitfulness of the one, for no fruit will come from goats; and the great profit from the other, for indeed from sheep great is the profit, as well from the milk, as from the wool, and from the young, of all which things the goat is destitute.

But while animals have from nature their unfruitfulness and fruitfulness, people have it from choice, which is why some are punished, and the others crowned. And he does not punish them until he

1. From *Nicene and Post-Nicene Fathers, Series One*, Volume X (Grand Rapids: Christian Classics Ethereal Library), edited by Philip Schaff and first published in Edinburgh, 1888. A number of modernizing changes have been made to this translation.

has pleaded with them, put them in their place, and mentioned the charges against them. And they speak with meekness, but they have no advantage from it now; and very reasonably, because they passed by a work so much to be desired. For indeed the prophets are everywhere saying this, "I will have mercy and not sacrifice,"[2] and the lawgiver by all means urged them to this, both by words, and by works; and nature herself taught it.

But mark them, how they are destitute not of one or two things only, but of all. For not only did they fail to feed the hungry, or clothe the naked; but they did not even visit the sick, which was an easier thing. And notice how easy his judgments are. He did not say, "I was in prison, and you set me free; I was sick, and you raised me up again"; but, "you visited me," and, "you came to me." And neither in hunger is the thing commanded grievous. For he did not seek a costly table, but only what is needful, and his necessary food, and he sought in a beggar's garb, so that all things were enough to bring punishment on them; the easiness of the request, for it was bread; the pitiable character of him that requests, for he was poor; the sympathy of nature, for he was a man; the desirableness of the promise, for he promised a kingdom; the fearfulness of the punishment, for he threatened hell . . .

For further back also he said that they who receive not such as these will suffer more grievous things than Sodom;[3] and here he says, "Whatever you did not do for one of the least of these my brethren, you did not do for me." What are you saying? They are your brethren; and how do you call them least? Why, for this reason they are brethren: because they are lowly, because they are poor, because they are out-cast. For such does he most invite to brotherhood, the unknown, the contemptible, not . . . monks only, and them that have occupied the mountains, but every believer; though he be a secular person, yet if he be hungry, and famishing, and naked, and a stranger, God's will is that he should have the benefit of all this care. For baptism renders a man a brother, and the partaking of the divine mysteries.

2. Then, in order that you may see in another way the justice of the sentence, Jesus first praises them that have done right, and says,

2. Hosea 6:6.
3. Matthew 11:22.

"Come, you blessed of my Father, inherit the kingdom prepared for you before the foundation of the world. For I was hungry, and you gave me food," and all that follows.[4] So that they could not say that they were incapable of this service, Jesus condemns them [the goats] by their fellow-servants; like the virgins were condemned alongside the faithful virgins, and the servant that was drunken and gluttonous alongside the faithful servant, and the man that buried his talent alongside the man that invested his two, and each one of those who continue in sin alongside those that have done right.

And this comparison is sometimes made in the case of an equal, as here, and in the instance of the virgins. Sometimes the comparison is made of people who have an advantage, as when Jesus said, "The men of Nineveh will rise up and will condemn this generation, because they believed at the preaching of Jonah; and, behold, a greater than Jonah is here"; and, "The queen of the south will condemn this generation, because she came to hear the wisdom of Solomon";[5] and of an equal again, "They will be your judges";[6] and again of one at advantage, "Know you not, that we will judge angels, much more things that pertain to this life?"[7]

And here, however, it is of an equal; for he compares rich with rich, and poor with poor. And not only in this way does Jesus show the sentence justly passed, by the example of their fellow-servants having done what was right when in the same circumstances, but also by their disobedient in these things in which poverty was no hindrance; as, for instance, in giving drink to the thirsty, in visiting him that is in bonds, in visiting the sick. And when he had commended them that had done right, he shows how great was originally his bond of love towards them. For, "Come," he says, "you blessed of my Father, inherit the kingdom prepared for you from the foundation of the world." To how many good things is this equivalent, to be blessed, and blessed of the Father? And why were they counted worthy of such great honors?

4. Matthew 25:34–40.
5. Matthew 12:41–42.
6. Matthew 12:27.
7. 1 Corinthians 6:3.

What is the cause? "I was hungry, and you gave me bread; I was thirsty, and you gave me drink"; and what follows.

Of what honor, of what blessedness are these words? He did not say to "take," but, to "inherit," as one's own, as your Father's, as yours, as is due to you from the first. He says, before you existed these things had been prepared, and made ready for you, for I knew you would be such as you are.

And in return for what do they receive such things? For the covering of a roof, for a garment, for bread, for cold water, for visiting, for going into the prison. For indeed in every case it is for what is needed; and sometimes not even for that. For surely, as I have said, the sick and he that is in bonds seeks not for this only, but the one to be loosed, the other to be delivered from his infirmity. But he, being gracious, requires only what is within our power, or rather even less than what is within our power, leaving to us to exert our generosity in doing more.

But to the others he says, "Depart from me, you cursed," (no longer of the Father; for it was not he that laid a curse on them, but their own works), "into the everlasting fire, prepared," not for you, but "for the devil and his angels." For concerning the kingdom indeed, when he had said, "Come, inherit the kingdom," he added, "prepared for you before the foundation of the world"; but concerning the fire, no longer so, but, "prepared for the devil." I, he says, prepared the kingdom for you, but the fire not for you, but "for the devil and his angels"; but you have chosen this lot for yourselves. And not only in this way but also in what follows he reveals the causes for their punishment, as though the Son of Man were excusing himself.

"For I was hungry and you gave me no food," For even if the one who came to you had been your enemy, would not his sufferings have been enough to have overcome and subdued you? The merciless hunger, and cold, and bonds, and nakedness, and sickness and to wander everywhere houseless; these things are sufficient even to destroy enmity. But you did not even do these things for a friend, being at once friend, and benefactor, and Lord. Even if it is only a dog that we see hungry, we are often overcome; and though we are looking at a wild beast, we feel compassion; but seeing the Lord, do you feel no compassion?[8] And wherein are these things worthy of defense?

For if it were this only, would it not be sufficient for compensation? (I speak not of hearing such a voice, in the presence of the world, from he that sits on the Father's throne, and of obtaining the kingdom), but were not the very doing it sufficient for a reward? But now even in the presence of the world, and at the appearing of that unspeakable glory, he proclaims and crowns you, and acknowledges you as his sustainer and host, and is not ashamed of saying such things, that he may make the crown brighter for you.

So for this cause, while the one group is punished justly, the others are crowned by grace. For though they had done ten thousand things, they were generous with grace, that in return for services so small and cheap, such a heaven, and a kingdom, and so great honor, should be given them. "And it came to pass, when Jesus had finished these sayings, he said unto his disciples, you know that after two days is the Passover, and the Son of Man is betrayed to be crucified."[9] With good timing he again speaks of the passion, reminding them of the kingdom, and of the reward there, and of the deathless punishment; as though he had said, "Why are you afraid at the dangers that are for a season, when such good things await you?" . . .

4. Consider how many things of which you are guilty; and how far you are from forgiving those that have injured you, you wilt even run to them that have grieved you, in order that you may have a ground for pardon, that you may find a remedy for your own evil deeds. . . .

But if you say that you burn with the memory of the insult; call to mind if any good has been done to you by him that has offended you, and how many ills you have occasioned to others. Has he spoken ill of you, and disgraced you? Consider also that you have spoken thus of others. How then will you obtain a pardon which you do not bestow

---

8. This illusion to the feeding of pets is reminiscent of the stern admonishment of Clement concerning the well-fed nature of exotic pets relative to the starvation of the poor.

9. Matthew 26:1–2.

on others? But have you spoken ill of no one? But you have heard men speaking ill of one another, and allowed it. Neither is this guiltless.

Will you learn how good a thing it is not to remember injuries, and how this more than anything pleases God? Them that Those who exult over persons . . . He punishes . . . . [N]evertheless, it is His will that we sympathize even with these. For if we, being evil, when we are punishing a servant, if we should see one of his fellow slaves laughing, we at the same time are provoked the more, and turn our anger against him; much more will God punish them that exult over those whom He chastises. But if upon them that are chastised by God it is not right to trample, but to grieve with them, much more with them that have sinned against us. For this is love's sign; God prefers love to all things. For as in the royal purple, those are precious among the flowers and dyes, which make up this robing; so here too, these virtues are the precious ones, which preserve love. But nothing maintains love so much as the not remembering them that have sinned against us.

Why? Did not God guard the other side also? Why? Did He not drive him that hath done the wrong to him that is wronged? Does He not send him from the altar to the other, and so after the reconciliation invite him to the table? But do not therefore wait for the other to come, since thus you have lost all. For to this intent most especially does He appoint you to an unspeakable reward, that you may prevent the other, since, if you are reconciled by his entreaties, the amity is no longer the result of the divine command, but of the other party's diligence. In this case, also, you go away uncrowned, while he receives the rewards.

What are you saying? Have you an enemy, and are you not ashamed? Why is not the devil enough for us? Must we bring upon ourselves enemies of our own race also? . . . Do you know how great the pleasure is after reconciliation? . . . For that it is sweeter to love him that does us wrong than to hate him, after the enmity is done away you will be able to learn full well.

5. Why then do we imitate the mad, devouring one another, warring against our own flesh? Hear even under the Old Testament, how

great regard there was for this, "The ways of revengeful men are unto death."[10] "One man keeps anger against another, and does he seek healing of God?"[11] And "yet He allowed, 'eye for eye,' and 'tooth for tooth,' how then doth He find fault?" Because He allowed even those things, not that we should do them one to another, but that through the fear of suffering, we might abstain from the commission of crime. And besides, those acts are the fruits of a short-lived anger, but to remember injuries is the part of a soul that practices itself in evil.

But have you suffered evil? yet nothing so great, as you will do to yourself by remembering injuries. And besides, it is not possible for a good man to suffer any evil. For suppose there to be any man, having both children and a wife, and let him practice virtue, and let him have many occasions of being injured, as well abundance of possessions, as sovereign power, and many friends, and let him enjoy honor; only let him practice virtue, for this must be added, and let us in supposition lay plagues upon him. And let some wicked man come unto him, and involve him in losses. What then is that to him who accounts money nothing? Let him kill his children. What is this to him, who learns to be wise touching the resurrection? Let him slay his wife; what is this to him who is instructed not to sorrow for them that are fallen asleep? let him cast him into dishonor. What is this to him who accounts the things present, the flower of the grass? If you will, let him also torture his body, and cast him into prison, what is this to him that has learned, "Though our outward man perish, yet the inward man is renewed";[12] and that "suffering produces perseverance?"[13]

Now I had undertaken that he should receive no harm; but the account as it proceeded has shown that he is even advantaged, being renewed, and becoming approved.

Let us not then vex ourselves with others, injuring ourselves, and rendering our souls weak. For the vexation is not so much from our neighbors' wickedness, as from our weakness. Because of this, should anyone insult us, we weep, and frown; should any one rob us, we suf-

10. Proverbs 12:28, from the Septuagint.
11. Sirach 28:3.
12. 2 Corinthians 4:16.
13. Romans 5:3–4.

fer the same like those little children, which the more clever of their companions provoke for nothing, grieving them for small causes; but nevertheless these too, if they should see them vexed, continue to tease them, but if laughing, they on the contrary leave off. But we are more foolish even than these, lamenting for these things, about which we ought to laugh.

Therefore I beg, let us let go of this childish mind, and lay hold of Heaven. For indeed, Christ wills us to be human, perfect humans. This is why Paul also command, "Brethren, be not children in understanding," he said, "but in evil be like children."[14] Let us therefore be children in malice, and flee wickedness, and lay hold on virtue, that we may attain also to the good things eternal, by the grace and love towards man of our Lord Jesus Christ, to whom be glory and might, world without end. Amen.

14. 1 Corinthians 14:20.

Reading Questions

1. Who are "the least of these" in this sermon?

2. Who are the "goats"? What are they like?

3. How does Chrysostom connect this parable to the issue of forgiveness?

4. Chrysostom emphasizes God's love and the power of forgetting the wrongs done against us. Reflect on the phrase "forgive and forget" in light of Chrysostom's sermon.

5. What do you think of Chrysostom's Job-like character, the hypothetical man who loses his family and is tortured? Do you agree with his opinion about suffering?

For Further Reading

Clark, Elizabeth A. *Jerome, Chrysostom, and Friends: Essays and Translations.* Studies in Women and Religion 2. Lewiston, NY: Mellen, 1979.

Kelly, J. N. D. *Golden Mouth: The Story of John Chrysostom, Ascetic, Preacher, Bishop.* 1995. Reprinted, Grand Rapids: Baker, 1998.

Mayer, Wendy. *John Chrysostom.* Early Church Fathers. London: Routledge, 2000.

Palladius. *Dialogue on the Life of St. John Chrysostom.* Edited and translated by Robert T. Mayer. Ancient Christian Writers 45. New York: Newman, 1985.

Sterk, Andrea. *Renouncing the World Yet Leading the Church: The Monk-Bishop in Late Antiquity.* Cambridge: Harvard University Press, 2004.

Wilken, Robert L. "John Chrysostom." In *Encyclopedia of Early Christianity,* edited by Everett Ferguson, 495–97. New York: Garland, 1990.

———. *John Chrysostom and the Jews: Rhetoric and Reality in the Late Fourth Century.* The Transformation of the Classical Heritage 4. 1983. Reprinted, Eugene, OR: Wipf & Stock, 2004.

11

St. Ambrose

❅

The following is an excerpt from a guide written by St. Ambrose (340–397) for the clergy in his diocese. Very concerned about the example that ministers must set for their people, St. Ambrose emphasized the importance of high moral values for clergy. There is a consistent emphasis in this book on the ways that Christian clergy differ from secular leaders. In this passage St. Ambrose is exhorting ministers to consider themselves deeply obligated to Christians who are being held captive. Fearing that they will be badly mistreated in captivity, or that they will be exposed to pagan religious idols, Ambrose is encouraging clergy to go to great lengths to embrace their obligation toward these captives.

An interesting biographical note is relevant here. When Ambrose was asked to become the Bishop of Milan he refused at first, not considering himself worthy of such a position. He accepted eventually, but only to quell violence that erupted over the struggle for a new bishop. He was not even baptized when he was selected, but when he finally agreed to become bishop he was baptized, ordained, and consecrated as a bishop all on the same day, December 7, 374! Also on that busy day (or shortly thereafter), he gave all of his considerable wealth to the poor and to the church, partly for the good his wealth could accomplish for the needy, and partly to be an example to his new flock.

. . .

On the Duties of the Clergy: Chapter 28[1]

Mercy must be freely shown even though it brings odium of its own. With regard to this, reference is made to the well-known story about the sacred vessels which were broken up by Ambrose to pay for the redemption of captives; and very beautiful advice is given about the right use of the gold and silver which the Church possesses. Next, after showing from the action of holy Lawrence what are the true treasures of the Church, certain rules are laid down which ought to be observed in melting down and employing for such uses the consecrated vessels of the Church.

136. It is a very great incentive to mercy to share in others' misfortunes, to help the needs of others as far as our means allow, and sometimes even beyond them. For it is better for mercy's sake to take up a case, or to suffer odium rather than to show hard feeling. So I once brought odium on myself because I broke up the sacred vessels to redeem captives—a fact that could displease the Arians. Not that it displeased them as an act, but as being a thing in which they could take hold of something for which to blame me. Who can be so hard, cruel, iron-hearted, as to be displeased because a man is redeemed from death, or a woman from barbarian impurities, things that are worse than death, or boys and girls and infants from the pollution of idols, whereby through fear of death they were defiled?

137. Although we did not act thus without good reason, yet we have followed it up among the people so as to confess and to add again and again that it was far better to preserve souls than gold for the Lord. For He Who sent the apostles without gold also brought together the churches without gold. The Church has gold, not to store up, but to lay out, and to spend on those who need. What necessity is there to guard what is of no good? Do we not know how much gold and silver the Assyrians took out of the temple of the Lord?[2] Is it not much better that the priests should melt it down for the sustenance of the poor, if

---

1. From *Nicene and Post-Nicene Fathers of the Christian Church,* Volume X, Second Series (Grand Rapids: Christian Classics Ethereal Library). Text translated by H. DeRomestin, edited by Philip Schaff and Henry Wace. This translation has been modified and modernized by the editor of this volume.

2. 2 Kings 24:13.

other supplies fail, than that a sacrilegious enemy should carry it off and defile it? Would not the Lord Himself say: Why did you suffer so many needy to die of hunger? Surely you had gold? You should have given them sustenance. Why are so many captives brought on the slave market, and why are so many unredeemed left to be slain by the enemy? It had been better to preserve living vessels than gold ones.

138. To this no answer could be given. For what would you say: I feared that the temple of God would need its ornaments? He would answer: The sacraments need not gold, nor are they proper to gold only—for they are not bought with gold. The glory of the sacraments is the redemption of captives. Truly they are precious vessels, for they redeem men from death. That, indeed, is the true treasure of the Lord which effects what His blood affected. Then, indeed, is the vessel of the Lord's blood recognized, when one sees in either redemption, so that the chalice redeems from the enemy those whom His blood redeemed from sin. How beautifully it is said, when long lines of captives are redeemed by the Church: These Christ has redeemed. Behold the gold that can be tried, behold the useful gold, behold the gold of Christ which frees from death, behold the gold whereby modesty is redeemed and chastity is preserved.

139. These, then, I preferred to hand over to you as free men, rather than to store up the gold. This crowd of captives, this company surely is more glorious than the sight of cups. The gold of the Redeemer ought to contribute to this work so as to redeem those in danger. I recognize the fact that the blood of Christ not only glows in cups of gold, but also by the office of redemption has impressed upon them the power of the divine operation.

140. Such gold the holy martyr Lawrence preserved for the Lord. For when the treasures of the Church were demanded from him, he promised that he would show them. On the following day he brought the poor together. When asked where the treasures were which he had promised, he pointed to the poor, saying: "These are the treasures of

the Church." And truly they were treasures, in whom Christ lives, in whom there is faith in Him. So, too, the Apostle says: "We have this treasure in earthen vessels."[3] What greater treasures has Christ than those in whom He says He Himself lives? For thus it is written: "I was hungry and you gave Me to eat, I was thirsty and you gave Me to drink, I was a stranger and you took Me in."[4] And again: "What you did to one of these, you did it to Me."[5] What better treasures has Jesus than those in which He loves to be seen?

141. These treasures Lawrence pointed out, and prevailed, for the persecutors could not take them away. Jehoiachim,[6] who preserved his gold during the siege and spent it not in providing food, saw his gold carried off, and himself led into captivity. Lawrence, who preferred to spend the gold of the Church on the poor, rather than to keep it in hand for the persecutor, received the sacred crown of martyrdom for the unique and deep-sighted vigor of his meaning. Or was it perhaps said to holy Lawrence: "You should not spend the treasures of the Church, or sell the sacred vessels"?

142. It is necessary that every one should fill this office, with genuine good faith and clear-sighted forethought. If any one derives profit from it for himself it is a crime, but if he spends the treasures on the poor, or redeems captives, he shows mercy. For no one can say: Why does the poor man live? None can complain that captives are redeemed, none can find fault because a temple of the Lord is built, none can be angry because a plot of ground has been enlarged for the burial of the bodies of the faithful, none can be vexed because in the tombs of the Christians there is rest for the dead. In these three ways it is allowable to break up, melt down, or sell even the sacred vessels of the Church.

143. It is necessary to see that the mystic cup does not go out of the Church, lest the service of the sacred chalice should be turned over to base uses. Therefore vessels were first sought for in the Church which had not been consecrated to such holy uses. Then broken up

3. 2 Corinthians 4:7.
4. Matthew 25:35.
5. Matthew 25:40.
6. 2 Kings 23:35.

and afterwards melted down, they were given to the poor in small payments, and were also used for the ransom of captives. But if new vessels fail, or those which never seem to have been used for such a holy purpose, then, as I have already said, I think that all might be put to this use without irreverence.

Reading Questions

1. Who are "the least of these" in this passage? How are their needs to be addressed? How do the concerns of St. Ambrose enlighten our understanding of their persecution?

2. What sort of temptations are St. Ambrose steering ministers away from?

3. From this passage and the biographical note above, construct a "philosophy of money" (gold) according to St. Ambrose.

4. This treatise was probably composed around 391 in Milan, Italy. What social and political factors are at play in that setting?

For Further Reading

Burrus, Virginia. *"Begotten, not Made": Conceiving Manhood in Late Antiquity.* Figurae: Reading Medieval Culture. Stanford: Stanford University Press, 2000.

Dudden, F. Holmes. *The Life and Times of St. Ambrose.* Oxford: Clarendon, 1935.

McLinn, Neil. *Ambose of Milan: Church and Court in a Christian Capital.* The Transformation of the Classical Heritage 22. Berkeley: University of California Press, 1994.

Paredi, Angelo. *Saint Ambrose: His Life and Times.* Translated by M. Joseph Costelloe. Notre Dame: University of Notre Dame Press, 1964.

Swift, Louis J. "Ambrose." In *Encyclopedia of Early Christianity,* edited by Everett Ferguson, 30–32. New York: Garland, 1990.

12

Jerome

Jerome's biography crosses paths with a number of important figures during his lifetime (ca. 347–420). He studied for years under Gregory of Nazianzus, was compelled to study Scripture by Apollinaris (before Apollinaris was suspected of heresy), and wrote prolifically and with a careful eye for theological detail. Jerome made a translation of the Bible from Hebrew and Greek into Latin. This translation, called the Vulgate, continues to be the official translation for the Roman Catholic Church and has exerted a great deal of influence on our contemporary understanding of Scripture.

A great deal of Christian theology occurs in the very practical format of letters. Most of the books of the New Testament are written in the form of a letter; letters are remarkably revealing media for understanding both authors and recipients. In the following letter Jerome writes to a widow named Furia, who has struggled with the various options open to her as a Christian widow. Should she remarry or not? Jerome has counseled her to use her "widowhood" for Christ rather than remarry, which Jerome considered to be a spiritual mistake. In this letter he attempts to lay out for her a way of life that will help her preserve the nobility of her character as a Christian widow. You may see why the well-adorned wife of the emperor disliked Jerome in the strict treatment of makeup and flashy clothing in the letter below.

. . .

Letter 54: To Furia[1]

1. You beg and implore me in your letter to write to you—or rather write back to you—what mode of life you ought to adopt to preserve the crown of widowhood and to keep your reputation for chastity unsullied. My mind rejoices, my reins exult, and my heart is glad that you desire to be after marriage what your mother Titiana of holy memory was for a long time in marriage.[2] Her prayers and supplications are heard. She has succeeded in winning afresh in her only daughter that which she herself when living possessed. It is a high privilege of your family that from the time of Camillus[3] few or none of your house are described as contracting second marriages. Therefore it will not redound so much to your praise if you continue a widow as to your shame if being a Christian you fail to keep what heathen women have jealously guarded for so many centuries. . . .

4. What troubles matrimony involves you have learned in the marriage state itself; you have been surfeited with quails' flesh[4] even to loathing; your mouth has been filled with the gall of bitterness; you have expelled the indigestible and unwholesome food; you have relieved a heaving stomach. Why will you again swallow what has disagreed with you? "The dog is turned to his own vomit again and the sow that was washed to her wallowing in the mire."[5] Even brute beasts and flying birds do not fall into the same snares twice. Do you fear extinction for the line of Camillus if you do not present your father with some little fellow to crawl upon his breast and slobber his neck? As if all who marry have children! and as if when they do come, they always resemble their forefathers! Did Cicero's son exhibit his father's eloquence? . . . It is ridiculous to expect as certain the offspring which many, as you can see, have not got, while others who have had it have

---

1. From *Nicene and Post-Nicene Fathers*, Volume VI (Grand Rapids: Christian Classics Ethereal Library). Text translated by W. H. Fremantle and edited by Philip Schaff and Henry Wace, first published in Edinburgh, 1892. A number of modernizing changes have been made to this translation.

2. Jerome is praising her for her choice to be celibate.

3. Lucius Furius Camillus was an important Roman consul, AD 349.

4. Numbers 11:20, 31–34.

5. 1 Peter 2:22.

lost it again. To whom then are you to leave your great riches? To Christ who cannot die. Whom will you make your heir? The same who is already your Lord. Your father will be sorry but Christ will be glad; your family will grieve but the angels will rejoice with you. Let your father do what he likes with what is his own. You are not his to whom you have been born, but His to whom you have been born again, and who has purchased you at a great price with His own blood.[6]

5. Beware of nurses and waiting maids and similar venomous creatures who try to satisfy their greed by sucking your blood. They advise you to do not what is best for you but what is best for them. They are for ever dinning into your ears Virgil's lines:

> Will you waste all your youth in lonely grief
> And children sweet, the gifts of love, forswear?[7]

Wherever there is holy chastity, there is also frugal living; and wherever there is frugal living, servants lose by it. What they do not get is in their minds so much taken from them. The actual sum received is what they look to, and not its relative amount. The moment they see a Christian they at once repeat the hackneyed saying:—"The Greek! The impostor!" They spread the most scandalous reports and, when any such emanates from themselves, they pretend that they have heard it from others, managing thus at once to originate the story and to exaggerate it. A lying rumor goes forth; and this, when it has reached the married ladies and has been fanned by their tongues, spreads through the provinces. You may see numbers of these—their faces painted, their eyes like those of vipers, their teeth rubbed with pumice-stone—raving and carping at Christians with insane fury. . . . Hereupon the rest chime in and every bench expresses hoarse approval. They are backed up by men of my own order who, finding themselves assailed, assail others. Always fluent in attacking me, they are dumb in their own defense; just as though they were not monks themselves, and as though

6. Acts 20:28.

7. From Virgil, *The Aeneid* 4. The following is an alternative translation of this verse by John Dryden:

> Will you to grief your blooming years bequeath, Condemn'd to waste in woes your lonely life, Without the joys of mother or of wife?

every word said against monks did not tell also against their spiritual progenitors the clergy. Harm done to the flock brings discredit on the shepherd. On the other hand we cannot but praise the life of a monk who holds up to veneration the priests of Christ and refuses to detract from that order to which he owes it that he is a Christian. . . .

7. In the gospel a harlot wins salvation. How? She is baptized in her tears and wipes the Lord's feet with that same hair with which she had before deceived many. She does not wear a waving headdress or creaking boots, she does not darken her eyes with antimony. Yet in her squalor she is lovelier than ever. What place have rouge and white lead on the face of a Christian woman? The one simulates the natural red of the cheeks and of the lips; the other the whiteness of the face and of the neck. They serve only to inflame young men's passions, to stimulate lust, and to indicate an unchaste mind. How can a woman weep for her sins whose tears lay bare her true complexion and mark furrows on her cheeks? Such adorning is not of the Lord; a mask of this kind belongs to Antichrist. With what confidence can a woman raise features to heaven which her Creator must fail to recognize? It is idle to allege in excuse for such practices girlishness and youthful vanity. A widow who has ceased to have a husband to please, and who in the apostle's language is a widow indeed,[8] needs nothing more but perseverance only. She is mindful of past enjoyments; she knows what gave her pleasure and what she has now lost. By rigid fast and vigil she must quench the fiery darts of the devil.[9] If we are widows, we must either speak as we are dressed, or else dress as we speak. Why do we profess one thing, and practice another? The tongue talks of chastity, but the rest of the body reveals incontinence.

9. . . . I seek to remove from youths and girls what are incentives to sensual pleasure. Neither the fiery Etna nor the country of Vulcan,[10] nor Vesuvius, nor Olympus, burns with such violent heat as the youthful marrow of those who are flushed with wine and filled with food. Many trample covetousness under foot, and lay it down as readily as they lay down their purse. An enforced silence serves to make amends

8. 1 Timothy 5:5.
9. Ephesians 6:16.
10. The volcanic island of Lemnos.

for a railing tongue. The outward appearance and the mode of dress can be changed in a single hour. All other sins are external, and what is external can easily be cast away. Desire alone, implanted in men by God to lead them to procreate children, is internal; and this, if it once oversteps its own bounds, becomes a sin, and by a law of nature cries out for sexual intercourse. It is therefore a work of great merit, and one which requires unremitting diligence to overcome that which is innate in you; while living in the flesh not to live after the flesh; to strive with yourself day by day and to watch the foe shut up within you with the hundred eyes of the fabled Argus. . . .

12. Make to yourself friends of the mammon of unrighteousness that they may receive you into everlasting habitations.[11] Give your riches not to those who feed on pheasants but to those who have none but common bread to eat, such as stays hunger while it does not stimulate lust. Consider the poor and needy. Give to everyone that asks of you, but especially unto them who are of the household of faith.[12] Clothe the naked, feed the hungry, visit the sick. Every time that you hold out your hand, think of Christ.[13] See to it that you do not, when the Lord your God asks alms of you, increase riches which are none of His. . . .

14. You have wealth and can easily therefore supply food to those who want it. Let virtue consume what was provided for self-indulgence; one who means to despise matrimony need fear no degree of want. Have about you troops of virgins whom you may lead into the king's chamber. Support widows that you may mingle them as a kind of violets with the virgins' lilies and the martyrs' roses. Such are the garlands you must weave for Christ in place of that crown of thorns in which he bore the sins of the world. Let your most noble father thus find in you his joy and support, let him learn from his daughter the lessons he used to learn from his wife. His hair is already gray, his knees tremble, his teeth fall out, his brow is furrowed through years, death is nigh even at the doors, the pyre is all but laid out hard by. Whether we like it or not, we grow old. Let him provide for himself the provision

11. Luke 16:9.
12. Galatians 6:10.
13. Matthew 25:35–36.

which is needful for his long journey. Let him take with him what otherwise he must unwillingly leave behind, nay let him send before him to heaven what if he declines it, will be appropriated by earth.

15. Young widows, of whom some "are already turned aside after Satan, when they have begun to wax wanton against Christ"[14] and wish to marry, generally make such excuses as these. "My little patrimony is daily decreasing, the property which I have inherited is being squandered, a servant has spoken insultingly to me, a maid has neglected my orders. Who will appear for me before the authorities? Who will be responsible for the rents of my estates? Who will see to the education of my children, and to the bringing up of my servants?" Thus, shameful to say, they put that forward as a reason for marrying again, which alone should deter them from doing so. For by marrying again a mother places over her sons not a guardian but a foe, not a father but a tyrant. Inflamed by her passions she forgets the fruit of her womb, and among the children who know nothing of their sad fate the lately weeping widow dresses herself once more as a bride. Why these excuses about your property and the insolence of servants? Confess the shameful truth. No woman marries to avoid cohabiting with a husband. At least, if passion is not your motive, it is mere madness to play the harlot just to increase wealth. You do but purchase a paltry and passing gain at the price of a grace which is precious and eternal! If you have children already, why do you want to marry? If you have none, why do you not fear a recurrence of your former sterility? Why do you put an uncertain gain before a certain loss of self-respect?

A marriage-settlement is made in your favor today but in a short time you will be constrained to make your will. Your husband will feign sickness and will do for you what he wants you to do for him. Yet he is sure to live and you are sure to die. Or if it happens that you have sons by the second husband, domestic strife is certain to result and intestine disputes. You will not be allowed to love your first children, nor to look kindly on those to whom you have yourself given birth. You will have to give them their food secretly; yet even so your present husband will bear a grudge against your previous one and, unless you hate your sons, he will think that you still love their father. But your

14. 1 Timothy 5:15, 11.

husband may have issue by a former wife. If so when he takes you to his home, though you should be the kindest person in the world, all the commonplaces of rhetoricians and declamations of comic poets and writers of mimes will be hurled at you as a cruel stepmother. If your stepson fall sick or have a headache you will be calumniated as a poisoner. If you refuse him food, you will be cruel, while if you give it, you will be held to have bewitched him. I ask you what benefit has a second marriage to confer great enough to compensate for these evils?

. . . That I may not exceed the limits of a letter, I will only give you this one last piece of advice. Think every day that you must die, and you will then never think of marrying again.

Reading Questions

1. What are the pressures on Furia? Are they familiar to contemporary widows?

2. Does it seem like Furia's first marriage was a happy one? Why or why not?

3. Why is Matthew 25:31–41 invoked here? Who are "the least of these"?

4. What do you think of Jerome's evaluation of sexuality and sexual desire?

5. What are the "fiery darts of the devil"?

For Further Reading

Adams, Jeremy DuQuesnay. *The Populus of Augustine and Jerome: A Study in the Patristic Sense of Community.* New Haven: Yale University Press, 1971.

Clark, Elizabeth A. *Jerome, Chrysostom, and Friends: Essays and Translations.* Studies in Women and Religion 2. Lewiston, NY: Mellen, 1979.

Kelly, J. N. D. *Jerome: His Life, Writings, and Controversies.* 1975. Reprinted, Peabody, MA: Hendrickson, 1998.

McHugh, Michael P. "Jerome." In *Encyclopedia of Early Christianity,* edited by Everett Ferguson, 484–87. New York: Garland, 1990.

Rebenich, Stefan. *Jerome.* Early Church Fathers. London: Routledge, 2002.

Sparks, H. F. D. "Jerome as Biblical Scholar." In *The Cambridge History of the Bible,* edited by P. R. Ackroyd, 1:510–41. Cambridge: Cambridge University Press, 1970.

13

Theodoret

Theodoret (393–457) played an important role in the divisive conflict surrounding the condemnation of Nestorius. Cyril of Alexandria was determined to condemn Nestorius as a heretic. Theodoret, a bishop who was deeply concerned about the plight of the poor and overtaxed, attempted to show that a compromise could be made between the orthodox faith and Nestorius. Theodoret was a casualty of these doctrinal skirmishes, being named a heretic himself and banished for many years before eventually being rehabilitated.

This short note below was written by Theodoret to Longinus, whose identity is unknown. It seems to have been written near the end of Theodoret's period in exile (450), where he wrote a number of letters to the Pope and to his friends in attempts to be reconciled with the church.

.   .   .

Letter 131: To Longinus, Archimandrite of Doliche[1]

You have shown alike your zeal for the true religion, and your love for your neighbor, both of which are at the present time clearly connected, for it is for the sake of the apostolic decrees that I am being attacked, because I refuse to give up the heritage of my fathers, and prefer to undergo any suffering to looking lightly on the robbery of one tittle from the faith of the Gospel. You have accepted fellowship in my sufferings, not only by comforting me by means of your letter, but further by sending to me the very honorable and pious Matthew and Isaac. You will hear, I am well assured, from the lips of the righteous Lord, "I was in prison, and you visited me."[2] We are small and of no account, and burdened by a great load of sins, but the Lord is bountiful and generous. He remembers the small rather than the great, and says, "Inasmuch as you have done it unto one of the least of these"[3] "which believe in me"[4] "you have done it unto me."[5] I pray you in that you are conspicuous for right doctrine, and shine by worthiness of life, and therefore have great boldness before God, help me in your prayers, that I may be able "to stand," to use the words of the Apostle, "against the wiles of error,"[6] escape the sins of the destroyer, and stand, though with little boldness, in the day of the appearing before the righteous Judge.

1. From *Nicene and Post-Nicene Fathers*, Second Series, Volume III (Grand Rapids: Christian Classics Ethereal Library). Text translated by Blomfield Jackson and edited by Philip Schaff, first published in Edinburgh, 1892.

2. Matthew 25:36.

3. Matthew 25:40.

4. Matthew 18:6.

5. Matthew 25:40.

6. Ephesians 4:14; 6:11. Theodoret is probably quoting from memory.

Reading Question

1. What does Theodoret see in the Parable of the Sheep and the Goats that unites love for God and love for neighbor?

2. Twice in this short letter Theodoret uses a controversial method of quoting Scripture. In his "least of these" reference, he inserts a line from Matthew 18, replacing "my brethren" with "which believe in me." Later in the same note he blends together two references from Ephesians as though Paul offered them as a single statement. Is this an acceptable way of using Scripture? Why or why not?

For Further Reading

Ellington, Gerald H. "Theodoret of Cyrus." In *Encyclopedia of Early Christianity*, edited by Everett Ferguson, 889–91. New York: Garland, 1990.

Pásztori-Kupán, István. *Theodoret of Cyrus*. The Early Church Fathers. London: Routledge, 2006.

Urbainczyk, Theresa. *Theodoret of Cyrrhus: The Bishop and the Holy Man*. Ann Arbor: University of Michigan Press, 2002.

14

Augustine

✿

Augustine (354–430) is considered by many Christians, particularly in the West, to be the most influential theologian in Christian history. From his probing self-reflection in this book Confessions, to his political dealings with the Donatists, to his resounding rejection of Pelagianism, Augustine remains theologically and historically pivotal. His influence on Western Christianity can hardly be overestimated.

Augustine makes mention of the Matthean parable more than one hundred times in his vast corpus,[1] so there are plenty of places where we can access his various interpretations of this parable. In the sermon below Augustine preaches against the hording of wealth and for a lifestyle of almsgiving. Augustine finds fascinating ways to weave his theology into the practical concerns of the people who listen to him preach.

. . .

1. Gray, *The Least of My Brothers*, 69.

Sermon 60: On the Words of the Gospel, Matthew 4:19, "Lay not up for yourselves treasures upon earth." An exhortation on alms deeds[2]

1. Every man who is in any trouble, and his own resources fail him, looks out for some prudent person from whom he may take counsel, and so know what to do. Let us suppose then the whole world to be as it were one single man. He seeks to escape evil, yet is slow in doing good; and as in this way tribulations thicken, and his own resources fail, whom can he find more prudent to receive counsel from than Christ? By all means, at least, let him find a better, and do what he will. But if he cannot find a better, let him come to Him whom he may find everywhere: let him consult and take advice from Him, keep the good commandment, escape the great evil. For present temporal ills of which men are so sore afraid, under which they murmur exceedingly, and by their murmuring offend Him who is correcting them, so that they find not His saving help; present ills I say without a doubt are but passing; either they pass through us, or we pass through them; either they pass away whilst we live, or they are left behind us when we die. Now that is not in the matter of tribulation great, which in duration is short. Whoever thinks about tomorrow, fails to recall the remembrance of yesterday. When the day after tomorrow comes, this tomorrow also will be yesterday; But now if men are so disquieted with anxiety to escape temporal tribulations which pass, or rather fly over, what thought ought they to take that they may escape those which abide and endure without end?

2. A hard condition is the life of man. What else is it to be born, but to enter on a life of toil? Of our toil that is to be, the infant's very cry is witness. From this cup of sorrow no one may be excused. The cup that Adam has pledged must be drunk. We were made, it is true, by the hands of Truth, but because of sin we were cast forth upon days of vanity. "We were made after the image of God," but we disfigured it by sinful transgression. Therefore does the Psalm remind us how we

2. From *Nicene and Post-Nicene Fathers* (Grand Rapids: Christian Classics Ethereal Library). Text edited by Philip Schaff and published in Edinburgh, 1887. A number of modernizing changes have been made to this translation.

were made, and to what a state we have come. For it says "Though a man walk in the image of God." See, what he was made. From where has he come? Listen to what follows, "Yet will he be disquieted in vain." He walks in the image of truth, and will be disquieted in the counsel of vanity. Finally, see his disquiet, see it, and as it were in a glass, be displeased with yourself. "Though," he says, "man walk in the image of God," and therefore be something great, "yet will he be disquieted in vain";[3] and as though we might ask, How: I pray, how is man disquieted in vain? "He heaps up treasure," he says, "and knows not for whom he gathers it." See then, this man, that is the whole human race represented as one man, who is without resource in his own case, and has lost counsel and wandered out of the way of a sound mind . . . What is more mad, what more unhappy? But surely he is doing it for himself? Not so. Why not for himself? Because he must die, because the life of man is short, because the treasure lasts, but he who gathers it quickly passes away. As pitying therefore the man who "walks in the image of God," who confesses things that are true, yet follows after vain things, he says, "He will be disquieted in vain." I grieve for him; "he heaps up treasure, and knows not for whom he gathers it." Does he gather it for himself? No. Because the man dies while the treasure endures. For whom then? If you have any good counsel, give it to me. But you have no counsel to give me, and so you have none for yourself. Wherefore if we are both without it, let us both seek it, let us both receive it, and both consider the matter together. He is disquieted, he heaps up treasure, he thinks, and toils, and is kept awake by anxiety. All day long you are harassed by labor, all night agitated by fear. So that your coffer may be filled with money, your soul is in a fever of anxiety.

3. I see it, I am grieved for you; you are disquieted, and as He who cannot deceive, assures us, "You are disquieted in vain." For you are heaping up treasures: supposing that all your undertakings succeed, to say nothing of losses, of so great perils and deaths in the prosecution of every several kind of gain (I speak not of deaths of the body, but of evil thoughts, for that gold may come in, uprightness goes out; that you may be clothed outwardly, you are made naked within), but to pass

3. Psalm 39:6, from the Septuagint.

over these, and other such things in silence, to pass by all the things that are against you, let us think only of the favorable circumstances. See, you are laying up treasures, gains flow into you from every quarter, and your money runs like fountains; everywhere where want presses, there flows abundance. Have you not heard, "If riches increase, set not your heart upon them?" You are getting, you are disquieted, not fruitlessly indeed, still in vain. "How," you will ask "am I disquieted in vain? I am filling my coffers, my walls will scarce hold what I get, how then am I disquieted in vain?" "You art heaping up treasure, and do not know for whom you gather it." Or if you do know, I pray you tell me. I will listen to you. For whom is it? If you are not disquieted in vain, tell me for whom you are heaping up your treasure? "For myself," you say. Do you dare say so, who must so soon die? "For my children." Do you dare say this of them who must so soon die? It is a great duty of natural affection (it will be said) for a father to lay up for his sons; rather it is a great vanity, one who must soon die is laying up for those who must soon die also. If it is for yourself, why do you gather, seeing you leave all when you die? This is the case also with your children; they will succeed you, but not to abide long. I say nothing about what sort of children they may be, whether debauchery may not waste what covetousness has amassed. So another by dissoluteness squanders what you by much toil have gathered together. But I pass over this. It may be they will be good children, they will not be dissolute, they will keep what you have left, will increase what you have kept, and will not dissipate what you have heaped together. Then will your children be equally vain with yourself, if they do so, if in this they imitate you their father. I would say to them what I said just now to you. I would say to your son, to him for whom you are saving, "You are heaping up treasure, and know not for whom you gather it." For as you knew not, neither does he know. If the vanity has continued in him, has the truth lost its power with respect to him?

4. I forbear to urge, that it may be even during your life you are but laying up for thieves. In one night they may come and find all ready the gathering of so many days and nights. It may be you are lay-ing up for a robber, or a highwayman. I will say no more on this, lest I call to mind and re-open the wound of past sufferings. How many

things which an empty vanity has heaped together, has the cruelty of an enemy found ready to its hand. It is not my place to wish for this: but it is the concern of all to fear it. May God avert it! May His own scourges be sufficient. May He to whom we pray, spare us! But if He asks you for whom are we are . . . [storing up treasure for], what will we answer? How then, O man, whoever you are, that are heaping up treasure in vain, how will you answer me, as I handle this matter with you, and with you seek counsel in a common cause? For you did speak and make answer, "I am laying up for myself, for my children, for my posterity." I have said already how many grounds of fear there are, even as to those children themselves. But I pass over the consideration, that your children may so live as to be a curse to you, and as your enemy would wish them; grant that they live as the father himself would have them. Yet how many have fallen into those bad fortunes, I have declared, and reminded you of already. You shuddered at them, though you did not amend yourself. For what have you to answer but this, "Perhaps it may not be so"? Well, I said so too; perhaps I say you are but laying up for the thief, or robber, or highwayman. I did not say certainly, but perhaps. Where there is a perhaps, there is a perhaps-not; so then you know not what will be, and therefore you "are disquieted in vain." You see now how truly spoken the Truth, how vainly vanity is disquieted. You have heard and at length learned wisdom, because when you say, "Perhaps it is for my children," but do not dare to say, "I am sure that it is for my children," you do not in fact know for whom you are gathering riches. So then, as I see, and have said already, you are yourself without resource; you find nothing wherewith to answer me, nor can I to answer you.

5. Let us both therefore seek and ask for counsel. We have opportunity of consulting not any wise man, but Wisdom Herself. Let us then both give ear to Jesus Christ, "to the Jews a stumbling stone, and to the Gentiles foolishness, but to them who are called, both Jews and Greeks, Christ the Power of God and the Wisdom of God."[4] Why are you preparing a strong defense for your riches? Hear the Power of God; nothing is stronger than He. Why are you preparing wise counsels to protect your riches? Hear the Wisdom of God, nothing is Wiser

4. 1 Corinthians 1:23–24.

than He. Perhaps when I say what I have to say, you will be offended, and so you will be a Jew, "because to the Jews is Christ an offence."[5] Or perhaps, when I have spoken, it will appear foolish to you, and so will you be a Gentile, "for to the Gentiles is Christ foolishness." Yet you are a Christian; you have been called. "But to them who are called, both Jews and Greeks, Christ is the Power of God and the Wisdom of God." Be not sad then when I have said what I have to say; be not offended; mock not my folly, as you deem it, with an air of disdain. Let us give ear. For what I am about to say, Christ has said. If you despise the herald, yet fear the Judge. What shall I say then? The reader of the Gospel has but just now relieved me from this embarrassment. I will not read anything fresh, but will only recall to you what has just been read. You were seeking counsel, failing in your own resources; see then what the Fountain of right counsel said, the Fountain from whose streams is no fear of poison, fill from It what you may.

6. "Lay not up for yourselves treasures on earth, where moth and rust destroy, and where thieves break through and steal: But lay up for yourselves treasures in heaven, where no thief approaches, nor moth corrupts: For where your treasure is, there will your heart be also." What more do you wait for? The thing is plain . . . For plunder does not cease its ravages; avarice does not cease to defraud; maliciousness does not cease to swear falsely. And all for what? that treasure may be heaped together. To be laid up where? In the earth, and rightly indeed, by earth for earth. For to the man who sinned[6] and who pledged us, as I have said, our cup of toil, was it said, "Earth you are, and to earth you will return."[7] With good reason is the treasure in earth, because the heart is there. Where then is that, "we lift them up unto the Lord?" Sorrow for your case, you who have understood me; and if you sorrow truly, amend yourselves. How long will you be applauding and not doing? What you have heard is true, nothing truer. Let that then which is true be done. One God we praise, yet we change not, that we may not in this very praise be disquieted in vain.

---

5. 1 Corinthians 1:23.

6. Adam.

7. Genesis 3:19, from the Septuagint.

7. Therefore, "Lay not up for yourselves treasures on earth"; whether you have found by experience how what is laid up in the earth is lost, or whether you have not so experienced it. . . . Let experience reform he who words will not reform. One cannot rise up now, one cannot go out, but all together with one voice are crying, "Woe to us, the world is falling."[8] If it be falling, why do you not remove? If an architect were to tell you that your house would soon fall, would you not remove yourself before you indulged in your vain lamentations? The Builder of the world tells you the world will soon fall, and will you not believe it? Hear the voice of Him who foretells it; hear the counsel of Him who gives you warning. The voice of prediction is, "Heaven and earth will pass away."[9] The voice of warning is, "Lay not up for yourselves treasure on earth."[10] If then you believe God in His prediction; if you despise not His warning, let what He says be done. He who has given you such counsel does not deceive you. You will not lose what you have given away, but will follow what you have sent before yourself. Therefore my counsel is, "Give to the poor, and you will have treasure in heaven."[11] You will not remain without treasure; but what you have on earth with anxiety, you will possess in heaven free from care. Therefore, transport your goods. I am giving you counsel for keeping, not for losing. "You will have," He said, "treasure in heaven, and come, follow Me," that I may bring you to your treasure. This is not a wasting, but a saving. Why do men keep silence? Let them hear, and having at last by experience found what to fear, let them do that which will give them no cause of fear, let them transport their goods to heaven. You put wheat in the low ground; and your friend comes, who knows the nature of the corn and the land, and instructs your unskillful work, and says to you, "What have you done?" You have put the corn in the flat soil, in the lower land; the soil is moist; it will all rot, and you will lose your labor. You answer, "What then must I do?" "Remove it," he says, "into the higher ground." Do you then

8. There must have been some violent turmoil occurring when Augustine spoke these words.

9. Matthew 24:35.

10. Matthew 6:19.

11. Matthew 19:21.

give ear to a friend who gives you counsel about your corn and despise God who gives you counsel about your heart? You are afraid to put your corn in the low earth, and will you lose your heart in the earth? Behold the Lord your God when He gave you counsel touching your heart, said, "Where your treasure is, there will your heart be also." Lift up your heart to heaven, He said, that it not rot in the earth. It is His counsel, who wishes to preserve your heart, not to destroy it.

8. If then this be so, what must be their repentance who have not listened and obeyed? How must they now reproach themselves! We might have had in heaven what we have now lost in earth. The enemy has broken up our house; but could he break heaven open? He has killed the servant who was set to guard; but could he kill the Lord who would have kept them "where no thief approaches, neither moth corrupts."[12] How many now are saying, "There we might have hidden our treasures safely, where after a little while we might have followed them securely. Why have we not hearkened to our Lord? Why have we despised the admonitions of the Father, and so have experienced the invasion of the enemy?"

If then this be good counsel, let us not be slow in taking heed to it; and if what we have must be transported, let us transfer it into that place, from where we cannot lose it. What are the poor to whom we give, but our couriers, by whom we convey our goods from earth to heaven? Give then: you are but giving to your courier, he carries what you give to heaven. How, you say, does he carry it to heaven? For I see that he makes an end of it by eating. No doubt, he carries it, not by keeping it, but by making it his food. What? Have you forgotten, "Come, you blessed of My Father, receive the kingdom; for I was hungry, and you gave Me meat"[13] and," Inasmuch as you did it to one of the least of Mine, you did it to Me." If you have not despised the beggar that stands before you, consider to Whom what you gaves him has come. "Inasmuch," said he, "as you did it to one of the least of Mine, you did it to Me."[14] He has received it, who gave you the

12. Matthew 6:19–21.
13. Matthew 25:34–35.
14. Matthew 25:40.

capacity to give. He has received it, who in the end will give His Own Self to you.

9. For this have I at many times called to your remembrance, Beloved, and I confess to you it astonishes me much in the Scriptures of God, and I ought repeatedly to call your attention to it. I pray you to think of what our Lord Jesus Christ Himself said, that at the end of the world, when He will come to judgment, He will gather together all nations before Him, and will divide men into two parts; that He will place some at His right hand, and others on His left; and will say to those on the right hand, "Come, you blessed of My Father, receive the kingdom prepared for you from the foundation of the world."[15] But to those on the left, "Depart into everlasting fire, prepared for the devil and his angels."[16] Search out the reasons either for so great a reward, or so great a punishment. "Receive the kingdom," and "Go into everlasting fire." Why will the first receive the kingdom? "For I was hungry, and you gave Me meat." Why will the other depart into everlasting fire? "For I was hungry, and you gave Me no meat." What does this mean, I ask? . . . Those who are to receive the kingdom gave as good and faithful Christians, not despising the words of the Lord, and with sure trust hoping for the promises they did accordingly; because had they not done so, this very barrenness would not surely have accorded with their good life. For it may be they were chaste, not cheats nor drunkards, and kept themselves from evil works. Yet if they had not added good works, they would have remained barren. For they would have kept, "Depart from evil," but they would not have kept, "and do good."[17] Notwithstanding, even to them He does not say, "Come, receive the kingdom," for you have lived in chastity; you have defrauded no man, you have not oppressed any poor man, you have invaded no one's landmark, you have deceived no one by oath. He said not this, but, "Receive the kingdom, because I was hungry, and you gave Me meat." How excellent is this above all, when the Lord made no mention of the rest, but named this only! And again to the others, "Depart into everlasting fire, prepared for the devil and his angels." How many

15. Matthew 25:34.
16. Matthew 25:41.
17. Psalm 34:14.

things could He urge against the ungodly, were they to ask, "Why are we going into everlasting fire!" Why? Do you ask, you adulterers, murderers, cheats, sacrilegious blasphemers, unbelievers. Yet none of these did He name, but, "Because I was hungry, and you gave Me no meat."

10. I see that you are surprised as I am. And indeed it is a marvelous thing. But I gather as best I can the reason of this thing so strange, and I will not conceal it from you. It is written, "As water quenches fire, so alms quench sin."[18] Again it is written, "Shut up alms in the heart of a poor man, and it will make supplication for you before the Lord."[19] Again it is written, "Hear, O king, my counsel, and redeem your sins by alms." And many other testimonies of the Divine oracles are there, whereby it is shown that alms avail much to the quenching and effacing of sins. To those whom He is about to condemn, yes, rather to those whom He is about to crown, He will impute alms only, as though He would say, "It were a hard matter for me not to find occasion to condemn you, were I to examine and weigh you accurately and with much exactness to scrutinize your deeds; but, "Go into the kingdom, for I was hungry, and you gave Me meat." You will therefore go into the kingdom, not because you have not sinned, but because you have redeemed your sins by alms. And again to the others, "Go into everlasting fire, prepared for the devil and his angels." They too, guilty as they are, old in their sins, late in their fear for them, in what respect, when they turn their sins over in their minds, could they dare to say that they are undeservedly condemned, that this sentence is pronounced against them undeservedly by so righteous a Judge? In considering their consciences, and all the wounds of their souls, in what respect could they dare to say, "we are unjustly condemned." Of whom it was said before in wisdom, "Their own iniquities will convince them to their face."[20] Without doubt they will see that they are justly condemned for their sins and wickedness; yet it will be as though He said to them, It is not in consequence of this that you think, but "because I was hungry, and you gave Me no meat." For if

18. Sirach 3:30.
19. Sirach 29:12, from the Latin Vulgate.
20. Wisdom of Solomon 4:20.

turning away from all these your deeds, and turning to Me, you had redeemed all those crimes and sins by alms, those alms would now deliver you, and absolve you from the guilt of so great offences; for, "Blessed are the merciful, for to them will be shown mercy."[21] But now go away into everlasting fire. "He will have judgment without mercy on he who has shown no mercy."[22]

11. O that I may have induced you, my brethren, to give away your earthly bread, and to knock for the heavenly! The Lord is that Bread. He said, "I am the Bread of life." But how will He give to you, who do not give to him that is in need? There is before you one in need, and you are in need before Another, and since you are in need before Another, and another is in need before you, that other is in need before him who is in need himself. For He before whom you are in need, needs nothing. Do then to others as you would have done to you. For it is not in this case as with those friends who are eager to upbraid one another with their kindnesses; as, "I did this for you," and the other answers, "and I this for you," that He wishes us to do Him some good office, because He has first done such an office for us. He is in want of nothing, and therefore is He the very Lord. I said unto the Lord, "You are my God, for You need not my goods." Notwithstanding, though He be the Lord, and the Very Lord, and need not our goods, yet that we might do something even for Him, has He vouchsafed to be hungry in His poor. "I was hungry," said He, "and you gave Me meat. Lord, when did we see You hungry? Forasmuch as you did it to one of the least of Mine, you did it to Me." To be brief then, let men hear, and consider as they ought, how great a merit it is to have fed Christ when He hungered, and how great a crime it is to have despised Christ when He hungered.

12. Repentance for sins changes men, it is true, for the better; but it does not appear as if even it would profit ought, if it should be barren of works of mercy. The Truth testifies by the mouth of John, who said to them that came to him, "O generation of vipers, who has warned you to flee from the wrath to come? Bring forth therefore fruits worthy of repentance; And do not say we have Abraham to our father;

21. Matthew 5:7.
22. James 2:13.

for I say unto you that God is able of these stones to raise up children unto Abraham. For now is the axe laid unto the root of the trees. Every tree therefore that does not bring forth good fruit will be cut down, and cast into the fire."[23] Touching this fruit he said above, "Bring forth fruits worthy of repentance." Whoever then does not bring forth these fruits has no cause to think that he will attain pardon for his sins by a barren repentance. Now what these fruits are, he shows afterwards himself. For after these words the multitude asked him, saying, "What will we do then?" That is, what are these fruits, which you exhort us with such alarming force to bring forth? "But he answering said unto them, he that has two coats, let him give to him that has none; and he that has meat, let him do likewise." My brethren, what is more plain, what more certain, or express than this? What other meaning then can that have which he said above, "Every tree therefore that does not bring forth good fruit will be cut down, and cast into the fire"; but that same which they on the left will hear, "Go you into everlasting fire, for I was hungry, and you gave Me no meat." So then it is but a small matter to depart from sins, if you will neglect to cure what is past, as it is written, "Son, you have sinned, do so no more." And that he might not think to be secure by this only, he said, "And for your former sins pray that they may be forgiven." But what will it profit you to pray for forgiveness, if you will not make yourself to be heard, by not bringing forth fruits for repentance, that you should be cut down as a barren tree, and be cast into the fire? If then you will be heard when you pray for pardon of your sins, "Forgive, and it will be forgiven you; Give, and it will be given you."[24]

23. Luke 3:7.
24. Luke 6:37–38.

Reading Questions

1. In Augustine's theology, how does sin relate to Adam?

2. Who are "the least of these"? How are they evident to the Christian community?

3. For Augustine, how does our commitment to almsgiving relate to salvation?

4. How does Augustine work forgiveness into this sermon? How does it relate to salvation and divine forgiveness?

5. What are, in your opinion, the strong and weak points of Augustine's arguments?

6. What is the theological link between the Lord's Supper and almsgiving?

For Further Reading

Brown, Peter. *Augustine of Hippo: A Biography.* New ed. Berkeley: University of California Press, 2000.

Byassee, Jason. *Reading Augustine: A Guide to the Confessions.* Cascade Companions. Eugene, OR: Cascade, 2006.

Ellingson, Mark. *The Richness of Augustine: His Contextual and Pastoral Theology.* Louisville: Westminster John Knox, 2005.

Knowles, Andrew, and Pachomios Pinkette. *Augustine and His World.* IVP Histories. Downers Grove, IL: InterVarsity, 2004.

Miles, Margaret R. "Augustine." In *Encyclopedia of Early Christianity,* edited by Everett Ferguson, 121–26. New York: Garland, 1990.

O'Donnell, James J. *Augustine: A New Biography.* New York: Ecco, 2005.

TeSelle, Eugene. *Augustine.* Abingdon Pillars of Theology. Nashville: Abingdon, 2006.

15

John Cassian

✳

John Cassian (360–435) was a considered a "Desert Father" because of his lead-
ership in monastic Christianity and mystical spirituality. The establishment of
stable monastic communities was an extremely important development in early
Christianity. During the Middle Ages monasteries were among the few places
where theology continued to develop. Cassian helped influence monasteries to have
a concern for the poor, an emphasis that appears in the reading below. In this pas-
sage he recounts an interaction with the famous Antony, who is considered to be
the founder of Christian monasticism and was immortalized by Athanasius' book,
The Life of Antony.

. . .

Second Conference of Abba Moses, Chapter 2[1]

And so I remember that while I was still a boy, in the region of Thebaid, where the blessed Antony lived, the elders came to him to inquire about perfection: and though the conference lasted from evening till morning, the greatest part of the night was taken up with this question. For it was discussed at great length what virtue or observance could preserve a monk always unharmed by the snares and deceits of the devil, and carry him forward on a sure and right path, and with firm step to the heights of perfection. And when each one gave his opinion according to the bent of his own mind, and some made it consist in zeal in fasting and vigils, because a soul that has been brought low by these, and so obtained purity of heart and body will be the more easily united to God, others in despising all things, as, if the mind were utterly deprived of them, it would come the more freely to God, as if henceforth there were no snares to entangle it: others thought that withdrawal from the world was the thing needful, i.e., solitude and the secrecy of the hermit's life; living in which a man may more readily commune with God, and cling more especially to Him; others laid down that the duties of charity, i.e., of kindness should be practiced, because the Lord in the gospel promised more especially to give the kingdom to these; when He said "Come you blessed of My Father, inherit the kingdom prepared for you from the foundation of the world. For I was an hungry and you gave Me to eat, I was thirsty and you gave Me to drink, etc.:"[2] and when in this fashion they declared that by means of different virtues a more certain approach to God could be secured, and the greater part of the night had been spent in this discussion, then at last the blessed Antony spoke and said: All these things which you have mentioned are indeed needful, and helpful to those who are thirsting for God, and desirous to approach Him. But countless accidents and the experience of many people will not allow us to conclude that the most important of gifts consist in

1. From *Nicene and Post-Nicene Fathers of the Christian Church* (Grand Rapids, MI: Christian Classics Ethereal Library). Text translated by Edgar C. S. Gibson and first published in New York, 1884. A few modernizing changes have been made to the original translation.

2. Matthew 25:35–36.

them. For often when men are most strict in fasting or in vigils, and nobly withdraw into solitude, and aim at depriving themselves of all their goods so absolutely that they do not suffer even a day's allowance of food or a single penny to remain to them, and when they fulfill all the duties of kindness with the utmost devotion, yet still we have seen them suddenly deceived, so that they could not bring the work they had entered upon to a suitable close, but brought their exalted fervor and praiseworthy manner of life to a terrible end. Wherefore we will be able clearly to recognize what it is which mainly leads to God, if we trace out with greater care the reason of their downfall and deception.

For when the works of the above mentioned virtues were abounding in them, discretion alone was wanting, and allowed them not to continue even to the end. Nor can any other reason for their falling off be discovered except that as they were not sufficiently instructed by their elders they could not obtain judgment and discretion, which passing by excess on either side, teaches a monk always to walk along the royal road, and does not suffer him to be puffed up on the right hand of virtue, i.e., from excess of zeal to transgress the bounds of due moderation in foolish presumption, nor allows him to be enamored of slackness and turn aside to the vices on the left hand, i.e., under pretext of controlling the body, to grow slack with the opposite spirit of luke-warmness. For this is discretion, which is termed in the gospel the "eye," "and light of the body," according to the Savior's saying: "The light of your body is your eye: but if your eye be single, your whole body will be full of light, but if your eye be evil, your whole body will be full of darkness:"[3] because as it discerns all the thoughts and actions of men, it sees and overlooks all things which should be done. But if in any man this is "evil," i.e., not fortified by sound judgment and knowledge, or deceived by some error and presumption, it will make our whole body "full of darkness," i.e., it will darken all our mental vision and our actions, as they will be involved in the darkness of vices and the gloom of disturbances. For, says He, "if the light

3. Matthew 6:22–23.

which is in you be darkness, how great will that darkness be!"[4] For no one can doubt that when the judgment of our heart goes wrong, and is overwhelmed by the night of ignorance, our thoughts and deeds, which are the result of deliberation and discretion, must be involved in the darkness of still greater sins.

Reading Questions

1. Cassian is advocating caution in this passage. What are we to watch out for?

2. What is the character of the "darkness" that he refers to?

3. What is unique about Cassian's treatment of the Matthew 25 parable?

For Further Reading

Burns, Paul C. "Cassian, John." In *Encyclopedia of Early Christianity*, edited by Everett Ferguson, 180–81. New York: Garland, 1990.

Chadwick, Owen. *John Cassian: A Study in Primitive Monasticism.* 2d ed. London: Cambridge University Press, 1968.

Driver, Steven D. *John Cassian and the Reading of Egyptian Monastic Culture.* Studies in Medieval History and Culture 8. London: Routledge, 2002.

Rousseau, P. "Cassian, Contemplation and the Cenobitic Life." *Journal of Ecclesiastical History* 26 (1975) 113–26.

Stewart, Columba. *Cassian the Monk.* Oxford Studies in Historical Theology. New York: Oxford University Press, 1998.

4. Ibid.

16

Leo the Great

✳

The papacy of Leo the Great was among the most important in Christian antiquity. Leo reigned from 440–461 during a critical time in the establishment of Christian doctrine. Leo the Great spent much of his papacy battling a variety of heresies, including monophysitism and persistent supporters of Pelagius, Eutyches, and others. Leo considered it his most important role as pope to sustain the unity of the church; heresies were divisive for the way they contort Christian theological claims, but perhaps even more so for the way they create disunity.

Leo moved to strengthen his control by centralizing authority in a time of great disorder, interpreting his papal supremacy to derive from divine and scriptural authority. He left a great literary legacy, with 143 letters and 97 sermons that have survived.

. . .

Sermon 41: On the Fast of the Seventh Month, VI[1]

I. Abstinence must include discipline of the soul as well as of the body.

There is nothing, dearly-beloved, in which the Divine Providence does not assist the devotions of the faithful. For the very elements of the world also minister to the exercise of mind and body in holiness, seeing that the distinctly varied revolution of days and months opens for us the different pages of the commands, and thus the seasons also in some sense speak to us of that which the sacred institutions enjoin. And hence, since the year's course has brought back the seventh month to us, I feel certain that your minds are spiritually aroused to keep the solemn fast; since you have learnt by experience how well this preparation purifies both the outer and the inner parts of men, so that by abstaining from the lawful, resistance becomes easier to the unlawful. But do not limit your plan of abstinence, dearly-beloved, to the mortifying of the body, or to the lessening of food alone. For the greater advantages of this virtue belong to that chastity of the soul, which not only crushes the lusts of the flesh, but also despises the vanities of worldly wisdom, as the Apostle says, "take heed that no one deceive you through philosophy and empty deceit, according to the tradition of men."[2]

II. And in particular we must abstain from heresy, and that of Eutyches as well as that of Nestorius.

We must restrain ourselves, therefore, from food, but much more must we fast from errors that the mind, given up to no carnal pleasure, may be taken captive by no falsehood: because as in past days, so also in our own, there are not wanting enemies of the Truth, who dare to stir

---

1. From *Nicene and Post-Nicene Fathers,* Second Series, Volume VII (Grand Rapids: Christian Classics Ethereal Library). Text translated by Charles Lett Feltoe and edited by Philip Schaff, first published in Edinburgh, 1894. A number of modernizing changes have been made to this translation.

2. Colossians 2:8.

up civil wars within the catholic Church,[3] in order that by leading the ignorant into agreement with their ungodly doctrines they may boast of increase in numbers through those whom they have been able to sever from the Body of Christ. For what is so opposed to the Prophets, so repugnant to the Gospels, so at variance with the Apostles' teaching as to preach one single Nature in the Lord Jesus Christ born of Mary, and without respect to time co-eternal with the Eternal Father? If it is only man's nature which is to be acknowledged, where is the Godhead which saves? If only God's, where is the humanity which is saved? But the catholic Faith, which withstands all errors, refutes these blasphemies also at the same time, condemning Nestorius, who divides the Divine from the human, and denouncing Eutyches, who nullifies the human in the Divine; seeing that the Son of True God, Himself True God, possessing unity and equality with the Father and with the Holy Ghost, has vouchsafed likewise to be true Man, and after the Virgin Mother's conception was not separated from her flesh and child-bearing, so uniting humanity to Himself as to remain immutably God; so imparting Godhead to man as not to destroy but enhance him by glorification. For He, Who became "the form of a slave," ceased not to be "the form of God," and He is not one joined with the other, but One in Both, so that ever since "the Word became Flesh" our faith is disturbed by no vicissitudes of circumstance, but whether in the miracles of power, or in the degradation of suffering, we believe Him to be both God, Who is Man, and Man, Who is God.

III. The truth of the incarnation is proved both by the Eucharistic Feast and by the Divine institution of almsgiving.

Dearly-beloved, utter this confession with all your heart and reject the wicked lies of heretics, that your fasting and almsgiving may not be polluted by any contagion with error: for then is our offering of the sacrifice clean and our gifts of mercy holy, when those who perform them understand that which they do. For when the Lord says, "unless you have eaten the flesh of the Son of Man, and drunk His blood, you

3. Leo may be referring to a problem with the infiltration of supporters of the Eutychian or Monophysite heresies.

will not have life in you,"[4] you ought so to be partakers at the Holy Table, as to have no doubt whatever concerning the reality of Christ's Body and Blood. For that is taken in the mouth which is believed in Faith, and it is vain for them to respond Amen who dispute that which is taken.[5] But when the Prophet says, "Blessed is he, who considers the poor and needy,"[6] he is the praiseworthy distributor of clothes and food among the poor, who knows he is clothing and feeding Christ in the poor: for He Himself says, "as long as you have done it to one of My brethren, you have done it to Me."[7] And so Christ is One, True God and True Man, rich in what is His own, poor in what is ours, receiving gifts and distributing gifts, Partner with mortals, and the Quickener of the dead, so that in the "name of Jesus every knee should bow, of things in heaven, of things on earth, and of things under the earth, and that every tongue should confess that the Lord Jesus Christ is in the glory of God the Father,"[8] living and reigning with the Holy Spirit for ever and ever. Amen.

Reading Questions

1. Reflect on the heresies directly mentioned by Leo here. How might these heresies be poisonous to the church as he envisions it?

2. What does Leo consider to be the purpose of fasting?

3. What is the relationship here between Eucharist and almsgiving? Who are "the least of these" in this sermon?

4. Some say that the Eucharist tastes sour in a divided church. What pollutes the Eucharist for Leo the Great?

4. John 6:53.

5. Leo means, perhaps, the response of "Amen" one gives after receiving the elements and hearing the words, "The Body of Christ, the Blood of Christ."

6. Psalm 41:1.

7. Matthew 25:40.

8. Philippians 2:10–11.

For Further Reading

Armitage, J. Mark. *A Twofold Solidarity: Leo the Great's Theology of Solidarity.* Early Christian Studies 9. Strathfield, NSW: St. Paul's Publication, 2005.

Jalland, Trevor. *The Life and Times of Leo the Great.* London: SPCK, 1941.

Ullmann, Walter. "Leo I and the Theme of Papal Primacy." *Journal of Theological Studies* 11 (1960) 25–51.

Zinn, Grover A. Jr. "Leo I, the Great." In *Encyclopedia of Early Christianity,* edited by Everett Ferguson, 534–35. New York: Garland, 1990.

17

John of Damascus

John of Damascus (676–749) is sometimes considered the last of the Church Fathers. He was born and raised in Muslim Damascus by a Christian family, excelling as a student in many areas. He succeeded his father as a high-ranking official in the Muslim court of Caliph (the word for a Muslim leader or king) Abd al-Malik. From this external position he was able to exert daring influence on Christianity, particularly with respect to the conflicts surrounding the use of icons in worship. In the writing below he takes up the characters of Barlaam and Joasaph from a popular story which appears to be a Christianized version of the story of Guatama Buddha. Joasaph, like the Buddha, is a prince who rejects the wealth and benefits of royal life and chooses instead spiritual fulfillment. He learns the great truths of Christianity from the elder Barlaam.

. . .

The Life of Barlaam and Joasaph: Chapter 9[1]

Joasaph said to him, "Great and marvelous, sir, are the things you tell me, fearful and terrible, if indeed these things be so, and, if there be after death and dissolution into dust and ashes, a resurrection and re-birth, and rewards and punishments for the deeds done during life. But what is the proof thereof? And how have you come to learn that which you have not seen, that you have so steadfastly and undoubtingly believed it? As for things that have already been done and made manifest in deed, though you saw them not, yet have you heard them from the writers of history. But, when it is of the future that you preach tidings of such vast import, how have you made your conviction on these matters sure?"

Barlaam said, "From the past I gain certainty about the future; for they that preached the Gospel, without erring from the truth, but establishing their sayings by signs and wonders and many miracles, they themselves also spoke of the future. So, as in the one case they taught us nothing amiss or false, but made all that they said and did to shine clearer than the sun, so also in the other matter they gave us true doctrine, even that which our Lord and Master Jesus Christ himself confirmed both by word and deed. 'Truly,' he spoke, 'I say unto you, the hour is coming in the which all that are in the graves will hear the voice of the Son of God and they that hear will live':[2] and again, 'The hour comes when the dead will hear his voice, and will come forth, they that have done good unto the resurrection of life, and they that have done evil unto the resurrection of damnation.' And again he said concerning the resurrection of the dead, 'Have you not read that which was spoken unto you by God, saying, I am the God of Abraham, and the God of Isaac, and the God of Jacob. God is not the God of the dead but of the living.'[3] 'For as the tares are gathered and burned in the fire, so will it be in the end of this age. The Son of God will send forth his Angels, and they will gather all things that offend, and them

---

1. From *St. John Damascene: Barlaam and Iosaph,* trans. G. R. Woodward and H. Mattingly (Cambridge: Harvard University Press, 1914). A number of modernizing changes have been made to this translation.

2. John 5:28.

3. Mark 20:27; Luke 20:38.

which do iniquity, and will cast them into the furnace of fire; there will be wailing and gnashing of teeth. Then will the righteous shine forth as the sun in the kingdom of their father.' Thus he added this, 'He who has ears to hear, let him hear.'[4]

"In such words and many more did the Lord make manifest the resurrection of our bodies, and confirm his words in deed, by raising many that were dead. And, toward the end of his life upon earth, he called from the grave one Lazarus his friend, that had already been four days dead and stank, and thus he restored the lifeless to life. Moreover, the Lord himself became the first-fruits of that resurrection which is final and no longer subject to death, after he had in the flesh tasted of death; and on the third day he rose again, and became the first-born from the dead. For other men also were raised from the dead, but died once more, and might not yet attain to the likeness of the future true resurrection. But he alone was the leader of that resurrection, the first to be raised to the resurrection immortal.

"This was the preaching also of them that from the beginning were eye-witnesses and ministers of the word; for thus said blessed Paul, whose calling was not of men, but from heaven, 'Brethren, I declare unto you the Gospel which I preached unto you. For I delivered unto you first of all that which I also received, how that Christ died for our sins according to the Scriptures. Now if Christ be preached that he rose from the dead, how say some among you that there is no resurrection of the dead? For if the dead rise not, then is not Christ raised. And if Christ be not raised, your faith is vain, you are yet in your sins. If in this life only we have hope in Christ, we are of all men most miserable. But now is Christ risen from the dead and become the first-fruits of them that slept. For since by man came death, by man came also the resurrection of the dead. For as in Adam all die, even so in Christ will all be made alive.'[5] And after a little while, 'For this corruptible must put on incorruption, and this mortal must put on immortality. So when this corruptible will have put on incorruption, and this mortal will have put on immortality, then will be brought to pass the saying that is written, Death is swallowed up in victory. O

4. Matthew 13:40.
5. 1 Corinthians 15:11–22.

death where is your sting? O grave, where is your victory?'[6] For then the power of death is utterly annulled and destroyed, no longer working in us, but for the future there is given unto men immortality and incorruption for evermore.

"Beyond all question, therefore, there will be a resurrection of the dead, and this we believe undoubtingly. Moreover we know that there will be rewards and punishments for the deeds done in our life-time, on the dreadful day of Christ's coming, 'wherein the heavens will be dissolved in fire and the elements will melt with fervent heat,'[7] as said one of the inspired clerks of God; 'nevertheless we, according to his promise, look for new heavens and a new earth.'[8] For that there will be rewards and punishments for men's works, and that absolutely nothing, good or bad, will be overlooked, but that there is reserved a requital for words, deeds and thoughts, is plain. The Lord said, 'Whosoever will give to drink unto one of these little ones a cup of cold water only, in the name of a disciple, he will in no wise lose his reward.' And again he said, 'When the Son of man will come in his glory, and all the holy Angels with him, then before him will be gathered all nations, and he will separate them one from another, as a shepherd divides his sheep from the goats. And he will set the sheep on his right hand, but the goats on the left. Then will the King say unto them on his right hand, 'Come you blessed of my Father, inherit the kingdom prepared for you from the foundation of the world. For I was an hungry, and you gave me meat: I was thirsty, and you gave me drink: I was a stranger, and you took me in: naked, and you clothed me: I was sick, and you visited me: I was in prison, and you came unto me.' [Does] he count the kind acts we do unto the needy as done to himself? And in another place he said, 'whoever will confess me before men, him will I also confess before my Father which is in heaven.'[9]

6. 1 Corinthians 15:53–55.
7. 2 Peter 3:12.
8. 2 Peter 3:13.
9. Matthew 25:34–41.

"Lo, by all these examples and many more he proves that the rewards of good works are certain and sure. Further, that punishments are in store for the bad, he foretold by parables strange and wonderful, which he, the Well of Wisdom most wisely put forth. At one time he brought into his tale a certain rich man which was clothed in purple and fine linen, and fared sumptuously every day, but who was so selfish and pitiless toward the destitute as to overlook a certain beggar named Lazarus laid at his gate, and not even to give him of the crumbs from his table. So when one and other were dead, the poor man, full of sores, was carried away, he said, into Abraham's bosom, for thus he described the habitation of the righteous—but the rich man was delivered to the fire of bitter torment in hell. To him said Abraham, 'You in your lifetime received your good things, and likewise Lazarus his evil things, but now he is comforted, and you art tormented.'[10]

"And elsewhere he likened the kingdom of heaven to a certain king which made a marriage-feast for his son where he declared future happiness and splendor. For just as he tended to speak to humble and earthly minded men, he would draw his parables from homely and familiar things. Not that he meant that marriages and feasts exist in that world; but in condescension to men's grossness, he employed these names when he would make known to them the future. So, as he tells, the king with high proclamation called all to come to the marriage to take their fill of his wondrous store of good things. But many of them that were called made light of it and came not, and busied themselves: some went to their farms, some to their merchandize and others to their newly wedded wives, and thus deprived themselves of the splendor of the bride chamber. Now when these had, of their own choice, absented themselves from this joyous merriment, others were bidden to come, and the wedding was furnished with guests. And when the king came in to see the guests, he saw there a man which had not on a wedding garment, and he said unto him, "Friend, how did you get in here, not having a wedding garment?"[11] And he was speechless. Then Said the king to the servants, "Bind him hand and foot, and take him away, and cast him into outer darkness; there will be weeping and

10. Luke 16:24.
11. Matthew 22:12.

gnashing of teeth.'[12] Now they who made excuses and paid no heed to the call are they that hasten not to the faith of Christ, but continue in idolatry or heresy. But he that had no wedding garment is he that believeth, but has soiled his spiritual garment with unclean acts, and was rightly cast forth from the joy of the bride chamber.

"And he put forth yet another parable, in harmony with this, in his picture of the Ten Virgins, 'five of whom were wise, and five were foolish. They that were foolish took their lamps and took no oil with them, but the wise took oil.' By the oil he signifies the acquiring of good works. 'And at midnight,' he said, 'there was a cry made, "Behold the bridegroom is coming, go you out to meet him."' By midnight he denotes the uncertainty of that time. Then all those virgins arose. 'They that were ready went forth to meet the bridegroom and went in with him to the marriage, and the door was shut.' But they that were un-ready (whom rightly he calls foolish), seeing that their lamps were going out, went forth to buy oil. Afterward they drew close, the door being now shut, and cried, saying, 'Lord, Lord, open to us.' But he answered and said, 'Verily I say unto you, I know you not.'[13] Wherefore from all this it is manifest that there is a requital not only for overt acts, but also for words and even secret thoughts; for the Savior said, 'I say unto you, that for every idle word that men will speak they will give account thereof in the day of judgment.'[14] And again he said, 'But the very hairs of your head are numbered,'[15] by the hairs meaning the smallest and slightest fantasy or thought. And in harmony herewith is the teaching of blessed Paul, 'For the word of God,' said he, 'is quick and powerful, and sharper than any two-edged sword, and piercing even to the dividing asunder of soul and spirit, and of the joints and marrow, and is a discerner of the thoughts and intents of the heart. Neither is there any creature that is not manifest in his sight: but all things are naked and laid bare unto the eyes of him with whom we have to do.'[16]

12. Matthew 22:1–14.
13. Matthew 25:2–12.
14. Matthew 12:36.
15. Matthew 10:30.
16. Hebrews 4:12–13.

"These things also were proclaimed with wondrous clearness by the prophets of old time, illumined by the grace of the Spirit. For Esay said, 'I know their works and their thoughts,' and will repay them. 'Behold, I come to gather all nations and all tongues; and they will come and see my glory. And the heaven will be new, and the earth, which I make before me. And all flesh will come to worship before me, said the Lord. And they will go forth, and look upon the carcasses of the men that have transgressed against me: for their worm will not die, neither will their fire be quenched; and they will be a spectacle unto all flesh."[17] And again he said concerning that day, "And the heavens will be rolled together as a scroll, and all the stars will fall down as leaves from the vine. For behold, the day of the Lord comes, cruel with wrath and fierce anger, to lay the whole world desolate and to destroy the sinners out of it. For the stars of heaven and Orion and all the constellations of heaven will not give their light, and there will be darkness at the sun's rising, and the moon will not give her light. And I will cause the arrogance of the sinners to cease, and will lay low the haughtiness of the proud.'[18] And again he said, 'Woe unto them that draw their iniquities as with a long cord, and their sins as with a heifer's cart-rope! Woe unto them that call evil good, and good evil; that put darkness for light, and light for darkness; that put bitter for sweet, and sweet for bitter! Woe unto those of you that are mighty, that are princes, that mingle strong drink, which justify the wicked for reward, and take justice from the just, and turn aside the judgment from the needy, and take away the right from the poor, that the widow may be their spoil and the fatherless their prey! And what will they do in the day of visitation, and to whom will they flee for help? And where will they leave their glory, that they fall not into arrest? Like as stubble will be burnt by live coal of fire, and consumed by kindled flame, so their root will be as foam, and their blossom will go up as dust, for they would not the law of the Lord of hosts, and provoked the oracle of the Holy One of Israel."[19]

17. Isaiah 66:22–24.
18. Isaiah 13:9–11.
19. Isaiah 5:18–24.

"In tune with this said also another prophet, 'The great day of the Lord is near, and hastens greatly. The bitter and austere voice of the day of the Lord has been appointed. A mighty day of wrath is that day, a day of trouble and distress, a day of waste and desolation, a day of blackness and gloominess, a day of clouds and thick darkness, a day of the trumpet and alarm. And I will bring distress upon the wicked, and they will walk like blind men, because they have sinned against the Lord. Neither their silver nor their gold will be able to deliver them in the day of the Lord's wrath; for the whole land will be devoured by the fire of his jealousy, for he will make a riddance of all them that dwell in the land.'[20] Moreover David, the king and prophet, cried out, 'God will come visibly, even our God, and will not keep silence: a fire will be kindled before him, and a mighty tempest round about him. He will call the heaven from above, and the earth, that he may judge his people.'[21] And again he said, 'Arise, O God, judge you the earth, because "the fierceness of man will turn to your praise." And you will "reward every man according to his works."' And many other such things have been spoken by the Psalmist, and all the Prophets inspired by the Holy Ghost, concerning the judgment and the recompense to come. Their words also have been most surely confirmed by the Savior who has taught us to believe the resurrection of the dead, and the recompense of the deeds done in the flesh, and the unending life of the world to come."

15. Said Joasaph to the elder, "How then will I be able to send before me treasures of money and riches, that, when I depart hence, I may find these unharmed and unwasted for my enjoyment? How must I show my hatred for things present and lay hold on things eternal? Please make this plain to me."

Barlaam said, "The sending of money to that eternal home is wrought by the hands of the poor. For one of the prophets, Daniel the wise, said to the king of Babylon, 'O Prince, let my counsel be acceptable unto you, and redeem your sins by almsgiving, and your iniquities by showing mercy to the poor.'[22] The Savior also said, 'Make to

---

20. Zephaniah 1:14–18.

21. Psalm 50:3–4.

22. Daniel 4:27.

yourselves friends of the mammon of unrighteousness; that, when you fail, they may receive you into everlasting habitations.'[23] And, in many places, the Master makes much mention of almsgiving and liberality to the poor, as we learn in the Gospel. Thus will you most surely send all your treasure before yourself by the hands of the needy, for whatever you will do for these the Master counts done unto himself,[24] and will reward you manifold; for, in the recompense of benefits, he ever surpasses them that love him. So in this manner by seizing for awhile the treasures of the darkness of this world, in whose slavery for a long time past you have been miserable, you will by these means make good provision for your journey, and by plundering another's goods you will store all up for yourself, with things fleeting and transient purchasing for yourself things that are stable and enduring. Afterwards, God working with you, you will perceive the uncertainty and inconstancy of the world, and saying farewell to all, will . . . anchor in the future, and, passing by the things that pass away, you will hold to the things that we look for, the things that endure. You will depart from darkness and the shadow of death, and hate the world and the ruler of the world; and, counting your perishable flesh your enemy, you will run toward the light that is unapproachable, and taking the Cross on your shoulders, will follow Christ without looking back, that you may also be glorified with him, and be made inheritor of the life that never changes nor deceives."

Joasaph asked, "When you spoke a minute ago of despising all things, and taking up such a life of toil, was that an old tradition handed down from the teaching of the Apostles, or is this a late invention of your wits, which you have chosen for yourselves as a more excellent way?"

The elder answered and said, "I teach you no law introduced but yesterday, God forbid! but one given to us of old. For when a certain rich young man asked the Lord, 'What will I do to inherit eternal life?' and boasted that he had observed all that was written in the Law, Jesus said unto him, 'One thing you lack yet. Go sell all that you have and distribute it to the poor, and you will have treasure in heaven, and

23. Luke 16:9.
24. Matthew 25:40.

come, take up your cross and follow me. But when the young man heard this he was very sorrowful, for he was very rich. And when Jesus saw that he was very sorrowful, he said, 'How hardly will they which have riches enter into the kingdom of God! For it is easier for a camel to go through the eye of a needle, than for a rich man to enter into the kingdom of God!'[25] So, when all the Saints heard this command, they thought fit by all means to withdraw from this hardness of riches. They parted with all their goods, and by this distribution of their riches to the poor laid up for themselves eternal riches; and they took up their Cross and followed Christ, some being made perfect by martyrdom, even as I have already told you; and some by the practice of self-denial falling not a whit short of those others in the life of the true philosophy. Know you, then, that this is a command of Christ our King and God, which leads us from things corruptible and makes us partakers of things everlasting."

Joasaph said, "If, then, this kind of philosophy be so ancient and so beneficial, why it that so few folk now-a-day follow it?"

The elder answered, "Many have followed, and do follow it; but the most people hesitate and draw back. For few, said the Lord, are the travelers along the strait and narrow way, but along the wide and broad way there are many. For they that have once been taken prisoners by the love of money, and the evils that come from the love of pleasure, and are given up to idle and vain glory, are hardly to be torn from these, seeing that they have of their own free will sold themselves as slaves to a strange master, and setting themselves on the opposite side to God, who gave these commands, are held in bondage to that other. For the soul that has once rejected her own salvation, and given the reins to unreasonable lusts, is carried about here and there. Therefore, said the prophet, mourning the folly that encompasses such souls, and lamenting the thick darkness that lies on them, 'O you sons of men, how long will you be of heavy heart? Why do you love vanity . . . ?' And in the same tone as he, but adding something of his own, one of our wise teachers, a most holy man, cried aloud to all, as from some, 'O you sons of men, how long will you be of heavy heart? Why love you vanity and seek after leasing? Do you think that this present life,

25. Matthew 19:16–24; Mark 10:17–25; Luke 18:18–25.

and luxury, and these shreds of glory, and petty lordship and false prosperity are any great thing?'—things which no more belong to those that possess them than to them that hope for them, nor to these latter any more than to those who never thought of them: things like the dust carried and whirled about to and fro by the tempest, or vanishing as the smoke, or delusive as a dream, or intangible as a shadow; which, when absent, need not be despaired of by them that have them not, and, when present, cannot be trusted by their owners.

"This then was the commandment of the Savior; this was the preaching of the Prophets and Apostles; in such wise do all the Saints, by word and deed, constrain us to enter the unerring road of virtue. And though few walk therein and more choose the broad way that leads to destruction, yet not for this will the life of this divine philosophy be diminished in fame. But as the sun, rising to shine on all, does bounteously send forth his beams, inviting all to enjoy his light, even so does our true philosophy, like the sun, lead with her light those that are her lovers, and warm and brighten them. But if any shut their eyes, and will not behold the light thereof, not for that must the sun be blamed, or scorned by others: still less will the glory of his brightness be dishonored through their silliness. But while they, self-deprived of light, grope like blind men along a wall, and fall into many a ditch, and scratch out their eyes on many a bramble bush, the sun, firmly established on his own glory, will illuminate them that gaze upon his beams with unveiled face. Even so the light of Christ shines on all men abundantly, imparting to us some of his luster. But every man shares in proportion to his desire and zeal. For the Sun of righteousness disappoints none of them that would fix their gaze on him, yet he does not compel those who willingly choose darkness; but every man, so long as he is in this present life, is committed to his own free will and choice."

Joasaph asked, "What is free will and what is choice?"

The elder answered, "Free will is the willing of a reasonable soul, moving without hindrance toward whatever it wishes, whether to virtue or to vice, the soul being thus constituted by the Creator. Free will again is the sovereign motion of an intelligent soul. Choice is desire accompanied by deliberation, or deliberation accompanied by desire for things that lie in our power; for in choosing we desire that which we have deliberately preferred. Deliberation is a motion towards enquiry about actions possible to us; a man deliberates whether he ought to pursue an object or no. Then he judges which is the better, and so arises judgment. Then he is inclined towards it, and loves that which was so judged by the deliberative faculty, and this is called resolve; for, if he judge a thing, and yet be not inclined toward the thing that he has judged, and love it not, it is not called resolve. Then, after inclination toward it, there arises choice or rather selection. For choice is to choose one or other of two things in view, and to select this rather than that. And it is manifest that choice is deliberation plus discrimination, and this from the very etymology. For that which is the 'object of choice' is the thing chosen before the other thing. And no man prefers a thing without deliberation, nor makes a choice without having conceived a preference. For, since we are not zealous to carry into action all that seems good to us, choice only arises and the deliberately preferred only becomes the chosen, when desire is added. Thus we conclude that choice is desire accompanied by deliberation for things that lie in our power; in choosing we desire that which we have deliberately preferred. All deliberation aims at action and depends on action; and thus deliberation goes before all choice, and choice before all action. For this reason not only our actions, but also our thoughts, inasmuch as they give occasion for choice, bring in their train crowns or punishments. For the beginning of sin and righteous dealing is choice, exercised in action possible to us. Where the power of activity is ours, there too are the actions that follow that activity in our power. Virtuous activities are in our power, therefore in our power are virtues also; for we are absolute masters over all our souls' affairs and all our deliberations. Since then it is of free will that men deliberate, and of free will that men choose, a man partakes of the light divine, and advances in the practice of this philosophy in exact measure of his choice, for there are differences of choice. And even as water-springs, issuing from the hollows of the earth, sometimes gush forth from the surface soil, and sometimes from a lower source, and at other times from a great depth, and even as some of these waters bubble forth continuously, and their taste is sweet, while others that come from deep wells are brackish or sulfurous, even as some pour forth in abundance while others flow drop by drop, thus, understand you, is it also with our choices. Some choices are swift and exceeding fervent, others languid and cold: some have a bias entirely toward virtue, while others incline with all their force to its opposite. And like in nature to these choices are the ensuing impulses to action."

Reading Questions

1. How would you answer for today Joasaph's question, "If, then, this kind of philosophy be so ancient and so beneficial, why it that so few folk now-a-day follow it?"

2. Who are "the least of these" in this passage?

3. The concept of "free will" is considered near the end of this section. What is free will for John of Damascus? How does it influence salvation?

4. What is the "divine light"? Is it available to all or just some?

For Further Reading

Berthold, George C. "John of Damascus." In *Encyclopedia of Early Christianity,* edited by Everett Ferguson, 498–99. New York: Garland, 1990.

Louth, Andrew. *St. John Damascene: Tradition and Originality in Byzantine Theology.* Oxford: Oxford University Press, 2002.

Sweeney, L. "John Damascene and the Divine Infinity." *New Scholasticism* 35 (1961) 76–106.

18

Gregory the Great

Gregory the Great (540–604) was pope for the last fourteen years of his life, a highly political papacy with much involvement in military disputes of his day. He is an enigmatic character both politically and in writing; his are the only significant set of writings we have by any pope between the fifth and eleventh centuries. He was the first pope to be from a monastic background, and the admonitions below show his ongoing monk-like concern for the poor. At the same time, he is not considered an accomplished theologian and appears to have been given to far-fetched and mystical interpretations of Scripture. In this portion of his Book of Pastoral Rule *he reveals his intimate knowledge with Scripture and monastic concern for the danger of riches.*

. . .

Book of Pastoral Rule: Chapter 20, How to Be
Admonished are Those Who Give Away What is Their
Own, and Those Who Seize What Belongs to Others[1]

Differently to be admonished are those who already give compassionately of their own, and those who still would dare seize even what
belongs to others. For those who already give compassionately of their
own are to be admonished not to lift themselves up in swelling thought
above those to whom they impart earthly things; not to esteem themselves better than others because they see others to be supported by
them. For the Lord of an earthly household, in distributing the ranks
and ministries of his servants, appoints some to rule, but some to be
ruled by others. Those he orders to supply to the rest what is necessary,
these to take what they receive from others. And yet it is for the most
part those that rule who offend, while those that are ruled remain
in favor with the good man of the house. Those who are dispensers
incur wrath; those who subsist by the dispensation of others continue
without offence. Those, then, who already give compassionately of
the things which they possess are to be admonished to acknowledge
themselves to be placed by the heavenly Lord as dispensers of temporal supplies, and to, impart the same all the more humbly from their
understanding that the things which they dispense are not their own.
And, when they consider that they are appointed for the service of
those to whom they impart what they have received, by no means let
vain glory elate their minds, but let fear depress them. Whence also it
is needful for them to take anxious thought test they distribute what
has been committed to them unworthily; lest they bestow something
on those on whom they ought to have spent nothing, or nothing on
those on whom they ought to have spent something, or much on those
on whom they ought to have spent little, or little on those on whom
they ought to have spent much; lest by precipitancy they scatter unprofitably what they give; lest by tardiness they mischievously torment

---

1. From *Nicene and Post-Nicene Fathers*, Second Series, Volume VII (Grand Rapids:
Christian Classics Ethereal Library). Text translated by Charles Lett Feltoe and edited
by Philip Schaff, first published in Edinburgh, 1894. A number of modernizing
changes have been made to this translation.

petitioners; lest the thought of receiving a favor in return creep in; lest craving for transitory praise extinguish the light of giving; lest accompanying moroseness beset an offered gift; lest in case of a gift that has been well offered the mind be exhilarated more than is fit; lest, when they have fulfilled all aright, they give something to themselves, and so at once lose all after they have accomplished all.

For, that they may not attribute to themselves the virtue of their liberality, let them hear what is written, If any man administer, let him do it as of the ability which God administers.[2] That they may not rejoice immoderately in benefits bestowed, let them hear what is written, When you will have done all those things which are commanded you, say, We are unprofitable servants, we have done that which was our duty to do.[3] That moroseness may not spoil liberality, let them hear what is written, God loves a cheerful giver.[4] That they may not seek transitory praise for a gift bestowed, let them hear what is written, Let not your left hand know what your right hand does.[5] That is, let not the glory of the present life mix itself with the largess of piety, nor let desire of favor know anything of the work of rectitude. That they may not require a return for benefits bestowed, let them hear what is written, When you make a dinner or a supper, call not your friends, nor your brethren, neither your kinsmen, nor your rich neighbors, lest they also bid you again, and a recompense be made you. But, when you make a feast, call the poor, the maimed, the lame, the blind: and you will be blessed; for they have not whereof to recompense you.[6] That they may not supply too late what should be supplied at once, let them hear what is written, Say not to your friend, go and come again, and tomorrow I will give, when you mightest give immediately.[7] Lest, under pretence of liberality, they should scatter what they possess unprofitably, let them hear what is written, Let your alms sweat in your hand. Lest, when much is necessary, little be given, let them hear what

2. 1 Peter 4:11.
3. Luke 17:10.
4. 2 Corinthians 9:7.
5. Matthew 6:3.
6. Luke 14:12.
7. Proverbs 3:28.

is written, He that sows sparingly will reap also sparingly.[8] Lest, when they ought to give little, they give too much, and afterwards, badly enduring want themselves, break out into impatience, let them hear what is written, Not that other men be eased, and you burdened, but by an quality, that your abundance may supply their want, and that their abundance may be a supply to your want.[9] For, when the soul of the giver knows not how to endure want, then, in withdrawing much from himself, he seeks out against himself occasion of impatience. For the mind should first be prepared for patience, and then either much or all be bestowed in bounty, lest, the inroad of want being borne with but little equanimity, both the reward of previous bounty be lost, and subsequent murmuring bring worse ruin on the soul. Lest they should give nothing at all to those on whom they ought to bestow something, let them hear what is written, Give to every man that asks of you.[10] Lest they should give something, however little to those on whom they ought to bestow nothing at all, let them hear what is written. Give to the good man, and receive not a sinner: do well to him that is lowly, and give not to the ungodly.[11] And again, set out your bread and wine on the burial of the just, but eat and drink not thereof with sinners.[12]

For he who gives his bread and wine to sinners gives assistance to the wicked. . . . [S]ome of the rich of this world nourish players with profuse bounties, while the poor of Christ are tormented with hunger. He, however, who gives his bread to one that is needy, though he be a sinner, not because he is a sinner, but because he is a man, does not in truth nourish a sinner, but a poor righteous man, because what he loves in him is not his sin, but his nature. Those who already distribute compassionately what they possess are to be admonished also that they study to keep careful guard, lest, when they redeem by alms the sins they have committed, they commit others which will still require redemption; lest they suppose the righteousness of God to be saleable, thinking that if they take care to give money for their sins, they can

8. 2 Corinthians 9:6.
9. 2 Corinthians 8:13–14.
10. Luke 6:30.
11. Sirach 12:4.
12. Tobit 4:17.

sin with impunity. For the soul is more than meat, and the body than raiment.[13] He, therefore, who bestows meat or raiment on the poor, and yet is polluted by iniquity of soul or body, has offered the lesser thing to righteousness, and the greater thing to sin; for he has given his possessions to God, and himself to the devil.

But, on the other hand, those who still would seize what belongs to others are to be admonished to give anxious heed to what the Lord says when He comes to judgment. For He says, I was hungry, and you gave Me no meat: I was thirsty, and you gave Me no drink: I was a stranger, and you took Me not in: naked, and you clothed Me not; sick, and in prison, and you visited Me not.[14] And these he previously addresses saying, Depart from Me, you cursed, into eternal fire, which is prepared for the devil and his angels. Lo, they are in no way told that they have committed robberies or any other acts of violence, and yet they are given over to the eternal fires of hell. Hence, then, it is to be gathered with how great damnation those will be visited who seize what is not their own, if those who have indiscreetly kept their own are smitten with so great punishment. Let them consider in what guilt the seizing of goods must bind them, if not parting with them subjects to such a penalty. Let them consider what injustice inflicted must deserve, if kindness not bestowed is worthy of so great a chastisement.

When they are intent on seizing what is not their own, let them hear what is written, Woe to him that increases that which is not his! How long does he heap up against himself thick clay?[15] For, indeed, for a covetous man to heap up against him thick clay is to pile up earthly gains into a load of sin. When they desire to enlarge greatly the spaces of their habitation, let them hear what is written, Woe to you that join house to house and lay field to field, even till there be no place left. What, will you dwell alone in the midst of the earth?[16] As if to say plainly, How far do you stretch yourselves, you that cannot bear to have comrades in a common world? Those that are joined to you, you keep down, and ever find some against whom you may have power to

13. Matthew 6:25; Luke 7:23.
14. Matthew 25:42–43.
15. Habakkuk 2:6.
16. Isaiah 5:8.

stretch yourselves. When they are intent on increasing money, let them hear what is written: the covetous man is not filled with money; and he that loves riches will not reap fruit thereof.[17] For indeed he would reap fruit of them, were he minded, not loving them, to disperse them well. But whoever in his affection for them retains them, will surely leave such riches behind him here without fruit. When they burn to be filled at once with all manner of wealth, let them hear what is written, He that makes haste to be rich will not be innocent:[18] for certainly he who goes about to increase wealth is negligent in avoiding sin; and, being caught after the manner of birds, while looking greedily at the bait of earthly things, he is not aware in what a noose of sin he is being strangled, When they desire any gains of the present world, and are ignorant of the losses they will suffer in the world to come, let them hear what is written, An inheritance to which haste is made in the beginning in the last end will lack blessing.[19] For indeed we derive our beginning from this life, that we may come in the end to the lot of blessing. They, therefore, that make haste to an inheritance in the beginning cut off from themselves the lot of blessing in the end; since, while they crave to be increased in goods here through the iniquity of avarice, they become disinherited there of their eternal patrimony. When they either solicit very much, or succeed in obtaining all that they have solicited, let them hear what is written. What is a man profited, if he should gain the whole world, but lose his own soul?[20] As if the Truth said plainly, What is a man profited, though he gather together all that is outside himself, if this very thing only which is himself he damns? But for the most part the covetousness of spoilers is the sooner corrected, if it be shown by the words of such as admonish them how fleeting is the present life; if mention be made of those who have long endeavored to grow rich in this world, and yet have been unable to remain long among their acquired riches; from whom hasty death has taken away suddenly and all at once whatever, neither all at once nor suddenly, they have gathered together; who have not only left

17. Ecclesiastes 5.
18. Proverbs 28:20.
19. Proverbs 20:21.
20. Matthew 16:26.

here what they had seized, but have carried with them to the judgment arraignments for seizure. Let them, therefore, be told of examples of such as these, whom they would, doubtless, even themselves, in words condemn; so that, when after their words they come back to their own heart, they may blush at any rate to imitate those whom they judge.

Chapter 21: How Those are to Be Admonished Who Desire Not the Things of Others, But Keep Their Own; And Those Who Give of Their Own, Yet Seize on Those of Others

Differently to be admonished are those who neither desire what belongs to others nor bestow what is their own, and those who give of what they have, and yet desist not from seizing on what belongs to others. Those who neither desire what belongs to others nor bestow what is their own are to be admonished to consider carefully that the earth out of which they are taken is common to all men, and therefore brings forth nourishment for all in common. Vainly, then, do those suppose themselves innocent, who claim to their own private use the common gift of God; those who, in not imparting what they have received, walk in the midst of the slaughter of their neighbors; since they almost daily slay so many persons as there are dying poor whose subsidies they keep close in their own possession. For, when we administer necessaries of any kind to the indigent, we do not bestow our own, but render them what is theirs; we rather pay a debt of justice than accomplish works of mercy. Whence also the Truth himself, when speaking of the caution required in shelving mercy, says, Take heed that you do not your justice before men.[21] The Psalmist also, in agreement with this sentence, says, He has dispersed, he has given to the poor, his justice endures forever.[22]

For, having first mentioned bounty bestowed upon the poor, he would not call this mercy, but rather justice: for it is surely just that whosoever receive what is given by a common Lord should use it in

21. Matthew 6:1.
22. Psalm 112:9.

common. Hence also Solomon says, whoever is just will give and will not spare.[23] They are to be admonished also anxiously to take note how of the fig-tree that had no fruit the rigorous husbandman complains that it even cumbers the ground. For a fig-tree without fruit cumbers the ground, when the soul of the selfish one keeps unprofitably what might have benefited many. A fig-tree without fruit cumbers the ground, when the fool keeps barren under the shade of sloth a place which another might have cultivated under the sun of good works.

But these people sometimes say, "We use what has been granted us; we do not seek what belongs to others; and, if we do nothing worthy of the reward of mercy, we still commit no wrong." So they think, because in truth they close the ear of their heart to the words which are from heaven. For the rich man in the Gospel who was clothed in purple and fine linen, and feasted sumptuously every day, is not said to have seized what belonged to others, but to have used what was his own unfruitfully; and avenging hell received him after this life, not because he did anything unlawful but because by immoderate indulgence he gave up his whole self to what was lawful.

The selfish are to be admonished to take notice that they do God, in the first place, this wrong; that to Him Who gives them all they render in return no sacrifice of mercy. For hence the Psalmist says he will not give his propitiation to God, nor the price of the redemption of his soul.[24] For to give the price of redemption is to return good deeds for preventing grace. Hence John cries aloud saying, Now the axe is laid unto the raft of the tree. Every tree which does not brings forth good fruit will be hewn down and cast into the fire.[25] Let those, therefore, who esteem themselves guiltless because they do not seize on what belongs to others look forward to the stroke of the axe that is nigh at hand, and lay aside the torpor of improvident security, lest, while they neglect to bear the fruit of good deeds, they be cut off from the present life utterly, as it were from the greenness of the root.

But, on the other hand, those who both give what they have and desist not from seizing on what belongs to others are to be admonished

23. Proverbs 21:26.
24. Psalm 68:96.
25. Luke 3:9.

not to desire to appear exceeding munificent, and so be made worse from the outward show of good. For these, giving what is their own without discretion, not only, as we have said above, fall into the murmuring of impatience, but, when want urges them, are swept along even to avarice. What, then, is more wretched than the mind of those in whom avarice is born of bountifulness, and a crop of sins is sown as it were from virtue? First, then, they are to be admonished to learn how to keep what is theirs reasonably, and then in the end not to go about getting what is another's. For, if the root of the fault is not burnt out in the profusion itself, the thorn of avarice, exuberant through the branches, is never dried up. So then, cause for seizing is withdrawn, if the right of possession be first adjusted well. But then, further, let those who are admonished be told how to give mercifully what they have, when they have learnt not to confound the good of mercy by throwing into it the wickedness of robbery. For they violently exact what they mercifully bestow. For it is one thing to show mercy on account of our sins; another thing to sin on account of showing mercy; which can no longer indeed be called mercy, since it cannot grow into sweet fruit, being embittered by the poison of its pestiferous root. For hence it is that the Lord through the prophet rejects even sacrifices themselves, saying, I the Lord love judgment, and I hate robbery in a whole burnt offering.[26] Hence again He has said, The sacrifices of the ungodly are abominable, which are offered of wickedness.[27] Such persons also often withdraw from the indigent what they give to God.

But the Lord shows with what strong censure he disowns them, saying through a certain wise man, Whoever offers a sacrifice of the substance of the poor does as one that kills the son before the father's eyes.[28] For what can be more intolerable than the death of a son before his father's eyes? Wherefore it is shown with what great wrath this kind of sacrifice is beheld, in that it is compared to the grief of a bereaved father. And yet for the most part people weigh well how much they give; but how much they seize they neglect to consider. They count, as it were, their wage, but refuse to consider their defaults. Let them

26. Isaiah 61:8.
27. Proverbs 21:28.
28. Sirach 34:20.

hear therefore what is written, He that has gathered wages has put them into a bag with holes.[29] For indeed money put into a bag with holes is seen when it is put in, but when it is lost it is not seen. Those, then, who have an eye to how much they bestow, but consider not how much they seize, put their wages into a bag with holes, because in truth they look to them when they gather them together in hope of being secure, but lose them without looking.

Reading Questions

1. How does poverty influence righteousness? Are poor sinners the same as rich sinners?

2. In what way does Gregory fear that people might consider themselves to be sinning "with impunity"?

3. Summarize the arguments of the three main targets of Gregory's admonitions.

4. How does "the least of these" passage support Gregory's argument? How are love for God and love for neighbor fused in Gregory theology?

For Further Reading

Butler, E. C. *Western Mysticism.* 2d ed. New York: Harper & Row, 1966.

Dudden, F. Holmes. *Gregory the Great: His Place in History and Thought.* 1905. Reprinted, Eugene, OR: Wipf & Stock, 2004.

Evans, G. R. *The Thought of Gregory the Great.* Cambridge: Cambridge University Press, 1986.

Richards, J. *Consul of God: The Life and Times of Gregory the Great.* London: Routledge and Kegan Paul, 1980.

Zinn, Grover A. Jr. "Gregory I, the Great." In *Encyclopedia of Early Christianity,* edited by Everett Ferguson, 393–97. New York: Garland, 1990.

29. Haggai 1:6.

19

St. Benedict of Nursia

✳

Benedict (480–557) was born to an established Italian family in Nursia and was sent as a boy to Rome for his education. Rome was in the middle of a tumultuous era, and Benedict retreated from both his studies and society into seclusion. Stories circulated concerning miracles that occurred during his seclusion, and many people flocked to learn from him as a monastic leader. His Rule of Monastic Life *is rough and repetitive, but it became the guidebook for centuries of monastic communities.*

. . .

Rule of Monastic Life[1]

PROLOGUE: Listen, O my son, to the precepts of your master, and incline the ear of your heart, and cheerfully receive and faithfully execute the admonitions of your loving Father, that by the toil of obedience you may return to Him from whom by the sloth of disobedience you hast gone away.

To you, therefore, my speech is now directed, who, giving up your own will, take up the strong and most excellent arms of obedience, to do battle for Christ the Lord, the true King.

In the first place, beg of Him by most earnest prayer, that He perfect whatever good you dost begin, in order that He who hath been pleased to count us in the number of His children, need never be grieved at our evil deeds. For we ought at all times so to serve Him with the good things which He hath given us, that He may not, like an angry father, disinherit his children, nor, like a dread lord, enraged at our evil deeds, hand us over to everlasting punishment as most wicked servants, who would not follow Him to glory.

Let us then rise at length, since the Scripture arouses us, saying: "It is now the hour for us to rise from sleep";[2] and having opened our eyes to the deifying light, let us hear with awestruck ears what the divine voice, crying out daily, admonishes us, saying: "Today, if you will hear his voice, harden not your hearts."[3] And again: "He that has ears to hear let him hear what the Spirit says to the churches."[4] And what does He say?—"Come, children, listen to me, I will teach you the fear of the Lord."[5] "Walk while you have the light of life, that the darkness of death overtake you not."[6]

And the Lord seeking His workman in the multitude of the people, to whom He proclaims these words, says again: "Who is the man

1. From *Rule of St. Benedict* (Grand Rapids: Christian Classics Ethereal Library, 1947). This text was translated by Boniface Verheyen. A number of minor, modernizing changes have been made to this translation.

2. Romans 13:11.

3. Psalm 95:8.

4. Revelation 2:7.

5. Psalm 34:11.

6. John 12:35.

that desires life and loves to see good days?"[7] If hearing this you answer, "I am he," God says to you: "If you would have true and everlasting life, keep your tongue from evil, and your lips from speaking guile; turn away from evil and do good; seek after peace and pursue it."[8] And when you will have done these things, my eyes will be on you, and my ears hear your prayers. And before you will call on me I will say: "Behold, I am here."[9]

What, dearest brethren, can be sweeter to us than this voice of the Lord inviting us? See, in His loving kindness, the Lord shows us the way of life. Therefore, having our loins girded with faith and the performance of good works, let us walk His ways under the guidance of the Gospel, that we may be found worthy of seeing Him who has called us to His kingdom.[10]

If we desire to dwell in the tabernacle of His kingdom, we cannot reach it in any way, unless we run there by good works. But let us ask the Lord with the Prophet, saying to Him: "Lord, who will dwell in Your tabernacle, or who will rest in Your holy hill?"[11]

After this question, brethren, let us listen to the Lord answering and showing us the way to this tabernacle, saying: "He that walks without blemish and works justice; he that speaks truth in his heart; who has not used deceit in his tongue, nor has done evil to his neighbor, nor has taken up a reproach against his neighbor,"[12] who has brought to naught the foul demon tempting him, casting him out of his heart with his temptation, and has taken his evil thoughts while they were yet weak and has dashed them against Christ, who fearing the Lord are not puffed up by their goodness of life, but holding that the actual good which is in them cannot be done by themselves, but by the Lord, they praise the Lord working in them, saying with the Prophet: "Not to us, O Lord, not to us; by to Your name give glory."[13] Thus also the

7. Psalm 34:13.
8. Psalm 34:14–15.
9. Isaiah 58:9.
10. 1 Thessalonians 2:12.
11. Psalm 15:1.
12. Psalm 15:23.
13. Psalm 115:1.

Apostle Paul has not taken to himself any credit for his preaching, saying: "By the grace of God, I am what I am."[14] And again he says: "He that glories, let him glory in the Lord."[15]

Hence, the Lord also says in the Gospel: "He that hears these my words and does them, will be like a wise man who built his house upon a rock; the floods came, the winds blew, and they beat upon that house, and it fell not, for it was founded on a rock.[16]" The Lord fulfilling these words waits for us from day to day, that we respond to His holy admonitions by our works. Therefore, our days are lengthened to a truce for the amendment of the misdeeds of our present life; as the Apostle says: "Do you not know that the patience of God leads you to penance?"[17] For the good Lord says: "I will not the death of the sinner, but that he be converted and live."[18]

Now, brethren, that we have asked the Lord who it is that will dwell in His tabernacle, we have heard the conditions for dwelling there; and if we fulfill the duties of tenants, we will be heirs of the kingdom of heaven. Our hearts and our bodies must, therefore, be ready to do battle under the biddings of holy obedience; and let us ask the Lord that He supply by the help of His grace what is impossible to us by nature. And if, flying from the pains of hell, we desire to reach life everlasting, then, while there is yet time, and we are still in the flesh, and are able during the present life to fulfill all these things, we must make haste to do now what will profit us forever.

We are, therefore, about to found a school of the Lord's service, in which we hope to introduce nothing harsh or burdensome. But even if, to correct vices or to preserve charity, sound reason dictates anything that turns out somewhat stringent, do not at once fly in dismay from the way of salvation, the beginning of which cannot but be narrow. But as we advance in the religious life and faith, we will run the way of God's commandments with expanded hearts and unspeakable sweetness of love; so that never departing from His guidance and

14. 1 Corinthians 15:10.
15. 2 Corinthians 10:17.
16. Matthew 7:24–25.
17. Romans 2:4.
18. Ezekiel 33:11.

persevering in the monastery in His doctrine till death, we may by patience share in the sufferings of Christ, and be found worthy to be coheirs with Him of His kingdom.

Chapter 4: The Instruments of Good Works

(1) In the first place to love the Lord God with the whole heart, the whole soul, the whole strength . . .

(2) Then, one's neighbor as one's self (Matthew 22:37–39; Mark 12:30–31; Luke 10:27).

(3) Then, not to kill . . .

(4) Not to commit adultery . . .

(5) Not to steal . . .

(6) Not to covet (Romans 13:9).

(7) Not to bear false witness (Matthew 19:18; Mark 10:19; Luke 18:20).

(8) To honor all men (1 Peter 2:17).

(9) And what one would not have done to himself, not to do to another (Tobit 4:16; Matthew 7:12; Luke 6:31).

(10) To deny one's self in order to follow Christ (Matthew 16:24; Luke 9:23).

(11) To chastise the body (1 Corinthians 9:27).

(12) Not to seek after pleasures.

(13) To love fasting.

(14) To relieve the poor.

(15) To clothe the naked . . .

(16) To visit the sick (Matthew 25:36).

(17) To bury the dead.

(18) To help in trouble.

(19) To console the sorrowing.

(20) To hold one's self aloof from worldly ways.

(21) To prefer nothing to the love of Christ.

(22) Not to give way to anger.

(23) Not to foster a desire for revenge.

(24) Not to entertain deceit in the heart.

(25) Not to make a false peace.

(26) Not to forsake charity.

(27) Not to swear, lest perchance one swear falsely.

(28) To speak the truth with heart and tongue.

(29) Not to return evil for evil (I Thessalonians 5:15; 1 Peter 3:9).

(30) To do no injury, yea, even patiently to bear the injury done us.

(31) To love one's enemies (Matthew 5:44; Luke 6:27).

(32) Not to curse them that curse us, but rather to bless them.

(33) To bear persecution for justice sake (Matthew 5:10).

(34) Not to be proud . . .

(35) Not to be given to wine (Titus 1:7; 1 Timothy 3:3).

(36) Not to be a great eater.

(37) Not to be drowsy.

(38) Not to be slothful (Romans 12:11).

(39) Not to be a murmurer.

(40) Not to be a detractor.

(41) To put one's trust in God.

(42) To refer what good one sees in himself, not to self, but to God.

(43) But as to any evil in himself, let him be convinced that it is his own and charge it to himself.

(44) To fear the Day of Judgment.

(45) To be in dread of hell.

(46) To desire eternal life with all spiritual longing.

(47) To keep death before one's eyes daily.

(48) To keep a constant watch over the actions of our life.

(49) To hold as certain that God sees us everywhere.

(50) To dash at once against Christ the evil thoughts which rise in one's heart.

(51) And to disclose them to our spiritual father.

(52) To guard one's tongue against bad and wicked speech.

(53) Not to love much speaking.

(54) Not to speak useless words and such as provoke laughter.

(55) Not to love much or boisterous laughter.

(56) To listen willingly to holy reading.

(57) To apply one's self often to prayer.

(58) To confess one's past sins to God daily in prayer with sighs and tears, and to amend them for the future.

(59) Not to fulfill the desires of the flesh (Galatians 5:16).

(60) To hate one's own will.

(61) To obey the commands of the Abbot in all things, even though he himself (which Heaven forbid) act otherwise, mindful of that precept of the Lord: "What they say, do; what they do, do not" (Matthew 23:3).

(62) Not to desire to be called holy before one is; but to be holy first, that one may be truly so called.

(63) To fulfill daily the commandments of God by works.

(64) To love chastity.

(65) To hate no one.

(66) Not to be jealous; not to entertain envy.

(67) Not to love strife.

(68) Not to love pride.

(69) To honor the aged.

(70) To love the younger.

(71) To pray for one's enemies in the love of Christ.

(72) To make peace with an adversary before the setting of the sun.

(73) And never to despair of God's mercy.

Behold, these are the instruments of the spiritual art, which, if they have been applied without ceasing day and night and approved on judgment day, will merit for us from the Lord that reward which He hath promised: "The eye hath not seen, nor the ear heard, neither has it entered into the heart of man, what things God hath prepared for them that love Him."[19] But the workshop in which we perform all these works with diligence is the enclosure of the monastery, and stability in the community.

Chapter 53: Of the Reception of Guests

Let all guests who arrive be received as Christ, because He will say: "I was a stranger and you took Me in."[20] And let due honor be shown

19. 1 Corinthians 2:9.

20. Matthew 25:35.

to all, especially to those "of the household of the faith"[21] and to wayfarers.

When, therefore, a guest is announced, let him be met by the Superior and the brethren with every mark of charity. And let them first pray together, and then let them associate with one another in peace. This kiss of peace should not be given before a prayer has first been said, on account of satanic deception. In the greeting let all humility be shown to the guests, whether coming or going; with the head bowed down or the whole body prostrate on the ground, let Christ be adored in them as He is also received.

When the guests have been received, let them be accompanied to prayer, and after that let the Superior, or whom he will bid, sit down with them. Let the divine law be read to the guest that he may be edified, after which let every kindness be shown him. Let the fast be broken by the Superior in deference to the guest, unless, perchance, it be a day of solemn fast, which cannot be broken. Let the brethren, however, keep the customary fast. Let the Abbot pour the water on the guest's hands, and let both the Abbot and the whole brotherhood wash the feet of all the guests. When they have been washed, let them say this verse: "We have received Your mercy, O God, in the midst of Your temple."[22] Let the greatest care be taken, especially in the reception of the poor and travelers, because Christ is received more specially in them; whereas regard for the wealthy itself procures them respect.

Let the kitchen of the Abbot and the guests be apart, that the brethren may not be disturbed by the guests who arrive at uncertain times and who are never wanting in the monastery. Let two brothers who are able to fulfill this office well go into the kitchen for a year. Let help be given them as they need it, that they may serve without murmuring; and when they have not enough to do, let them go out again for work where it is commanded them. Let this course be followed, not only in this office, but in all the offices of the monastery—that whenever the brethren need help, it be given them, and that when they have nothing to do, they again obey orders. Moreover, let also a God-fearing brother have assigned to him the apartment of the guests,

21. Galatians 6:10.
22. Psalm 48:10.

where there should be sufficient number of beds made up; and let the house of God be wisely managed by the wise.

Reading Questions

1. How do "good works" relate to the Kingdom of God for Benedict?

2. How does the help of "grace" function here? Does Benedict strike a balance between grace and works?

3. Who are "the least of these" in the first section above (Chapter 4)? Who are they in the second (Chapter 53)?

4. Reflect on the litany of rules on Chapter 4. Do these sound unreasonable? What is the reasoning for them?

5. Reflect on monastic hospitality? How might this relate to the role of the monasteries during the middle ages?

For Further Reading

Chapman, J. *Saint Benedict and the Sixth Century.* 1929. Reprinted, Westport, CN: Greenwood, 1971.

Elder, L. Rozanne. *Benedictus: Studies in Honor of St. Benedict of Nursia.* Cistercian Studies Series 67. Kalamazoo, MI: Cistercian, 1981.

Matt, L. von, and S. Hilpisch. *Saint Benedict.* Chicago: Regnery, 1961.

Kardong, Terrence G. "Benedict of Nursia." In *Encyclopedia of Early Christianity,* edited by Everett Ferguson, 148–50. New York: Garland, 1990.

20

Bernard of Clairvaux

An eloquent and significant theologian arose in the twelfth century in the person of Bernard of Clairvaux (1090–1153). Bernard was a French monk who was instrumental in the development of the Cistercian monastic order and an important voice of stability and constancy during a tumultuous period in church history. Though he was born into a noble class and would have been able to secure high political positions within the church, Bernard insisted on becoming a monk. His eloquence and determined defense of the church quickly earned him fame and the trust of the popes. He is credited with using his influence to end a major controversy over papal succession in 1130. He also opposed the golden tongued theologian, Abelard, whom he prosecuted for heresy.

Two excerpts from his correspondence are included here, a long letter and a short one. In the first letter he addresses a man named Thomas who had taken his vows to join the Cistercian Order, which he was so instrumental in establishing. Thomas has become reluctant to join the monks at Clairvaux, and Bernard pens this eloquent correspondence to encourage him to overcome his hesitation. This letter is also a fascinating and thorough summary of Bernard's interpretation of faith, salvation, and the Christian life. The second letter is a brief but interesting use of Jesus' parable with respect to a very practical matter involving monks, hospitality, and road tolls.

. . .

Some Letters of Saint Bernard, Abbot of Clairvaux, Letter 15: To Thomas, Prior of Beverly[1]

To Thomas, Prior of Beverley

Bernard to his beloved son Thomas, as being his son.

1. What is the good of words? An ardent spirit and a strong desire cannot express themselves simply by the tongue. We want your sympathy and your bodily presence to speak to us; for if you come you will know us better, and we will better appreciate each other. We have long been held in a mutual bond as debtors one to another; for I owe you faithful care and you owe me submissive obedience. Let our actions and not our pens, if you please, prove each of us. I wish you would apply to yourself henceforth and carry out towards me those words of the Only Begotten: The works which the Father has given Me to finish, the same works bear witness of Me.[2] For, indeed, only thus does the spirit of the Only Son bear witness with our spirit that we also are the sons of God, when, quickening us from dead works, He causes us to bring forth the works of life. A good or bad tree is distinguished, not by its leaves or flowers, but by its fruit. So by their fruits, He says, you will know them.[3] Works, then, and not words, make the difference between sons of God and sons of unbelief. By works, accordingly, do you display your sincere desire and make proof of mine.

2. I long for your presence; my heart has long wished for you, and expected the fulfillment of your promises. Why am I so pressing? Certainly not from any personal or earthly feeling. I desire either to be profited by you or to be of service to you. Noble birth, bodily strength and beauty, the glow of youth, estates, palaces, and sumptuous furniture, external badges of dignity, and, I may also add, the world's wisdom—all these are of the world, and the world loves its own. But for how long will they endure? Forever? Assuredly not; for the world itself will not last forever; but these will not last even for long. In fact, the world will not be able long to keep these gifts for you, nor will you

---

1. Saint Bernard, Abbot of Clairvaux, *Some Letters of Saint Bernard, Abbot of Clairvaux* (Grand Rapids: Christian Classics Ethereal Library, 2002). This translation is in the public domain.

2. John 5:36.

3. Matthew 7:16.

dwell long in the world to enjoy them, for the days of man are short. The world passes away with its lusts, but it dismisses you before it quite passes away itself. How can you take unlimited pleasure in a love that soon must end? But I ever love you, not your possessions; let them go whence they were derived. I only require of you one thing: that you would be mindful of your promise, and not deny us any longer the satisfaction of your presence among us, who love you sincerely, and will love you forever. In fact, if we love purely in our life, we will also not be divided in death. For those gifts which I wish for in your case, or rather for you, belong not to the body or to time only; and so they fail not with the body, nor pass away with time; nay, when the body is laid aside they delight still more, and last when time is gone. They have nothing in common with the gifts above-mentioned, or such as they with which, I imagine, not the Father, but the world has endowed you. For which of these does not vanish before death, or at last fall a victim to it?

3. But, indeed, that is the best part, which will not be taken away forever. What is that? Eye hath not seen it, nor ear heard, neither hath it entered into the heart of man.[4] He who is a man and walks simply according to man's nature only, he who, to speak more plainly, is still content with flesh and blood, is wholly ignorant what that is, because flesh and blood will not reveal the things which God alone reveals through His Spirit. So the natural man is in no way admitted to the secret; in fact, he receives not the things of the Spirit of God.[5] Blessed are they who hear His words. I have called you friends, for all things that I have heard of My Father I have made known to you.[6] O, wicked world, which will not bless your friends except by making them enemies of God, and consequently unworthy of the council of the blessed. For clearly he who is willing to be your friend makes himself the enemy of God. And if the servant knows not what his Lord does, how much less the enemy? Moreover, the friend of the Bridegroom stands, and rejoices with joy because of the Bridegroom's voice; also it

4. 1 Corinthians 2:9.
5. 1 Corinthians 2:14.
6. John 15:15.

says, My soul failed when [my beloved] spoke[7]. And so the friend of the world is shut out from the council of the friends of God; who have received not the spirit of this world but the spirit which is of God, that they may know the things which are given to them of God. I thank You, O Father, because You have hidden these things from the wise and prudent, and have revealed them to babes; even so, Father, for so it seemed good in Your sight,[8] not because they of themselves deserved it. For all have sinned, and come short of Your glory, that You may freely send the Spirit of Your Son, crying in the hearts of the sons of adoption: Abba, Father. For those who are led by this Spirit, they are sons, and cannot be kept from their Father's council. Indeed, they have the Spirit dwelling within them, who searches even the deep things of God. In short, of what can they be ignorant whom grace teaches everything?

4. Woe to you, you sons of this world, because of your wisdom, which is foolishness! You know not the spirit of salvation, nor have share in the counsel, which the Father alone discloses alone to the Son, and to him to whom the Son will reveal Him. For who has known the mind of the Lord? Or who has been His counselor?[9] Not, indeed, on one; but only a few, only those who can truly say: The only begotten Son, which is in the bosom of the Father, He has declared Him. Woe to the world for its clamor! That same Only Begotten, like as the Angel of a great revelation, proclaims among the people: He who hath ears to hear let him hear. And since he finds not ears worthy to receive His words, and to whom He may commit the secret of the Father, he weaves parables for the crowd, that hearing they might not hear, and seeing they might not understand. But for His friends how different! With them He speaks apart: To you it is given to know the mysteries of the kingdom of God;[10] to whom also He says: Fear not, little flock, for it is your Father's good pleasure to give you the kingdom.[11] Who are these? These are they whom He foreknew and foreordained

7. Song of Songs 5:6.
8. Matthew 11:25–26.
9. Romans 11:34.
10. Luke 8:8–10.
11. Luke 12:32.

to be conformed to the image of His Son, that He might be the first born among many brethren. The Lord knows who are His. Here is His great secret and the counsel which He has made known unto men. But He judges no others worthy of a share in so great mystery, except those whom He has foreknown and foreordained as His own. For those whom He foreordained, them also He called. Who, except he be called, may approach God's counsel? Those whom He called, them also He justified. Over them a Sun arises, though not that sun which may daily be seen arising over good and bad alike, but He of whom the Prophet speaks when addressing himself to those alone who have been called to the counsel, he says: Unto you that fear My name will the Sun of Righteousness arise.[12] So while the sons of unbelief remain in darkness, the child of light leaves the power of darkness and comes into this new light, if once he can with faith say to God: I am a companion of all them that fear You.[13] Do you see how faith precedes, in order that justification may follow? Perchance, then, we are called through fear, and justified by love. Finally, the just will live by faith,[14] that faith, doubtless, which works by love.[15]

5. So at his call let the sinner hear what he has to fear; and thus coming to the Sun of Righteousness, let him, now enlightened, see what he must love. For what is that saying: The merciful goodness of the Lord endures from everlasting to everlasting upon them that fear Him.[16] From everlasting, because of predestination, to everlasting, because of glorification. The one process is without beginning, the other knows no ending. Indeed, those whom He predestines from everlasting, He glorifies to everlasting, with an interval, at least, in the case of adults, of calling and justification between. So at the rising of the Sun of Righteousness, the mystery, hidden from eternity, concerning souls that have been predestinated and are to be glorified, begins in some degree to emerge from the depths of eternity, as each soul, called by fear and justified by love, becomes assured that it, too,

12. Malachi 9:2.
13. Psalm 119:63.
14. Romans 1:17.
15. Galatians 5:6.
16. Psalm 103:17.

is of the number of the blessed, knowing well that whom He justified, them also He glorified.[17] What then? The soul hears that it is called when it is stricken with fear. It feels also that it is justified when it is surrounded with love. Can it do otherwise than be confident that it will be glorified? There is a beginning; there is continuation. Can it despair only of the consummation? Indeed, if the fear of the Lord, in which our calling is said to consist, is the beginning of wisdom, surely the love of God—that love, I mean, which springs from faith, and is the source of our justification—is progress in wisdom. And so what but the consummation of wisdom is that glorification which we hope for at the last from the vision of God that will make us like Him? And so one deep calls another because of the noise of the water-pipes,[18] when, with terrible judgments, that unmeasured Eternity and Eternal Immensity, whose wisdom cannot be told, leads the corrupt and inscrutable heart of man by Its own power and goodness forth into Its own marvelous light . . .

7. And then at length God, as it were, divides the light from the darkness, when a sinner, enlightened by the first rays of the Sun of Righteousness; casts off the works of darkness and puts on the armor of light. His own conscience and the sins of his former life alike doom him as a true child of Hell to eternal fires; but under the looks with which the Dayspring from on high deigns to visit him, he breathes again, and even begins to hope beyond hope that he will enjoy the glory of the sons of God. For rejoicing at the near prospect with unveiled face, he sees it in the new light, and says: Lord, lift up the light of Your countenance upon us; You have put gladness in my heart;[19] Lord, what is man that You have such respect for him, or the son of man that You so regard him?[20] Now, O good Father, vile worm and worthy of eternal hatred as he is, he yet trusts that he is loved, because he feels that he loves; nay, because he has a foretaste of Your love he does not blush to make return of love. Now in Your brightness it becomes clear, Oh! Light that no man can approach, what good things

17. Romans 8:30.
18. Psalm 42:9.
19. Psalm 4:7.
20. Psalm 144:3.

You have in store for so poor a thing as man, even though he be evil! He loves not undeservedly, because he was loved without his deserving it; and his love is for everlasting, because he knows that he has been loved from everlasting. He brings to light for the comfort of the sorrowful the great design which from eternity had lain in the bosom of eternity, namely, that God wills not the death of a sinner, but rather that he should be converted and live. As a witness of this secret, Oh! man, you have the justifying Spirit bearing witness with your spirit that you yourself also are the son of God. Acknowledge the counsel of God in your justification; confess it and say, Your testimonies are my delight and my counselor.[21] For your present justification is the revelation of the Divine counsel, and a preparation for future glory. Or rather, perhaps, predestination itself is the preparation for it, and justification is more the gradual drawing near unto it. Indeed, it is said, Repent, for the kingdom of heaven is at hand.[22] And hear also of predestination that it is the preparation: Come, inherit, He says, the kingdom prepared for you from the foundation of the world.[23]

8. Let none, therefore, doubt that he is loved who already loves. The love of God freely follows our love which it preceded. For how can He grow weary of returning their love to those whom He loved even while they yet loved Him not? He loved them, I say; yes, He loved. For as a pledge of His love you have the Spirit; you have also Jesus, the faithful witness, and Him crucified. Oh! Double proof, and that most sure, of God's love towards us. Christ dies, and deserves to be loved by us. The Spirit works, and makes Him to be loved. The One shows the reason why He is loved: the Other how He is to be loved. The One commends His own great love to us; the Other makes it ours. In the One we see the object of love; from the Other we draw the power to love. With the One, therefore, is the cause; with the Other the gift of charity. What shame to watch, with thankless eyes, the Son of God dying—and yet this may easily happen, if the Spirit be not with us. But now, since the love of God is shed abroad in our hearts by the Holy

21. Psalm 119:24.
22. Matthew 3:2.
23. Matthew 25:34.

Ghost which is given to us,[24] having been loved we love; and as we love, we deserve to be loved yet more. For if, says the Apostle, while we were yet enemies, we have been reconciled to God through the death of His Son; much more, being reconciled, will we be saved through His life.[25] For He that spared not His own Son, but delivered Him up for us all, how will He not with Him also freely give us all things?

9. Since, then, the token of our salvation is twofold, namely, a twofold outpouring, of the Blood and of the Spirit, neither can profit without the other. For the Spirit is not given except to such as believe in the Crucified; and faith avails not unless it works by love. But love is the gift of the Spirit. If the second Adam (I speak of Christ) not only became a living soul, but also an enlivening spirit, dying as being the one, and raising the dead as being the other, how can that which dies in Him profit me, apart from that which enlivens? Indeed, He Himself says: It is the spirit that gives life, the flesh counts for nothing.[26] Now, what does "gives life" mean except "justifies"? For as sin is the death of the soul (The soul that sins is the one who will die),[27] without doubt righteousness is its life; for the just will live by faith.[28] Who, then, is righteous, except he who returns to God, who loves him, His reward of love? And this never happens unless the Spirit by faith reveals to the man the eternal purpose of God concerning his future salvation. Such a revelation is simply the infusion of spiritual grace, by which, with the mortification of the deeds of the flesh, man is made ready for the kingdom which flesh and blood cannot inherit. And he receives by one and the same Spirit both the reason for thinking that he is loved and the power of returning love, lest the love of God for us should be left without return.

10. This, then, is that holy and secret counsel which the Son has received from the Father by the Holy Spirit. This by the same Spirit He imparts to His own whom He knows, in their justification, and by the imparting He justifies. Thus in his justification each of the faith-

24. Romans 5:5.
25. Romans 8:32.
26. John 6:63.
27. Ezekiel 18:4.
28. Romans 1:17.

ful receives the power to begin to know himself even as he is known: when, for instance, there is given to him some foretaste of his own future happiness, as he sees how it lay hid from eternity in God, who foreordains it, but will appear more fully in God, who is effecting it. But concerning the knowledge that he has now, for his part, attained, let a man glory at present in the hope, not in the secure possession of it. How must we pity those who possess as yet no token of their own calling to this glad assembly of the righteous! Lord, who has believed our report?[29] Oh! that they would be wise and understand. But unless they believe they will not understand.

11. But you, too, you unhappy and heedless lovers of the world, have your purpose far from that of the just. Scale sticks close to scale, and there is no airhole between you. You, too, oh sons of impiety, have your purpose communicated one to another, but openly against the Lord and against His Christ.[30] For if, as the Scripture says, The fear of God, that is piety,[31] of course anyone who loves the world more than God is convicted of impiety and idolatry, of worshipping and serving the creature rather than the Creator. But if, as has been said, the holy and impious have each their purpose kept for themselves, doubtless there is a great gulf fixed between the two. For as the just keeps himself aloof from the purpose and council of evil men,[32] so the impious never rise in the judgment, nor sinners in the purpose for the just. For there is a purpose for the just, a gracious rain which God has set apart for His heritage. There is a purpose really secret, descending like rain into a fleece of wool—a sealed fount whereof no stranger may partake—a Sun of Righteousness rising only for such as fear God.

12. Moreover, the prophet, noting that the rest remain in their own dryness and darkness, being ignorant of the rain and of the light of the just, mocks and brands their unfruitful gloom and confused perversity. This is a nation, he says, that obeys not the voice of the

29. Isaiah 53:1.

30. Psalm 2:2.

31. Job 28:28; the wording of Bernard's quotations from Scripture often bear the marks of quotation from memory.

32. Psalm 1:6.

Lord their God.[33] You are not ready, oh! miserable men, to say with David, I will listen what the Lord God will say with regard to me,[34] for being exhausted abroad upon [the quest of] vanity and false folly, you seek not for the deepest and best hearing of the truth. Oh! you sons of men, how long will you blaspheme my honor, and have such pleasure in vanity and seek after delusions?[35] You are deaf to the voice of truth, and you know not the purpose of Him who thinks thoughts of peace, who also speaks peace to His people, and to His saints, and to those who are converted in heart. Now, he says, you are clean through the word which I have spoken to you.[36] Therefore, they who hear not this word are unclean.

13. But do you, dearly beloved, if you are making ready your inward ear for this Voice of God that is sweeter than honey and the honey-comb, flee from outward cares, that with your inmost heart clear and free you also may say with Samuel, Speak, Lord, for your servant hears.[37] This Voice sounds not in the market-place, and is not heard in public. It is a secret purpose, and seeks to be heard in secret. It will of a surety give you joy and gladness in hearing it, if you listen with attentive ear. Once it ordered Abraham to get him out of his country and from his kindred, that he might see and possess the land of the living.[38] Jacob left his brother and his home, and passed over Jordan with his staff, and was received in Rachel's embrace.[39] Joseph was lord in Egypt, having been torn by a fraud from his father and his home. Thus the Church is bidden, in order that the King may have pleasure in her beauty, to forget her own people and her father's house.[40] The boy Jesus was sought by His parents among their kinsfolk and acquaintance, and was not found.[41] Do you also flee from your brethren, if you wish to

33. Jeremiah 7:28.
34. Psalm 85:8.
35. Psalm 4:2.
36. John 15:3.
37. 1 Samuel 3:9.
38. Genesis 12:1.
39. Genesis 29:11.
40. Psalm 45:11–12.
41. Luke 2:44–45.

find the way of salvation? Flee, I say, from the midst of Babylon, flee from before the sword of the northwind. A bare sustenance I am ready to offer for the help of every one that flees. You call me your abbot; I refuse not the title for obedience' sake—obedience, I say, not that I demand it, but that I render it in service to others, even as The Son of Man came not to be ministered to, but to minister and to give His life a ransom for many.[42] But if you deem me worthy, receive as your fellow-disciple him whom you choose for your master. For we both have one Master, Christ. And so let Him be the end of this Letter, who is the End of the law for righteousness to every one that believes.[43]

Some Letters of Saint Bernard, Abbot of Clairvaux, Letter 57: To the Duke and Duchess of Lorraine

To the Duke and Duchess of Lorraine, Bernard, Abbot of Clairvaux, sends greeting, and prays that they may so lovingly and purely rejoice in each other's affection that the love of Christ alone maybe supreme in them both.

Ever since the needs of our Order obliged me to send for necessaries into your land I have found great favor and kindness in the eyes of your Grace. You freely displayed the blessings of your bounty on our people when they needed it. You freely remitted to them when traveling their toll,[44] the dues on their purchases, and any other legal due of yours. For all these things your reward is surely great in heaven, if, indeed, we believe that to be true which the Lord promises in His Gospel: Inasmuch as you have done it unto one of the least of these my brethren you have done it unto me.[45] But why is it that you allow your servants to take away again what you bestow? It seems to me that it is worthy of you and for your honor, that when you have been pleased to bestow anything for the safety of your souls no one should venture to demand it back again. If, then (which God forbid), you do

42. Matthew 20:28.

43. Romans 10:4.

44. Like modern tolls, people in Bernard's day were often required to pay tolls when passing through a town or country.

45. Matthew 25:40.

not repent of your good deed, and your general intention in respect
to us is still the same, be pleased to order it to be a firm and unshaken
rule; that from now on our brethren may never fear to be disturbed in
this matter by any of your servants. But otherwise we do not refuse to
follow our Lord's example, who did not disdain to pay the dues. We
also are ready willingly to render to Cæsar the things that are Cæsar's,[46]
custom to whom custom, and tribute to whom tribute is due,[47] especially because, according to the Apostle, we ought not to seek our gift
so much as your gain.[48]

Reading Questions

1. Bernard writes much about love, and the role of love in conversion.
   Describe how love functions according to Bernard.

2. How do the Holy Spirit and the Son function with respect to the
   communication of God's love?

3. For Bernard, does "belief" or "understanding" come first? Why?

4. How is Matthew 25 invoked in the first reading? The second?

5. What are the sins and temptations which Bernard sees as most
   dangerous?

For Further Reading

Dumont, Charles. *Pathway of Peace: Cistercian Wisdom according to Saint
Bernard.* Translated by Elizabeth Connor. Cistercian Studies Series 187.
Kalamazoo, MI: Cistercian, 1999.

Evans, Gillian R. *Bernard of Clairvaux.* Great Medieval Thinkers. Oxford:
Oxford University Press, 2000.

McGuire, Brian Patrick. *The Difficult Saint: Bernard of Clairvaux and His Tradition.* Cistercian Studies Series 126. Kalamazoo, MI: Cistercian, 1991.

Sommerfeldt, John R. *Bernard of Clairvaux on the Spirituality of Relationship.*
New York: Newman, 2004.

46. Matthew 17:26.
47. Romans 13:7.
48. Philippians 4:17.

21

Thomas Aquinas

Christian theology was dramatically transformed by the work of Thomas Aquinas (1225–1274). Thomas managed to be faithful to the treasured theology of the Church Fathers while simultaneously introducing elements of the teaching of Aristotle in his understanding of God's nature, Scripture, and salvation history. His vast corpus offers a number of insightful references to Matthew 25:31–46. Several of these occur in his extremely influential work Summa Theologica, *which is the source for all five readings below. This sampling allows us to see the careful reasoning and theological exactness which made Thomas one of the most important theological minds in Christian history.*

. . .

Summa Theologica, Question 10, Article 3: Whether to be eternal belongs to God alone?[1]

Objection 1: It seems that it does not belong to God alone to be eternal. For it is written that "those who instruct many to justice," will be "as stars unto perpetual eternities."[2] Now if God alone were eternal, there could not be many eternities. Therefore God alone is not the only eternal.

Objection 2: Further, it is written "Depart, you cursed, into eternal 'everlasting' fire."[3] Therefore God is not the only eternal.

Objection 3: Further, every necessary thing is eternal. But there are many necessary things; as, for instance, all principles of demonstration and all demonstrative propositions. Therefore God is not the only eternal.

On the contrary, Jerome says that "God is the only one who has no beginning." Now whatever has a beginning is not eternal. Therefore God is the only one eternal.

I answer that, Eternity truly and properly so called is in God alone, because eternity follows on immutability; as appears from the first article. But God alone is altogether immutable, as was shown above. Accordingly, however, as some receive immutability from Him, they share in His eternity. Thus some receive immutability from God in the way of never ceasing to exist; in that sense it is said of the earth, "it stands forever."[4] Again, some things are called eternal in Scripture because of the length of their duration, although they are in nature corruptible;[5] thus the hills are called "eternal" and we read "of the fruits

---

1. Thomas Aquinas, *Summa Theologica*, translated by the Fathers of the English Dominican Province (Benziger Brothers, 1947 edition). This text is in the public domain. A number of minor and modernizing editorial changes have been made to this translation.

2. Daniel 12:3.

3. Matthew 25:41.

4. Ecclesiastes 1:4.

5. Psalm 75:5.

of the eternal hills."[6] Some again, share more fully than others in the nature of eternity, inasmuch as they possess unchangeableness either in being or further still in operation; like the angels, and the blessed, who enjoy the Word, because "as regards that vision of the Word, no changing thoughts exist in the Saints," as Augustine says.[7] Hence those who see God are said to have eternal life; according to that text, "This is eternal life, that they may know You the only true God," etc.[8]

Reply to Objection 1: There are said to be many eternities, accordingly as many share in eternity, by the contemplation of God.

Reply to Objection 2: The fire of hell is called eternal, only because it never ends. Still, there is change in the pains of the lost, according to the words "To extreme heat they will pass from snowy waters."[9] Hence in hell true eternity does not exist, but rather time; according to the text of the Psalm "Their time will be for ever."[10]

Reply to Objection 3: Necessary means a certain mode of truth; and truth, according to the Philosopher [Aristotle] is in the mind.[11] Therefore in this sense the true and necessary are eternal, because they are in the eternal mind, which is the divine intellect alone; hence it does not follow that anything beside God is eternal.

Question 5, Article 4:
Whether happiness once had can be lost?

Objection 1: It would seem that Happiness can be lost. For Happiness is a perfection. But every perfection is in the thing perfected according to the mode of the latter. Since then man is, by his nature, changeable,

---

6. Deuteronomy 33:15.
7. Augustine, *On the Trinity,* chapter 15.
8. John 17:3.
9. Job 24:19.
10. Psalm 80:16.
11. Aristotle, *Metaphysics,* chapter 6.

it seems that Happiness is participated by man in a changeable manner. And consequently it seems that man can lose Happiness.

Objection 2: Further, Happiness consists in an act of the intellect; and the intellect is subject to the will. But the will can be directed to opposites. Therefore it seems that it can desist from the operation whereby man is made happy: and thus man will cease to be happy.

Objection 3: Further, the end corresponds to the beginning. But man's Happiness has a beginning, since man was not always happy. Therefore it seems that it has an end.

On the contrary, It is written of the righteous that "they will go . . . into life everlasting,"[12] which, as above stated, is the Happiness of the saints. Now what is eternal ceases not. Therefore Happiness cannot be lost.

I answer that, If we speak of imperfect happiness, such as can be had in this life, in this sense it can be lost. This is clear of contemplative happiness, which is lost either by forgetfulness, for instance, when knowledge is lost through sickness; or again by certain occupations, whereby a man is altogether withdrawn from contemplation.

This is also clear of active happiness: since man's will can be changed so as to fall to vice from the virtue, in whose act that happiness principally consists. If, however, the virtue remain unimpaired, outward changes can indeed disturb such like happiness, in so far as they hinder many acts of virtue; but they cannot take it away altogether because there still remains an act of virtue, whereby man bears these trials in a praiseworthy manner. And since the happiness of this life can be lost, a circumstance that appears to be contrary to the nature of happiness, therefore did the Philosopher state that some are happy in this life, not simply, but "as men," whose nature is subject to change.[13]

---

12. Matthew 25:46.
13. Aristotle, *Nicomachean Ethics*, 1:10.

But if we speak of that perfect Happiness which we await after this life, it must be observed that Origen,[14] following the error of certain Platonists, held that man can become unhappy after the final Happiness. This, however, is evidently false, for two reasons. First, from the general notion of happiness. For since happiness is the "perfect and sufficient good," it must needs set man's desire at rest and exclude every evil. Now man naturally desires to hold to the good that he has, and to have the surety of his holding: else he must of necessity be troubled with the fear of losing it, or with the sorrow of knowing that he will lose it. Therefore it is necessary for true Happiness that man have the assured opinion of never losing the good that he possesses. If this opinion be true, it follows that he never will lose happiness: but if it be false, it is in itself an evil that he should have a false opinion: because the false is the evil of the intellect, just as the true is its good, as stated in [Aristotle's] Ethics[15]. . . . Consequently he will no longer be truly happy, if evil be in him.

Secondly, it is again evident if we consider the specific nature of Happiness. For . . . man's perfect Happiness consists in the vision of the Divine Essence. Now it is impossible for anyone seeing the Divine Essence, to wish not to see It. Because every good that one possesses and yet wishes to be without, is either insufficient, something more sufficing being desired in its stead; or else has some inconvenience attached to it, by reason of which it becomes wearisome. But the vision of the Divine Essence fills the soul with all good things, since it unites it to the source of all goodness; hence it is written: "I will be satisfied when Your glory appears";[16] and: "All good things came to me together with her,"[17] i.e. with the contemplation of wisdom. In like manner neither has it any inconvenience attached to it; because it is written of the contemplation of wisdom: "Her conversation has no bitterness, nor her company any tediousness." It is thus evident that the happy man cannot forsake Happiness of his own accord. Moreover, neither can he lose Happiness, through God taking it away from him. . . .

14. Origen, *Peri Archon*, 2:3.
15. Aristotle, *Nicomachean Ethics*.
16. Psalm 17:15.
17. Wisdom of Solomon 8:16.

Nor again can it be withdrawn by any other agent. Because the mind that is united to God is raised above all other things: and consequently no other agent can sever the mind from that union. Therefore it seems unreasonable that as time goes on, man should pass from happiness to misery, and vice versa; because such like vicissitudes of time can only be for such things as are subject to time and movement.

Reply to Objection 1: Happiness is consummate perfection, which excludes every defect from the happy. And therefore whoever has happiness has it altogether unchangeably: this is done by the Divine power, which raises man to the participation of eternity which transcends all change.

Reply to Objection 2: The will can be directed to opposites, in things which are ordained to the end; but it is ordained, of natural necessity, to the last end. This is evident from the fact that man is unable not to wish to be happy.

Reply to Objection 3: Happiness has a beginning owing to the condition of the participator: but it has no end by reason of the condition of the good, the participation of which makes man happy. Hence the beginning of happiness is from one cause, its endlessness is from another.

Question 24, Article 3: Whether charity is infused according to the capacity of our natural gifts?

Objection 1: It would seem that charity is infused according to the capacity of our natural gifts. For it is written that "He gave to every one according to his own ability."[18] Now, in man, none but natural virtue precedes charity, since there is no virtue without charity, as stated above. Therefore God infuses charity into man according to the measure of his natural virtue.

Objection 2: Further, among things ordained towards one another, the second is proportionate to the first: thus we find in natural things

18. Matthew 25:15.

that the form is proportionate to the matter, and in gratuitous gifts, that glory is proportionate to grace. Now, since charity is a perfection of nature, it is compared to the capacity of nature as second to first. Therefore it seems that charity is infused according to the capacity of nature.

Objection 3: Further, men and angels partake of happiness according to the same measure, since happiness is alike in both, according to Matthew 22:30 and Luke 20:36. Now charity and other gratuitous gifts are bestowed on the angels, according to their natural capacity, as the Master teaches. Therefore the same apparently applies to man.

On the contrary, It is written: "The Spirit breathes where He will,"[19] and: "All these things one and the same Spirit works, dividing to every one according as He will."[20] Therefore charity is given, not according to our natural capacity, but according as the Spirit wills to distribute His gifts.

I answer that, The quantity of a thing depends on the proper cause of that thing, since the more universal cause produces a greater effect. Now, since charity surpasses the proportion of human nature, as stated above it depends, not on any natural virtue, but on the sole grace of the Holy Ghost Who infuses charity. Wherefore the quantity of charity depends neither on the condition of nature nor on the capacity of natural virtue, but only on the will of the Holy Ghost Who "divides" His gifts "according as He will." Hence the Apostle says: "To every one of us is given grace according to the measure of the giving of Christ."[21]

Reply to Objection 1: The virtue in accordance with which God gives His gifts to each one, is a disposition or previous preparation or effort of the one who receives grace. But the Holy Ghost forestalls even this disposition or effort, by moving man's mind either more or less, ac-

19. John 3:8.
20. 1 Corinthians 12:11.
21. Ephesians 4:7.

cording as He will. Wherefore the Apostle says: "Who hath made us worthy to be partakers of the lot of the saints in light."[22]

Reply to Objection 2: The form does not surpass the proportion of the matter. In like manner grace and glory are referred to the same genus, for grace is nothing else than a beginning of glory in us. But charity and nature do not belong to the same genus, so that the comparison fails.

Reply to Objection 3: The angel's is an intellectual nature, and it is consistent with his condition that he should be borne wholly however he is born . . . Hence there was a greater effort in the higher angels, both for good in those who persevered, and for evil in those who fell, and consequently those of the higher angels who remained steadfast became better than the others, and those who fell became worse. But man's is a rational nature, with which it is consistent to be sometimes in potentiality and sometimes in act: so that it is not necessarily born wholly to whatever place it is born, and where there are greater natural gifts there may be less effort, and vice versa. Thus the comparison fails.

Question 32, Article 5:
Whether almsgiving is a matter of precept?[23]

Objection 1: It would seem that almsgiving is not a matter of precept. For the counsels are distinct from the precepts. Now almsgiving is a matter of counsel, according to Daniel: "Let my counsel be acceptable to the King; redeem your sins with alms."[24] Therefore almsgiving is not a matter of precept.

Objection 2: Further, it is lawful for everyone to use and to keep what is his own. Yet by keeping it he will not give alms. Therefore it is lawful not to give alms: and consequently almsgiving is not a matter of precept.

22. Colossians 1:12.
23. That which is a "matter of precept" is something mandatory.
24. Daniel 4:24.

Objection 3: Further, whatever is a matter of precept binds the transgressor at some time or other under pain of mortal sin, because positive precepts are binding for some fixed time. Therefore, if almsgiving were a matter of precept, it would be possible to point to some fixed time when a man would commit a mortal sin unless he gave an alms. But it does not appear how this can be so, because it can always be deemed probable that the person in need can be relieved in some other way, and that what we would spend in almsgiving might be needful to ourselves either now or in some future time. Therefore it seems that almsgiving is not a matter of precept.

Objection 4: Further, every commandment is reducible to the precepts of the Decalogue.[25] But these precepts contain no reference to almsgiving. Therefore almsgiving is not a matter of precept.

On the contrary, No man is punished eternally for omitting to do what is not a matter of precept. But some are punished eternally for omitting to give alms, as is clear from Matthew 25:41–43. Therefore almsgiving is a matter of precept.

I answer that, As love of our neighbor is a matter of precept, whatever is a necessary condition to the love of our neighbor is a matter of precept also. Now the love of our neighbor requires that not only should we be our neighbor's well-wishers, but also his well-doers, according to 1 John: "Let us not love in word, nor in tongue, but in deed, and in truth."[26] And in order to be a person's well-wisher and well-doer, we ought to succor his needs: this is done by almsgiving. Therefore almsgiving is a matter of precept.

Since, however, precepts are about acts of virtue, it follows that all almsgiving must be a matter of precept, in so far as it is necessary to virtue, namely, in so far as it is demanded by right reason. Now right reason demands that we should take into consideration something on the part of the giver, and something on the part of the recipient. On the part of the giver, it must be noted that he should give of his sur-

25. The Ten Commandments.
26. 1 John 3:18.

plus, according to Luke 11:41: "That which remains, give alms." This surplus is to be taken in reference not only to himself, so as to denote what is unnecessary to the individual, but also in reference to those of whom he has charge. Because each one must first of all look after himself and then after those over whom he has charge, and afterwards with what remains relieve the needs of others. Thus nature first, by its nutritive power, takes what it requires for the upkeep of one's own body, and afterwards yields the residue for the formation of another by the power of generation.

On the part of the recipient it is requisite that he should be in need, else there would be no reason for giving him alms: yet since it is not possible for one individual to relieve the needs of all, we are not bound to relieve all who are in need, but only those who could not be succored if we not did succor them. For in such cases the words of Ambrose apply, "Feed him that dies of hunger: if you have not fed him, you have slain him." Accordingly we are bound to give alms of our surplus, as also to give alms to one whose need is extreme: otherwise almsgiving, like any other greater good, is a matter of counsel.

Reply to Objection 1: Daniel spoke to a king who was not subject to God's Law, wherefore such things as were prescribed by the Law which he did not profess, had to be counseled to him. Or he may have been speaking in reference to a case in which almsgiving was not a matter of precept.

Reply to Objection 2: The temporal goods which God grants us, are ours as to the ownership, but as to the use of them, they belong not to us alone but also to such others as we are able to succor out of what we have over and above our needs. Hence Basil says: "If you acknowledge them," regarding your temporal goods, "as coming from God, is He unjust because He apportions them unequally? Why are you rich while another is poor, unless it be that you may have the merit of a good stewardship, and he the reward of patience? It is the hungry man's bread that you withhold, the naked man's cloak that you have stored away, the shoe of the barefoot that you have left to rot, the money of the needy that you have buried underground: and so you injure as many as you might help."[27] Ambrose expresses himself in the same way.

Reply to Objection 3: There is a time when we sin mortally if we omit to give alms; on the part of the recipient when we see that his need is evident and urgent, and that he is not likely to be succored otherwise—on the part of the giver, when he has superfluous goods, which he does not need for the time being, as far as he can judge with probability. Nor need he consider every case that may possibly occur in the future, for this would be to think about tomorrow, which Our Lord forbade us to do (Matthew 6:34), but he should judge what is superfluous and what necessary, according as things probably and generally occur.

Reply to Objection 4: All assistance given to our neighbor is reduced to the precept about honoring our parents. For thus does the Apostle interpret it (1 Timothy 4:8) where he says: "Dutifulness is profitable to all things, having promise of the life that now is, and of that which is to come," and he says this because the precept about honoring our parents contains the promise, "that you may be longlived upon the land"[28] and dutifulness comprises all kinds of almsgiving.

Question 133, Article 1—Whether cowardliness is a sin?[29]

Objection 1: It seems that cowardliness is not a sin. For every sin makes a man evil, just as every virtue makes a man good. But a fainthearted man is not evil, as the Philosopher says.[30] Therefore cowardliness is not a sin.

Objection 2: Further, the Philosopher says that "a fainthearted man is especially one who is worthy of great goods, yet does not deem himself

27. Basil the Great, *Homily on Luke 7:18.*

28. Exodus 20:12.

29. "Pusillanimity" is the normal translation for this word, but it has been replaced in the translation above by the more common word "cowardliness." What is somewhat lost in this replacement is the monetary stinginess somewhat implied by the word "pusillanimity." Ideally, this word should be rendered something like "monetary cowardliness" or "cheapness."

30. Aristotle, *Nicomachean Ethics,* 4:3.

worthy of them."[31] Now no one is worthy of great goods except the virtuous, since as the Philosopher again says, "none but the virtuous are truly worthy of honor."[32] Therefore the fainthearted are virtuous: and consequently cowardliness is not a sin.

Objection 3: Further, "Pride is the beginning of all sin."[33] But cowardliness does not proceed from pride, since the proud man sets himself above what he is, while the fainthearted man withdraws from the things he is worthy of. Therefore cowardliness is not a sin.

Objection 4: Further, the Philosopher says that "he who deems himself less worthy than he is, is said to be fainthearted."[34] Now sometimes holy men deem themselves less worthy than they are; for instance, Moses and Jeremias, who were worthy of the office God chose them for, which they both humbly declined.[35] Therefore cowardliness is not a sin.

On the contrary, Nothing in human conduct is to be avoided save sin. Now cowardliness is to be avoided: for it is written: "Fathers, provoke not your children to indignation, lest they be discouraged."[36] Therefore cowardliness is a sin.

I answer that, Whatever is contrary to a natural inclination is a sin, because it is contrary to a law of nature. Now everything has a natural inclination to accomplish an action that is commensurate with its power: as is evident in all natural things, whether animate or inanimate. Now just as presumption makes a man exceed what is proportionate to his power, by striving to do more than he can, so cowardliness makes a man fall short of what is proportionate to his power, by refusing to tend to that which is commensurate thereto. Wherefore as presumption is a sin, so is cowardliness. Hence it is that the servant who buried

31. Ibid.
32. Ibid.
33. Sirach 10:15.
34. Aristotle, *Nicomachean Ethics,* 4:3.
35. Exodus 3:11; Jeremiah 1:6.
36. Colossians 3:21.

in the earth the money he had received from his master, and did not trade with it through fainthearted fear, was punished by his master.[37]

Reply to Objection 1: The Philosopher calls those evil who injure their neighbor: and accordingly the fainthearted is said not to be evil, because he injures no one, save accidentally, by omitting to do what might be profitable to others. For Gregory says that if "they who demur to do good to their neighbor in preaching be judged strictly, without doubt their guilt is proportionate to the good they might have done had they been less retiring."[38]

Reply to Objection 2: Nothing hinders a person who has a virtuous habit from sinning venially and without losing the habit, or mortally and with loss of the habit of gratuitous virtue. Hence it is possible for a man, by reason of the virtue which he has, to be worthy of doing certain great things that are worthy of great honor, and yet through not trying to make use of his virtue, he sins sometimes venially, sometimes mortally. Again it may be replied that the fainthearted is worthy of great things in proportion to his ability for virtue, ability which he derives either from a good natural disposition, or from science, or from external fortune, and if he fails to use those things for virtue, he becomes guilty of cowardliness.

Reply to Objection 3: Even cowardliness may in some way be the result of pride: when, to wit, a man clings too much to his own opinion, whereby he thinks himself incompetent for those things for which he is competent. Hence it is written: "The sluggard is wiser in his own conceit than seven men that speak sentences."[39] For nothing hinders him from depreciating himself in some things, and having a high opinion of himself in others. Wherefore Gregory says of Moses that "perchance he would have been proud, had he undertaken the leadership of a

37. Matthew 25; Luke 19.
38. Gregory the Great, *Book of the Pastoral Rule,* Part I.
39. Proverbs 26:16.

numerous people without misgiving: and again he would have been proud, had he refused to obey the command of his Creator."[40]

Reply to Objection 4: Moses and Jeremiah were worthy of the office to which they were appointed by God, but their worthiness was of Divine grace: yet they, considering the insufficiency of their own weakness, demurred; though not obstinately lest they should fall into pride.

Reading Questions:

1. How does Thomas' define "eternity"?

2. According to Thomas, what are the different kinds of happiness that one can experience in life?

3. When Thomas uses the term "the Philosopher" he is referring to Aristotle. In the references above, what authority does Aristotle have? How does Aristotle influence Thomas' reasoning?

4. Where does our capacity to be charitable come from? Why is this an important question?

5. Thomas states above that "Whatever is contrary to a natural inclination is a sin." How does this statement compare to other definitions of what is sinful? According to Thomas, are humans sinful by nature?

For Further Reading

Davies, Brian. *Aquinas's Summa theologiae: Critical Essays.* Critical Essays on the Classics. Lanham, MD: Rowman & Littlefield, 2006.

Eschmann, Theodore. *The Ethics of Saint Thomas Aquinas: Two Courses.* Edited by Edward A. Synan. Toronto: Pontifical Institute of Mediaeval Studies, 1997.

---

40. Gregory the Great, *Book of the Pastoral Rule,* Part I.

22

Francis of Assisi

❋

Francis of Assisi (1182–1226) was born Giovanni Bernardone, one of several children of a wealthy cloth merchant. Though he enjoyed many of the benefits of being the child of a rich man, he developed a rebellious attitude toward his father's pursuit of wealth. He showed a compassionate concern for the poor, and after spending a year as a prisoner of war he began to have an increasingly sober attitude toward life, poverty, and spiritual insight. He became a wandering mystic and famous preacher, eventually founding the Franciscan Order and leaving a lasting impact on Christianity through his reverence for nature and heartfelt pursuit of spiritual enlightenment.

. . .

The Works of St. Francis of Assisi: That the Brothers shall appropriate nothing to themselves: and of seeking Alms and of the Sick Brothers [1]

The brothers shall appropriate nothing to themselves, neither a house nor place nor anything. And as pilgrims and strangers[2] in this world, serving the Lord in poverty and humility, let them go confidently in quest of alms, nor ought they to be ashamed, because the Lord made Himself poor for us in this world. This, my dearest brothers, is the height of the most sublime poverty which has made you heirs and kings of the kingdom of heaven: poor in goods, but exalted in virtue. Let that be your portion, for it leads to the land of the living;[3] cleaving to it unreservedly, my best beloved brothers, for the Name of our Lord Jesus Christ, never desire to possess anything else under heaven.

And wherever the brothers are and may find themselves, let them mutually show among themselves that they are of one household. And let one make known his needs with confidence to the other, for, if a mother nourishes and loves her carnal son, how much more earnestly ought one to love and nourish his spiritual brother! And if any of them should fall into illness, the other brothers must serve him as they would wish to be served themselves.

23. Prayer, Praise, and Thanksgiving

Almighty, most Holy, most High and Supreme God, Holy and Just Father, Lord King of heaven and earth, for Thyself we give thanks to Thee because by Thy holy will, and by Thine only Son, Thou hast created all things spiritual and corporal in the Holy Ghost and didst place us made to Thine image and likeness in paradise,[4] whence we fell by our own fault. And we give Thee thanks because, as by Thy Son Thou didst create us, so by the true and holy love with which Thou hast

---

1. From *The Writings of Saint Francis of Assisi*, newly translated into English with an Introduction and Notes by Father Paschal Robinson (Philadelphia: Dolphin, 1906).

2. 1 Peter 2:11

3. Psalm 141:6. St. Francis recited this Psalm on his deathbed.

4. Genesis 1:26; 2:15.

loved us,[5] Thou didst cause Him, true God and true Man, to be born of the glorious and ever-Virgin, most Blessed holy Mary, and didst will that He should redeem us captives by His Cross and Blood and Death. And we give thanks to Thee because Thy Son Himself is to come again in the glory of His Majesty to put the wicked who have not done penance for their sins, and have not known Thee, in eternal fire, and to say to all who have known Thee and adored Thee, and served Thee in penance: "Come, you blessed of My Father, possess the kingdom prepared for you from the beginning of the world."[6]

And since all we wretches and sinners are not worthy to name Thee, we humbly beseech Thee, that our Lord Jesus Christ, Thy beloved Son, in whom Thou art well pleased, together with the Holy Ghost, the Paraclete, may give thanks to Thee as it is pleasing to Thee and Them, for all; He suffices Thee always for all through whom Thou hast done so much for us. Alleluia. And we earnestly beg the glorious Mother, the most Blessed Mary ever-Virgin, Blessed Michael, Gabriel, Raphael, and all the choirs of the blessed spirits, seraphim, cherubim, and thrones, dominations, principalities and powers, virtues, angels and archangels, blessed John the Baptist, John the Evangelist, Peter, Paul, the blessed patriarchs and prophets, innocents, apostles, evangelists, disciples, martyrs, confessors, virgins, blessed Elias and Enoch, and all the Saints who have been and are, and shall be, for Thy love, that they may, as it is pleasing to Thee, give thanks for these things to the most high, true God, eternal and living, with Thy most dear Son, our Lord Jesus Christ, and the Holy Ghost, the Paraclete, for ever and ever. Amen. Alleluia.

And all we, brothers minor, useless servants, humbly entreat and beseech all those within the holy Catholic and Apostolic Church wishing to serve God, and all ecclesiastical Orders, priests, deacons, subdeacons, acolytes, exorcists, lectors, door-keepers, and all clerics; all religious men and women, all boys and children, poor and needy, kings and princes, laborers, husbandmen, servants and masters, all virgins, continent, and married people, laics, men and women, all infants, youths, young men and old, healthy and sick, all small and great,

5. John 17:26.
6. Matthew 25:34.

and all peoples, clans, tribes, and tongues, all nations and all men in all the earth, who are and shall be, that we may persevere in the true faith and in doing penance, for otherwise no one can be saved. Let us all love with all our heart, with all our soul, with all our mind, with all our strength and fortitude, with all our understanding and with all our powers,[7] with our whole might and whole affection, with our innermost parts, our whole desires, and wills, the Lord God, who has given, and gives to us all, the whole body, the whole soul, and our life; who has created and redeemed us, and by His mercy alone will save us; who has done and does all good to us, miserable and wretched, vile, unclean, ungrateful, and evil.

Let us therefore desire nothing else, wish for nothing else, and let nothing please and delight us except our Creator and Redeemer, and Savior, the only true God, who is full of good, all good, entire good, the true and supreme good, who alone is good,[8] merciful and kind, gentle and sweet, who alone is holy, just, true, and upright, who alone is benign, pure, and clean, from whom, and through whom, and in whom is all mercy, all grace, all glory of all penitents and of the just, and of all the blessed rejoicing in heaven. Let nothing therefore hinder us, let nothing separate us, let nothing come between us. Let us all, everywhere, in every place, at every hour, and at all times, daily and continually believe, truly and humbly, and let us hold in our hearts, and love, honor, adore, serve, praise and bless, glorify and exalt, magnify and give thanks to the most High and Supreme, Eternal God, in Trinity and Unity, to the Father, and Son, and Holy Ghost, to the Creator of all, to the Savior of all who believe and hope in Him, and love Him, who, without beginning or end, is immutable, invisible, unerring, ineffable, incomprehensible, unfathomable, blessed, praiseworthy, glorious, exalted, sublime, most high, sweet, amiable, lovable, and always wholly desirable above all forever and ever.

In the Name of the Lord, I beseech all the brothers that they learn the tenor and sense of those things that are written in this life for the salvation of our souls, and frequently recall them to mind. And I pray God that He who is Almighty, Three in One, may bless all who teach,

7. Deuteronomy 6:5; Mark 12:30, 33; Luke 10:27.
8. Luke 18:19.

learn, hold, remember, and fulfill those things as often as they repeat and do what is there written for our salvation. And I entreat all, kissing their feet, to love greatly, keep and treasure up these things. And on the part of Almighty God and of the Lord Pope, and by obedience, I, Brother Francis, strictly command and enjoin that no one subtract from those things that are written in this life, or add anything written to it over and above, and that the brothers have no other Rule.

Glory be to the Father, and to the Son, and to the Holy Ghost. As it was in the beginning, is now and ever shall be, world without end. Amen.

Reading Questions

1. What is the importance of "penance" in Assisi's prayers and admonitions?

2. Reflect on the poverty advocated by Francis for his Order in light of his wealthy upbringing.

3. Francis calls God "ineffable, incomprehensible" and "unfathomable." How does Christian theology discuss God in light of these restrictions on articulations?

For Further Reading

Boff, Leonardo. *Francis of Assisi: A Model for Human Liberation.* Translated by John W. Dierksmeier. Maryknoll, NY: Orbis, 2006.

Cunningham, Lawrence S. *Francis of Assisi: Performing the Gospel Life.* Grand Rapids: Eerdmans, 2004.

Galli, Mark. *Francis of Assisi and His World.* IVP Histories. Downers Grove, IL: InterVarsity, 2002.

Le Goff, Jacques. *Saint Francis of Assisi.* Translated by Christine Rhone. London: Routledge, 2004.

23

Julian of Norwich

✻

History provides little direct biographical information concerning Julian of Norwich (1342–1413), but her writings and her setting provide a powerful window into a creative and sometimes shocking theological imagination. Her name and family background are unknown to us. We know that she came to live in a small room adjacent to her English church at the age of thirty, taking on the name of the Julian, the patron saint of the church. The Black Plague was a daily reality for Julian, first hitting Norwich when Julian was a young child and devastating the population of Europe throughout her life, eventually claiming the lives of one-third of the European population. Some scholars have guessed that she may have been widowed by the plague or by war. Her age and the turmoil of her era make this a distinct possibility. Her home at the church is called an "anchorage," a small room in which the "anchoress" would enter for the purpose of lifelong prayer and meditation. Often the door was sealed or the wall finished, illustrating the permanence of this living situation. Julian had a small window into the church where she could observe the mass and a small window where she could receive food and gifts, dispose of waste, and communicate with people who came to her for prayer or advice. She spent more than forty years praying and writing in her anchorage before her death in 1413.

The passages below are taken from her "Showings," based on revelations she experienced while near death, her body wracked by a terrible sickness. She is considered a "mystic" because she reports direct experiences of Jesus, and a profoundly intimate communion with God. Though she makes no direct scriptural references in her "Revelations of Divine Love," she is clearly well versed in both theology and Scripture. Scholars marvel at her theological acumen. A small percentage of women during this difficult era would have had the level of literary and theological education evident in her writings. One of her revelations below has been tentatively aligned with Jesus' "least of these" parable, but it will be left to the reader to explore the validity of this connection. It cannot be denied that Julian's writings have pushed Christians to examine the significance of the relationship between pain, suffering, and divine love.

. . .

Revelations of Divine Love, Chapter 17: "How might any pain be more to me than to see Him that is all my life, and all my bliss, and all my joy suffer?"[1]

And in this dying was brought to my mind the words of Christ: I thirst.

For I saw in Christ a double thirst: one bodily; another spiritual

. . . .

For this word was shown for the bodily thirst: which I understood was caused by failing of moisture. For the blessed flesh and bones was left all alone without blood and moisture. The blessed body dried alone long time with wringing of the nails and weight of the body. For I understood that for tenderness of the sweet hands and of the sweet feet, by the greatness, hardness, and grievousness of the nails the wounds waxed wide and the body sagged, for weight by long time hanging. And [there was also the] piercing and pressing of the head, and binding of the Crown all baked with dry blood, with the sweet hair clinging, and the dry flesh, to the thorns, and the thorns to the flesh drying; and in the beginning while the flesh was fresh and bleeding, the continual sitting of the thorns made the wounds wide. And furthermore I saw that the sweet skin and the tender flesh, with the hair and the blood, was all raised and loosed about from the bone, with the thorns through it were rent in many pieces, as a cloth that were sagging, as if it would hastily have fallen off, for heaviness and looseness, while it had natural moisture. And that was great sorrow and dread to me: for I thought I would not for my life have seen it fall. How it was done I saw not; but understood it was with the sharp thorns and the violent and grievous setting on of the Garland of Thorns, unsparingly and without pity. This continued awhile, and soon it began to change, and I beheld and marveled how it might be. And then I saw it was because it began to dry, and stint a part of the weight, and set about the Garland.

---

1. Julian of Norwich, *Revelations of Divine Love* (Grand Rapids: Christian Classics Ethereal Library, 2002). Julian wrote in English, but the English language has changed quite a bit since the fourteenth century. The "translation" here, which is in the public domain, has been altered a points to further modernize Julian's language.

And thus it encircled all about, as it were garland upon garland. The Garland of the Thorns was dyed with the blood, and that other garland [of Blood] and the head, all was one color, as clotted blood when it is dry. The skin of the flesh that showed (of the face and of the body), was small-rimpled with a tanned color, like a dry board when it is aged; and the face more brown than the body.

I saw four manner of dryings: the first was bloodlessness; the second was pain following after; the third, hanging up in the air, as men hang a cloth to dry; the fourth, that the bodily Kind asked liquid and there was no manner of comfort ministered to Him in all His woe and distress. Ah! hard and grievous was his pain, but much more hard and grievous it was when the moisture failed and began to dry thus, shriveling.

These were the pains that showed in the blessed head: the first wrought to the dying, while it had moisture; and that other, slow, with shrinking drying, [and] with blowing of the wind from without, that dried and pained Him with cold more than mine heart can think. And other pains—for which pains I saw that all is too little that I can say: for it may not be told.

This Showing of Christ's pains filled me full of pain. For I knew well He suffered but once, but [this was as if] He would show it to me . . . And in all this time of Christ's pains I felt no pain but for Christ's pains. Then I thought: I knew but little what pain it was that I asked for; and, as a wretch, I repented, thinking: If I had known what it had been, I would have been loath to have prayed for it. For I thought it passed bodily death, my pains.

I thought: Is any pain like this? And I was answered in my reason: Hell is another pain: for there is despair. But of all pains that lead to salvation this is the most pain, to see thy Love suffer. How might any pain be more to me than to see Him that is all my life, all my bliss, and all my joy, suffer? Here felt I truly[2] that I loved Christ so much above myself that there was no pain that might be suffered like to that sorrow that I had to [see] Him in pain.

---

2. Julian used the archaic term "soothfastly."

CHAPTER 18: "When He was in pain, we were in pain"

Here I saw a part of the compassion of our Lady, Saint Mary: for Christ and she were so united[3] in love that the greatness of her loving was the cause of the greatness of her pain. For in this [Showing] I saw a Substance of Nature's Love, continued by Grace, that creatures have to Him: which Kind Love was most fully showed in His sweet Mother, and overpassing; for so much as she loved Him more than all other, her pains passed all other. For ever the higher, the mightier, the sweeter that the love be, the more sorrow it is to the lover to see that body in pain that is loved.

And all His disciples and all His true lovers suffered pains more than their own bodily dying. For I am sure by mine own feeling that the least of them loved Him so far above himself that it passes all that I can say.

Here I saw a great union between Christ and us, to mine understanding: for when He was in pain, we were in pain.

And all creatures that might suffer pain, suffered with Him: that is to say, all creatures that God has made to our service. The firmament, the earth, failed for sorrow in their Nature in the time of Christ's dying. For it belongs naturally to their property to know Him for their God, in whom all their virtue stands: when He failed, then it was proper for them, because of kindness [between creatures and Christ], to fail with Him, as much as they might, for [identification with the] sorrow of His pains.

And thus they that were His friends suffered pain for love . . . .

CHAPTER 24: "Our Lord looked unto His [pierced] Side, and beheld, rejoicing. . . . Lo! how I loved you"

Then with a glad cheer our Lord looked unto His Side and beheld [His wound], rejoicing. With His sweet looking He led forth the understanding of His creature by the same wound into His Side. And then he showed a fair, delectable place, and large enough for all mankind that shall be saved to rest in peace and in love. And therewith He

3. Julian used the term "oned."

brought to mind His worthy blood and precious water which he let pour all out for love. And with the sweet beholding He showed His blessed heart even torn in two.

And with this sweet enjoying, He showed unto my understanding, in part, the blessed Godhead, stirring then the poor soul to understand, as it may be said, that is, to think on, the endless Love that was without beginning, and is, and shall forever be. And with this our good Lord said blissfully: Lo, how I loved you, as if He had said: My darling, behold and see your Lord, your God that is your Maker and your endless joy, see what satisfying and bliss I have in your salvation; and for my love rejoice with me.

And also, for more understanding, this blessed word was said: Lo, how I loved you! Behold and see that I loved you so much before I died for you that I would die for you; and now I have died for you and suffered willingly that which I may. And now all my bitter pain and all my hard travail is turned to endless joy and bliss to me and to you. How should it now be that you would pray for anything that pleases me that I should not gladly grant you? For my pleasing is your holiness and your endless joy and bliss with me.

This is the understanding, simply as I can say it, of this blessed word: Lo, how I loved you. This showed our good Lord for to make us glad and merry.

CHAPTER 25: "I knew well that you would see my blessed Mother. . . ."

"Will you see in her how you are loved?"

And with this same cheer of mirth and joy our good Lord looked down on the right side and brought to my mind where our Lady stood in the time of His Passion; and said: Will you see her? And in this sweet word [it was] as if He had said: I knew well that you would see my blessed Mother: for, after myself, she is the highest joy that I might show you, and most pleasing and worship to me; and most she is desired to be seen of my blessed creatures. And for the high, marvelous, singular love that He hath to this sweet Maiden, His blessed Mother, our Lady Saint Mary, He showed her highly rejoicing, as by the meaning of these sweet words; as if He said: Will you see how I love her, that you might joy with me in the love that I have in her and she in me?

And also (to more understanding this sweet word) our Lord speaks to all mankind that shall be saved, as it were all to one person, as if He said: Will you see in her how you are loved? For your love I made her so high, so noble and so worthy; and this pleases me, and so I desire that this also please you.

For after Himself she is the most blissful sight. But hereof am I not learned to long to see her bodily presence while I am here, but the virtues of her blessed soul: her truth, her wisdom, her charity; whereby I may learn to know myself and reverently dread my God. And when our good Lord had showed this and said this word: Will you see her? I answered and said: Yes, good Lord, I thank You; yes, good Lord, if it be Your will. Oftentimes I prayed this, and I longed to have seen her in bodily presence, but I saw her not so. And Jesus in that word showed me ghostly sight of her: just as I had seen her before little and simple, so He showed her then high and noble and glorious, and pleasing to Him above all creatures.

And He wills that it be known; that all those that please them in Him should please them in her, and in the joy that He has in her and she in Him. And, to more understanding, He showed this example: As if a man loves a creature singularly, above all creatures, he desires to make all creatures to love and to have joy in that creature that he loves so greatly. And in this word that Jesus said: Will you see her? I thought it was the most pleasing word that He might have given me of her, with that ghostly Showing that He gave me of her. For our Lord showed me nothing in special but our Lady Saint Mary; and He showed her three times. The first was as she was with Child; the second was as she was in her sorrows under the Cross; the third is as she is now—in pleasing, worship, and joy.

CHAPTER 28: "Each brotherly compassion that man has on his fellow Christians, with charity, it is Christ in him"[4]

Thus I saw how Christ has compassion on us for the cause of sin. And just as I was filled with pain and compassion in the [Showing of the] Passion of Christ, so in this [sight] I was filled, in part, with compassion for fellow Christians—for that well beloved people that will be saved. For God's servants, Holy Church, shall be shaken in sorrow and anguish, tribulation in this world, as men shake a cloth in the wind.

And as to this our Lord answered in this manner: A great thing shall I make of this in Heaven of endless worship and everlasting joys.

Yes, so I saw, that our Lord rejoices in the tribulations of His servants, with pity and compassion. On each person that He loves, to bring [them] His bliss, He lays something that has no blame in His sight, whereby they are blamed and despised in this world, scorned, mocked, and outcasted. And this He does to hinder the harm that they should take from the pomp and the vain-glory of this wretched life, and make their way ready to come to Heaven, and raise them up in His bliss everlasting. For He says: I will wholly break you of your vain affections and your vicious pride; and after that I will gather you together, and make you mild and meek, clean and holy, by uniting [them] to me.

And then I saw that each kind compassion that man has on his fellow Christians with charity, it is Christ in him.

That same noughting[5] that was shown in His Passion, it was shown again here in this Compassion. There were two manners of understandings in our Lord's meaning. The one was the bliss that we are brought to, wherein He wills that we rejoice. The other is for comfort in our pain: for He wills that we perceive that it will all be turned to worship and profit by virtue of His passion, that we perceive that we

---

4. Matthew 25:40?

5. The term "noughting," related to the word "nothingness," is used by Julian to refer to the purification process by which our sins and sufferings are directed into the unifying desire for God. This term reveals the way that God turns the "nothingness" of suffering and even death into joy.

suffer not alone but with Him, and see Him to be our Ground, and that we see His pains and His noughting passes so far all that we may suffer, that it may not be fully thought.

The beholding of this will save us from murmuring and despair in the feeling of our pains. And if we see truly that our sin deserves it, yet His love excuses us, and of His great courtesy He does away [with] all our blame, and beholds us with compassion and pity as children innocent and unloathful.

Reading Questions

1. Do you find Julian's descriptions of Christ's suffering to be too graphic? Why or why not?

2. What is Julian's description of the deepest form of love? How can she tell that she loves Christ more than herself?

3. Why do you think Jesus makes the wound in his side big enough for all humankind? What tears Jesus' heart in two?

4. Is Mary a comforting figure? What role does Mary play in our understanding of love and suffering?

5. What is the role of "compassion" in Christian life? How are we to become Christ to one another?

For Further Reading

Dutton, Marsha L. "Julian of Norwich, Medieval Anglican." In *One Lord, One Faith, One Baptism: Studies in Christian Ecclesiality and Ecumenism in Honor of J. Robert Wright,* edited by Marsha L. Dutton and Patrick Terrell Gray, 99–119. Grand Rapids: Eerdmans, 2006.

Macquarrie, John. *Two Worlds Are Ours: An Introduction to Christian Mysticism.* Minneapolis: Fortress, 2005.

Magill, Kevin J. *Julian of Norwich: Mystic or Visionary?* Routledge Studies in Medieval Religion and Culture 4. London: Routledge, 2006.

Watson, Nicholas, and Jacqueline Jenkins, editors. *The Writings of Julian of Norwich: A Vision Showed to a Devout Woman and A Revelation of Love.* Medieval Women: Texts and Contexts 5. Turnhout: Brepols, 2006.

24

Catherine of Siena

※

Catherine of Siena (1347–1380) was a Dominican tertiary, a layperson that embraces many of the rules of the convent but continues to live at home. She was a mystic and a visionary, dedicating her virginity to Christ at the age of seven. Throughout her life she was deeply admired for her ability to abstain from food for prolonged periods of time. After experiencing what she called a "Mystical Marriage" to Jesus, she poured her life into tending the sick and serving the needy. Her major writing Dialogues, *part of which is reproduced below, was dictated to her secretaries when she was in a mystical state of "ecstasy."*

. . .

The Dialogue of Saint Catherine of Siena:[1]

How every virtue and every defect is obtained by means of our neighbor

I wish also that you should know that every virtue is obtained by means of your neighbor, and likewise, every defect; he, therefore, who stands in hatred of Me,[2] does an injury to his neighbor, and to himself, who is his own chief neighbor, and this injury is both general and particular. It is general because you are obliged to love your neighbor as yourself, and loving him, you ought to help him spiritually, with prayer, counseling him with words, and assisting him both spiritually and temporally, according to the need in which he may be, at least with your goodwill if you have nothing else. A man therefore, who does not love, does not help him, and thereby does himself an injury; for he cuts off from himself grace, and injures his neighbor, by depriving him of the benefit of the prayers and of the sweet desires that he is bound to offer for him to Me. Thus, every act of help that he performs should proceed from the charity which he has through love of Me.

And every evil also, is done by means of his neighbor, for, if he do not love Me, he cannot be in charity with his neighbor; and thus, all evils derive from the soul's deprivation of love of Me and her neighbor; whence, inasmuch as such a man does no good, it follows that he must do evil. To whom does he evil? First of all to himself, and then to his neighbor, not against Me, for no evil can touch Me, except in so far as I count done to Me that which he does to himself. To himself he does the injury of sin, which deprives him of grace, and worse than this he cannot do to his neighbor. Him he injures in not paying him the debt, which he owes him, of love, with which he ought to help him by means of prayer and holy desire offered to Me for him. This is an assistance which is owed in general to every rational creature; but its

---

1. From *The Dialogue of the Seraphic Virgin Catherine of Sienna* (London: Kegan Paul, Trench, Trubner & Co., 1907), dictated by her, while in a state of ecstasy, to her secretaries and completed in the year 1370. Translated from Latin by Algar Thorold.

2. Matthew 25:34–41. Catherine dictated these words in a "state of ecstasy"; she is speaking for Christ.

usefulness is more particular when it is done to those who are close at hand, under your eyes, as to whom, I say, you are all obliged to help one another by word and doctrine, and the example of good works, and in every other respect in which your neighbor may be seen to be in need; counseling him exactly as you would yourselves, without any passion of self-love; and he (a man not loving God) does not do this, because he has no love towards his neighbor; and, by not doing it, he does him, as you see, a special injury. And he does him evil, not only by not doing him the good that he might do him, but by doing him a positive injury and a constant evil. In this way sin causes a physical and a mental injury. The mental injury is already done when the sinner has conceived pleasure in the idea of sin, and hatred of virtue, that is, pleasure from sensual self-love, which has deprived him of the affection of love which he ought to have towards Me, and his neighbor, as has been said. And, after he has conceived, he brings forth one sin after another against his neighbor, according to the diverse ways which may please his perverse sensual will. Sometimes it is seen that he brings forth cruelty, and that both in general and in particular.

His general cruelty is to see himself and other creatures in danger of death and damnation through privation of grace, and so cruel is he that he reminds neither himself nor others of the love of virtue and hatred of vice. Being thus cruel he may wish to extend his cruelty still further, that is, not content with not giving an example of virtue, the villain also usurps the office of the demons, tempting, according to his power, his fellow-creatures to abandon virtue for vice; this is cruelty towards his neighbors, for he makes himself an instrument to destroy life and to give death. Cruelty towards the body has its origin in cupidity, which not only prevents a man from helping his neighbor, but causes him to seize the goods of others, robbing the poor creatures; sometimes this is done by the arbitrary use of power, and at other times by cheating and fraud, his neighbor being forced to redeem, to his own loss, his own goods, and often indeed his own person.

Oh, miserable vice of cruelty, which will deprive the man who practices it of all mercy, unless he turn to kindness and benevolence towards his neighbor! Sometimes the sinner brings forth insults on which often follows murder; sometimes also impurity against the person of his neighbor, by which he becomes a brute beast full of stench, and in this case he does not poison one only, but whoever approaches him, with love or in conversation, is poisoned.

Against whom does pride bring forth evils? Against the neighbor, through love of one's own reputation, whence comes hatred of the neighbor, reputing one's self to be greater than he; and in this way is injury done to him. And if a man be in a position of authority, he produces also injustice and cruelty and becomes a retailer of the flesh of men. Oh, dearest daughter, grieve for the offense against Me, and weep over these corpses, so that, by prayer, the bands of their death may be loosened!

See now, that, in all places and in all kinds of people, sin is always produced against the neighbor, and through his medium; in no other way could sin ever be committed either secret or open. A secret sin is when you deprive your neighbor of that which you ought to give him; an open sin is where you perform positive acts of sin, as I have related to you. It is, therefore, indeed the truth that every sin done against Me, is done through the medium of the neighbor.[3]

How virtues are accomplished by means of our neighbor, and how it is that virtues differ to such an extent in creatures

I have told you how all sins are accomplished by means of your neighbor, through the principles which I exposed to you, that is, because men are deprived of the affection of love, which gives light to every virtue. In the same way self-love, which destroys charity and affection towards the neighbor, is the principle and foundation of every evil. All scandals, hatred, cruelty, and every sort of trouble proceed from this perverse root of self-love, which has poisoned the entire world, and weakened the mystical body of the Holy Church, and the universal body of the believers in the Christian religion; and, therefore, I said

3. Matthew 25:45.

to you, that it was in the neighbor, that is to say in the love of him, that all virtues were founded; and, truly indeed did I say to you, that charity gives life to all the virtues, because no virtue can be obtained without charity, which is the pure love of Me.

Wherefore, when the soul knows herself, as we have said above, she finds humility and hatred of her own sensual passion, for she learns the perverse law, which is bound up in her members, and which ever fights against the spirit. And, therefore, arising with hatred of her own sensuality, crushing it under the heel of reason, with great earnestness, she discovers in herself the bounty of My goodness, through the many benefits which she has received from Me, all of which she considers again in herself. She attributes to Me, through humility, the knowledge which she has obtained of herself, knowing that, by My grace, I have drawn her out of darkness and lifted her up into the light of true knowledge.

When she has recognized My goodness, she loves it without any medium, and yet at the same time with a medium, that is to say, without the medium of herself or of any advantage accruing to herself, and with the medium of virtue, which she has conceived through love of Me, because she sees that, in no other way, can she become grateful and acceptable to Me, but by conceiving, hatred of sin and love of virtue; and, when she has thus conceived by the affection of love, she immediately is delivered of fruit for her neighbor, because, in no other way, can she act out the truth she has conceived in herself, but, loving Me in truth, in the same truth she serves her neighbor.

And it cannot be otherwise, because love of Me and of her neighbor are one and the same thing, and, so far as the soul loves Me, she loves her neighbor, because love towards him issues from Me. This is the means which I have given you, that you may exercise and prove your virtue therewith; because, inasmuch as you can do Me no profit, you should do it to your neighbor. This proves that you possess Me by grace in your soul, producing much fruit for your neighbor and making prayers to Me, seeking with sweet and amorous desire My honor and the salvation of souls. The soul, enamored of My truth, never ceases to serve the whole world in general, and more or less in a particular case according to the disposition of the recipient and the ardent desire of the donor, as I have shown above, when I declared to you that the endurance of suffering alone, without desire, was not sufficient to punish a fault.

When she has discovered the advantage of this unitive love in Me, by means of which, she truly loves herself, extending her desire for the salvation of the whole world, thus coming to the aid of its neediness, she strives, inasmuch as she has done good to herself by the conception of virtue, from which she has drawn the life of grace, to fix her eye on the needs of her neighbor in particular. Wherefore, when she has discovered, through the affection of love, the state of all rational creatures in general, she helps those who are at hand, according to the various graces which I have entrusted to her to administer; one she helps with doctrine, that is, with words, giving sincere counsel without any respect of persons, another with the example of a good life, and this indeed all give to their neighbor, the edification of a holy and honorable life. These are the virtues, and many others, too many to enumerate, which are brought forth in the love of the neighbor; but, although I have given them in such a different way, that is to say not all to one, but to one, one virtue, and to another, another, it so happens that it is impossible to have one, without having them all, because all the virtues are bound together. Wherefore, learn, that, in many cases I give one virtue, to be as it were the chief of the others, that is to say, to one I will give principally love, to another justice, to another humility, to one a lively faith, to another prudence or temperance, or patience, to another fortitude. These, and many other virtues, I place, indifferently, in the souls of many creatures; it happens, therefore, that the particular one so placed in the soul becomes the principal object of its virtue; the soul disposing herself, for her chief conversation, to this rather than to other virtues, and, by the effect of this virtue, the soul draws to herself all the other virtues, which, as has been said, are all bound together in the affection of love; and so with many gifts and graces of virtue, and not only in the case of spiritual things but also of temporal. I use the word temporal for the things necessary to the physical life of man; all these I have given indifferently, and I have not placed them all in one soul, in order that man should, perforce, have material for love of his fellow. I could easily have created men possessed of all that they should need both for body and soul, but I wish that one should have need of the other, and that they should be My ministers to administer the graces and the gifts that they have received from Me. Whether man will or no, he cannot help making an act of love. It is true, however, that that act, unless made through love of Me, profits him nothing so far as grace is concerned. See then, that I have made men My ministers, and placed them in diverse stations and various ranks, in order that they may make use of the virtue of love. "Wherefore, I show you that in My house are many mansions,"[4] and that I wish for no other thing than love, for in the love of Me is fulfilled and completed the love of the neighbor, and the law observed.[5] For he, only, can be of use in his state of life, who is bound to Me with this love.

How virtues are proved and fortified by their contraries

Up to the present, I have taught you how a man may serve his neighbor, and manifest, by that service, the love which he has towards Me. Now I wish to tell you further, that a man proves his patience on his neighbor, when he receives injuries from him. Similarly, he proves his humility on a proud man, his faith on an infidel, his true hope on one who despairs, his justice on the unjust, his kindness on the cruel, his gentleness and benignity on the irascible. Good men produce and prove all their virtues on their neighbor, just as perverse men all their vices; thus, if you consider well, humility is proved on pride in this way. The humble man extinguishes pride, because a proud man can do no harm to a humble one; neither can the infidelity of a wicked man, who neither loves Me, nor hopes in Me, when brought forth against one who is faithful to Me, do him any harm; his infidelity does not diminish the faith or the hope of him who has conceived his faith and hope through love of Me, it rather fortifies it, and proves it in the

4. John 14:2.
5. Matthew 25:34–41.

love he feels for his neighbor. For, he sees that the infidel is unfaithful, because he is without hope in Me, and in My servant, because he does not love Me, placing his faith and hope rather in his own sensuality, which is all that he loves. My faithful servant does not leave him because he does not faithfully love Me, or because he does not constantly seek, with hope in Me, for his salvation, inasmuch as he sees clearly the causes of his infidelity and lack of hope. The virtue of faith is proved in these and other ways.

Wherefore, to those, who need the proof of it, My servant proves his faith in himself and in his neighbor, and so, justice is not diminished by the wicked man's injustice, but is rather proved, that is to say, the justice of a just man. Similarly, the virtues of patience, benignity, and kindness manifest themselves in a time of wrath by the same sweet patience in My servants, and envy, vexation, and hatred demonstrate their love, and hunger and desire for the salvation of souls. I say, also, to you, that, not only is virtue proved in those who render good for evil, but, that many times a good man gives back fiery coals of love, which dispel the hatred and rancor of heart of the angry, and so from hatred often comes benevolence, and that this is by virtue of the love and perfect patience which is in him, who sustains the anger of the wicked, bearing and supporting his defects. If you will observe the virtues of fortitude and perseverance, these virtues are proved by the long endurance of the injuries and detractions of wicked men, who, whether by injuries or by flattery, constantly endeavor to turn a man aside from following the road and the doctrine of truth. Wherefore, in all these things, the virtue of fortitude conceived within the soul, perseveres with strength, and, in addition proves itself externally upon the neighbor, as I have said to you; and, if fortitude were not able to make that good proof of itself, being tested by many contrarieties, it would not be a serious virtue founded in truth.

Reading Questions

1. What are the indications that Catherine has Matthew 25 in mind?

2. What are the various meanings of the word "love" for Catherine?

3. Do you agree with the suggestion that all sins (defects) and virtues happen by means of the neighbor?

4. What contributions does Catherine bring to this text as a female theologian? What aspects of the study of theology have suffered for lack of attention to the theology of women?

5. Given the clues of the passage above, how might Catherine define "sin"?

For Further Reading

Cavallini, Giuliana. *Catherine of Siena*. Outstanding Christian Thinkers. London: Chapman, 1998.

————. *Things Visible and Invisible: Images in the Spirituality of St. Catherine of Siena*. Translated by Sister Mary Jeremiah. New York: Alba, 1996.

Hilkert, Mary Catherine. *Speaking with Authority: Catherine of Siena and the Voices of Women Today*. New York: Paulist, 2001.

Noffke, Suzanne. *Catherine of Siena: Vision through a Distant Eye*. Collegeville, MN: Liturgical, 1996.

25

Martin Luther

Fiery, sincere, and divisive, Martin Luther (1483–1546) led efforts to reform the Roman Catholic Church in the sixteenth century. Though this "reformation" turned into a major division within Christianity, creating the division between "Protestant" and "Catholic" Christian communions, this was not Martin Luther's initial intent. With an intimate knowledge of Scripture and an inability to stomach hypocrisy, Luther repeatedly challenged the popes and other Christian leaders. Eventually he was expelled as a heretic and established the "Lutheran" church. The following sermon was preached to this young and struggling flock. Like no other sermon in this volume, Luther shows how relevant Matthew 25:31–46 is to his contemporary context.

· · ·

The Sermons of Martin Luther: Matthew 25:31–46[1]

1. The words of this Gospel are in themselves clear and lucid; they have been given both for the comfort and encouragement of believing Christians, and for the warning and terror of others, if perchance, they might be of help to them. While most lessons almost exclusively teach and inculcate faith, this one treats only of the works, which Christ will examine at the last day, that it may be seen that he wishes them to be remembered and performed by those who wish to be Christians and be found in his kingdom.

2. And Christ himself gives this admonition here in the strongest terms that can be given, both in the consoling promise of a glorious, eternal reward, and in the most terrible threatenings of eternal wrath and punishment upon all who despise the admonition; so that whoever is not moved and aroused by these words can certainly never be moved by anything. For Christ says, he will himself come visibly in his majesty, at the last day, with all the angels, and that he will transplant all who have believed in him and have exercised love toward his followers, into his father's kingdom of eternal glory all who believe in him and love his saints; and that he will also cast into hell forever all who live not as Christians, and who separate themselves from him and all his saints.

3. Now, had it not been told us we should be inquisitive beyond measure to know what would happen on the last day, and what Jesus would say and do on that day. Here we are now told, and have set before us first of all, death, which no one can escape; but after that the Day of Judgment. Then it will come to pass that Christ will bring together by means of the resurrection all who have ever lived upon earth; and at the same time he will descend in great inexpressible majesty, sitting upon the throne of judgment, with all the heavenly host hovering around him; and all the good and bad will appear, so that we will all stand exposed before him, and no one will be able to conceal himself.

---

1. The following sermon is taken from *The Sermons of Martin Luther* (Minneapolis: Lutherans in all Lands, 1905), as *The Precious and Sacred Writings of Martin Luther*, vol. 14. This text is in the public domain.

4. The appearance of this glory and majesty will immediately become a great terror and pain to the condemned, as we read in today's Epistle lesson, lest they suffer punishment, even eternal destruction from the face of the Lord and from the glory of his might, when he comes to be glorified in his saints.[2] For even if there were no more than a single angel present, there would not remain in his presence one fickle, wicked conscience, were it possible to escape, any more than a thief and a rascal can bear to come before a human judge. If he could escape, he would much prefer it, if only for the purpose that he might escape public disgrace, to say nothing of his being compelled to hear the judgment passed upon him.

What a terrible sight this will be, when the ungodly sees not only all God's angels and creatures, but also the Judge in his divine majesty, and hears the verdict of eternal destruction and hell fire pronounced upon them forever! This ought surely to be a strong, powerful admonition for us to live as Christians, so that we may stand in honor and without fear at the right hand of this majestic Lord, where there will be no fear nor terror, but pure comfort and everlasting joy.

5. For he will then, as he says here himself, immediately separate the goats from the sheep. And this will take place publicly in the presence of all angels, men, and creatures, and before the whole rabble of an ungodly world, that it may be seen who have been pious, honest Christians, as well as who have been false hypocrites. This separation cannot take place in the world until that day, not even in the assembly that constitutes the Christian Church. The good and the bad must remain together in this world, as the parable of the wedding guests says;[3] or as Christ himself had to tolerate Judas among his Apostles. Christians are even now grieved that they must remain here in the midst of a crooked, perverse, ungodly people, which is the kingdom of Satan.[4]

6. While they have their sufferings here upon earth, they will have also their comfort on the coming day of judgment, when Christ will

2. 2 Thessalonians 1:9–10.
3. Matthew 22:10.
4. Philippians 2:15.

separate them from the other flock, so that after that day no false, ungodly men, nor death, nor devil can ever touch them or offend them.

7. Then he will pronounce the verdict in the very words in which he has already prepared it and set it forth, and he will certainly not change it. And the words are peculiar in this that he makes them depend upon the deeds and works here mentioned, which they have or have not done, and which are the basis and cause of his judgment. And all these words set forth at length the works which have been done as well as those which have been neglected. And all this will happen in the twinkling of an eye, when the hearts of all men will be revealed before all creatures; and as it is preached here, so there all will be forthwith executed.

8. You may ask why Christ there especially examines works called deeds of mercy, or the neglect of such works? Six different kinds are mentioned in the text, although many more might be given; yet were one to judge critically in the matter, there are no more works than those implied in the fifth commandment: Thou shalt not kill; in which we are commanded in general, as Christ himself explains it, not to be angry with our neighbor, but to be kind to him and ready to serve and assist him, supply his wants in times of need, whether in hunger, thirst, nakedness, suffering, imprisonment, sickness or other troubles, and to do this even to those who may have given us occasion for anger or for unmerciful acts, and thus do not appear to be worthy of our love and benevolence. For that is a poor virtue which does good only to those we love, or from whom we hope to receive kindness and thanks in return.

9. But one might, as has been said, add to those works of mercy many more from other commandments; for example from the sixth, that one is to assist his neighbor, to protect his wife, children and domestics, and to keep them under proper restraint and in honor; also from the seventh, eighth and last commandments, that is, to help save and maintain the goods and property, house, home and good report of his neighbor; also to help protect and defend the poor, the oppressed and the down-trodden . . . .

10. For Christ himself shows that he is speaking of the works of believing Christians, when he says: "I was hungry and you gave me to eat," etc.; "what you have done unto the least of these my brethren you have done unto me."[5] For there is no doubt that he who performs such works of mercy to Christians, must himself be a Christian and a believer; but he who does not believe in Christ, will certainly never be so kind toward a Christian, much less toward Christ, so that for his sake he would show mercy to the poor, and needy; therefore he will refer to these works at the judgment, and accordingly pronounce the verdict to both parties, to those who have done, and those who have not done these works, as a public testimony of the fruits of their faith or of their unbelief.

11. It seems as though he meant hereby to show that many Christians, after receiving the preaching of the Gospel, of the forgiveness of sins and grace through Christ, become even worse than the heathen. For he also says in, Matthew 19:30, "Many that are first will be last; and the last will be first." Thus it will also be at the end of the world; those who should be honest Christians, because they heard the Gospel, are much worse and more unmerciful than they were before, as we see too many examples of this even now.

Aforetime when we were to do good works under the seduction and false worship of the Papacy, every one was ready and willing; a prince, for example, or a city, could give more alms and a greater endowment than now all the kings and emperors are able to give. But now all the world seems to be learning nothing else than how to estimate values, to rake and scrape, to rob and steal by lying, deceiving, usury, overcharging, overrating, and the like; and every man treats his neighbor, not as though he were his friend, much less as his brother in Christ, but as his mortal enemy, and as though he intended to snatch all things to himself and begrudge everything to others.

12. This goes on daily, is constantly increasing, is a very common practice and custom. among all classes of people, among princes, the nobility, burghers, peasants, in all courts, cities, villages, yes in almost every home. Tell me, what city is now so strong and pious as to be able to raise an amount sufficient to support a schoolmaster or a preacher?

5. Matthew 25:40.

Yes, if we did not already have the liberal alms and endowments of our forefathers, the Gospel would long ago have disappeared in the cities on account of the burghers, and in the country because of the nobility and peasants, and poor preachers would have nothing to eat nor to drink. For we do not love to give, but would rather take even by force what others have given and endowed. Therefore it is no credit to us that a single pulpit or school is still maintained. Yea, how many there are among the great, the powerful, and the rich, especially in the Papacy, who would like to see nothing better than all preachers, schools, and arts exterminated.

13. Such are the thanks to the blessed Gospel, by which men have been freed from the bondage and plagues of the Pope, that they must become so shamefully wicked in these last times. They are now no more unmerciful, no more in a human, but in a satanic way; they are not satisfied with being allowed to enjoy the Gospel, and grow fat by robbing and stealing the revenues of the church, but they must also be scheming with all their power how they may completely starve out the Gospel. One can easily count upon his fingers, what they who enjoy the Gospel are doing and giving, here and elsewhere; and, were it only for us now living, there would long since have been no preacher or student from whom our children and descendants might know what we had taught and believed.

14. In short, what do you think Christ will say on that day, seated on his judgment throne, to such unmerciful Christianity? "Dear Sir, listen, you have also pretended to be a Christian and boasted of the Gospel; did you not also hear this sermon, that I myself preached, in which I told you what my verdict and decision would be: 'Depart from me, you cursed'? I was hungry and thirsty, naked and sick, poor and in prison, and you gave me no meat, no drink, clothed me not, took me not in, and visited me not. Why have you neglected this, and have been more shameless and unmerciful toward your own brethren than the Turk or heathen?

Will you excuse yourself by pleading: "Lord, when saw we you hungry or thirsty?" etc. Then he will answer you again through your own conscience: Dear Sir, were there no people who preached to you; or perhaps poor students who should have at the time been studying and learning God's Word, or were there no poor, persecuted Christians whom you ought to have fed, clothed and visited?

15, We ought really to be ashamed of ourselves, having had the example of parents, ancestors, lords and kings, princes and others, who gave so liberally and charitably, even in profusion, to churches, ministers, schools, endowments, hospitals and the like; and by such liberal giving neither they nor their descendants were made poorer. What would they have done, had they had the light of the Gospel, that is given unto us? How did the Apostles and their followers in the beginning bring all they had for their poor widows, or for those who had nothing, or who were banished and persecuted, in order that no one among them might suffer for the necessities of life! In this way poor Christians should at all times support one another. Otherwise, as I have said, the Gospel, the pulpit, churches and schools would already be completely exterminated, no matter how much the rest of the world did.

Were it not for the grace of God, by which he gives us here and there a pious prince, or godly government, which preserves the fragments still left, that all may not be destroyed by the graspers and vultures, thieves and robbers; were it not for this grace, I say, the poor pastors and preachers would not only be starved, but also murdered. Nor are there now any other poor people than those who serve, or are being trained to serve the church; and these can obtain no support elsewhere, and must leave their poor wives and children die of hunger because of an indifferent world; on the other hand the world is full of useless, unfaithful, wicked fellows among day-laborers, lazy mechanics, servants, maids, and idle, greedy beggars, who everywhere by lying, deceiving, robbing and stealing, take away the hard-earned bread and butter from those who are really poor, and yet go unpunished in the midst of their wantonness and insolence.

16. This I say, that we may see how Christ will upbraid the false liars and hypocrites among Christians, on the day of judgment, and having convicted them before all creatures will condemn them, because they have done none of the works which even the heathen do to

their fellows; who did much more in their false and erroneous religion, and would have done it even more willingly had they known better.

17. Since now this terrible condemnation is justly pronounced over those who neglected these works, what will happen to those who have not only neglected the same, have given nothing to the poor Christians, nor served them; but robbed them of what they had, drove them to hunger, thirst and nakedness, furthermore persecuted, scattered, imprisoned, and murdered them? These are so unutterably wicked, so utterly condemned to the bottomless pit with the devil and his angels, that Christ will not think or speak of them. But he will assuredly not forget these robbers, tyrants, and bloodhounds any more than he will forget or pass over unrewarded those who have suffered hunger thirst, nakedness, persecution and the like, especially for his and his Word's sake. He will not forget those to whom mercy has been shown, even though he speaks only to those who have shown mercy and have lent their aid; for he highly and nobly commends them, when he says. "Inasmuch as you did it to one of these my brethren, even these least, you did it to me."[6]

18. On account of this judgment fear and trembling might well seize our great spiritual prelates, as they call themselves, the popes, cardinals, bishops, canons, priests, and then whole diabolical rabble of the anti-Christian crowd at Rome, and everywhere, in their monasteries and brothels, if they were not altogether hardened and deliberately given to Satan, body and soul. They think and act as though they were especially appointed to snatch to themselves every thing that belongs to the poor church, and in their own wantonness to consume, spend, waste, squander, in dissipation, gambling and debauchery, in the most shameful and scandalous manner, whatever has been given for the maintenance of students, schools and the poor people. They mock God and man;[7] yes, they publicly murder innocent, pious people.

19. Yes, woe, another and eternal woe, to them and to all who side with them. For it had been, better for them, had they never been born, as Christ says of Judas. Therefore they ought rather to wish that their mothers had drowned them in their first bath, or that they had

6. Matthew 25:40.
7. 2 Peter 2:13.

never come forth from the womb, than that one of them should have become pope or cardinal or a popish priest. For they are nothing else than merely desperate and select ones, not highway robbers, but public country-thieves, who take, not the goods of the mighty and the powerful that really have something, but of the poor and wretched, of the parish churches, schools, and hospitals, whose morsels are snatched from their teeth, and whose drink is torn from their mouths, so that they are unable to maintain life.

20. Therefore let every man beware of the Pope, the bishops, and the priesthood, as he would beware of those who have already been condemned alive to the abyss of perdition. Truly Paul did not prophesy in vain,[8] that in the last days perilous times will come. Yet all the world moves along indifferently and gives no heed to this terrible judgment that has already been decided against such unmerciful robbers, thieves, and murderers of poor Christians, but especially against those who pretend to be Christians, who after having received grace slide back again, and like a dog eat their own vomit, or as the swine wallow in their own.

21. The second reason why Christ especially mentions these works of mercy and their omission, from the fifth commandment, is, that he wishes to remind us, who have been called to be Christians, have received mercy through our Lord, have been redeemed from the wrath of God and the guilt of the fifth commandment and from eternal death, and on the contrary have a gracious God, who is good to us in time and in eternity, to remind us, I say, to look upon all this and regard it as having been done not only for our salvation but also for an example. For, since he has shown us such mercy as to save us, we are also to act toward our neighbor in a manner as not to transgress against the fifth commandment, which especially demands love and mercy.

And we are not to do these things simply because of the commandment and of the threatening of judgment, but for the sake of the example of the excellent and great goodness God has shown. For this example cannot be without blessed results, as God's work of redemption is not without power and good fruit. Although most people become worse from having heard the Gospel, there must nevertheless

8. 2 Timothy 3:1.

be some who rightly understand it and remain faithful to it; for he says that he will separate them into two flocks; therefore there must also be pious ones who have kept this commandment.

22. Therefore see to it that you are among those who are kind and merciful here upon earth for Christ's sake, or who even suffer for his sake, then you may joyfully await the last day, and need not be afraid of the judgment; for he has already selected you and placed you among those who will stand at his right hand.

23. For we, who are Christians, should hope for the coming of this judgment and desire it with our whole heart; as we pray for it in the words: Thy kingdom come, thy will be done, deliver us from evil; so that we may also hear the glad and welcome words: Come, you blessed, into the kingdom of my Father. This is the verdict we await; for this reason we are Christians, and just for the sake of this hope we are so severely oppressed, first by Satan and by our own flesh, which would not have us believe this and rejoice over it; then by the tyranny and enmity of the world. For we must constantly see and hear the maliciousness which Satan and the world practice against the Gospel. There is so much misery upon earth that we ought to be tired of this life and cry aloud: Come, dear Lord, and deliver us.

24. For there are certainly souls who are joyfully and with a good conscience awaiting the judgement of Christ; for they are in the rank and fellowship of those who believe in Christ, and who show fruits of faith through charity and beneficence toward the poor, or through patience in suffering with them. For, as I have said, he who does not have faith will not do works of mercy to Christians, but he who does them, will do them because he believes that he has a faithful Savior and Redeemer in Christ, who has reconciled him to God. Therefore he must have also a kind, loving heart toward his neighbors, even toward his enemies, and serve them in every time of need. Yea, he endures also, as I have just said, those things which come upon him from the world and the devil on account of his faith.

Whosoever is thus minded, I say, let him be joyful and of good courage; for he has already the blessed and joyful verdict: Come, blessed one, for you have also been one of the least of my brethren, who have yourself suffered hunger and thirst, or who hast served the other hungry and thirsty ones, and have shown mercy, as I have done.

25. Behold, therefore, the separation of the sheep and goats is already made in this life, so that every one can experience it internally and must indicate and show it also externally. For they who have not faith will surely do none of these things—they will neither comfort themselves with the grace of Christ, nor think of exercising mercy; they pass by the Word of God and their neighbor, as though they neither saw nor heard anything; they do not care to know that there is a Lord whom they are to serve and who will demand such service from them. For if they would consider that they must die, and appear before this judgment seat, they would not at the time defraud any one of a farthing. But, on the contrary, they think best to turn their eyes away from death and to keep the heart from thinking of it . . .

28. Notice, however, as I said, that he wishes to distinguish the good works of the Christians from the works of the Turks and the heathen. For he speaks of the works done unto him, of which both parties claim to be ignorant, the wicked excusing themselves, because they had not seen him, etc. But herewith he has most beautifully explained the fifth commandment, that it means, he who fulfills it can be none else than a believing Christian, who did it unto Christ. Thus the woman who anointed his head and feet, fulfilled this commandment and is praised by him when he says: "She has done a good work to me. For you always have the poor with you, and if you wish you can always do good to them, but me you do not always have. Truly I tell you, wherever this Gospel is preached in the whole world, that which this woman has done will be told in remembrance of her." [9] Again in Matthew 10:42: "Whoever gives a cup of cold water to one of these little ones, who believe in me, he will certainly not lose his reward."

29. We should therefore impress the fact upon our hearts and consider that it is a great and fine thing to do good to a Christian; but on the contrary also, what it is to do evil to him, as I said of the Pope, the bishops, the tyrants, and feudal nobility, who take from the feet of Christ what they have not given him the food, the drink, the lodging and the support of the poor, who are poor for Christ's sake, because

9. Matthew 26:10–13.

they are not in the position, as ministers, sextons and school masters, to rule the world; nor are they able to engage, in any other business in which they might gain a livelihood; for then they would also have been made the partakers of power and would receive enough. But since they have no part in the government, the world gives them nothing for their services. As they receive nothing for God's nor Christ's sake, they can have nothing, and must leave behind them poor, wretched widows and orphans.

30. Those in other positions and offices, who have plenty in all respects, do not wish and cannot attend to the duties and the services of the church, neither do they know how. And when ministers and pastors engage in worldly trades and pursuits, they step outside of their proper calling. Therefore they must be supported, if they are to have anything to eat, from beggary, of which Christ here speaks; but he makes it so precious that whosoever gives meat or drink to the least of his members on earth, he recognizes the same as though it had been done and given to himself. Do we wish then to be Christians, and expect from Christ the honor to be praised and rewarded in the presence of all creatures, we must, indeed, cheerfully and gratuitously give to those who are to perform the duties of their office gratuitously, because they can have no share in secular matters. This we are to do in order to escape the curse and wrath that will come upon those who would not have mercy on their poor brethren, who had to suffer hunger, thirst, misery, and imprisonment in the world in order to bring us to Christ.

31. But how does it happen that the righteous do not recognize and know that they have done their works unto Christ? They say: Lord, when saw we thee hungry, or athirst, etc.? The reason is, that to give something to a poor minister, chaplain, teacher, sexton is regarded as a matter altogether of too small significance to be so precious in the sight of God. Yea, the world looks upon it as so much money thrown away. Yet will any one say that the world would be so much richer, were there no pupils, schools, hospitals? Or that it is on their account any poorer, unless it were entirely heathen, or it were, as heretofore, compelled to give enough for the devil's sake, and allow itself to be flayed to the bone by those who have cheated it of body and soul. In short, the churches and schools receive the very least from the world;

yet it is jealous, complains bitterly, and makes a great cry about what they already have, although it gives nothing, and claims to make much better use of its means, when at other times it gives a hundred times as much to shameless, dissolute villains and jugglers . . . . It never enters the brain of the world to think and believe that this means to give to Christ; nor is it easy for us to see it ourselves . . . .

33. The same conditions now exist everywhere. Every peasant, burgher, nobleman is simply gathering dollars, waits and saves, eats and drinks, is insolent and mischievous as though God were nothing at all. No one cares for the despised Jesus in his poverty; nay, he is even tread under foot, until all obedience, discipline and honor are destroyed among us, as they were in Sodom and Gomorrah, and matters become so bad, as to become unbearable, because all admonition and preaching seem to be of no avail.

34. Right unwillingly do I prophesy; for I have often experienced how it came true; but the same conditions, alas, prevail now everywhere; and I fear and must almost resign myself that Germany may have the same experience as Sodom and Jerusalem, and will be a thing of the past; it will either be destroyed by the Turks or it will crumble by its own hand, unless the last day overtake it soon. For the present conditions are altogether unbearable and so exceedingly bad that they cannot become worse; and if there be still a God, he cannot thus let matters go on unpunished . . . May God preserve us, and grant us and our little flock that we may escape this terrible wrath, and be found among those who honor and serve our dear Christ, and await the judgment at his right hand joyously and blissfully. Amen.

Reading Questions

1. What pressures on Luther's fledgling church are evident from this sermon?

2. Who are "the least of these"?

3. How is the Pope characterized? For what reasons?

4. Are there doctrinal differences with the Roman Catholic Church evident in this sermon?

5. What social issues in Germany are evident from this sermon?

6. How were the people in Luther's congregation to respond to this message?

For Further Reading

Atkinson, James. *Martin Luther: Prophet to the Catholic Church.* 1983. Reprinted, Eugene, OR: Wipf & Stock, 2004.

Gritsch, Eric W. *The Wit of Martin Luther.* Facets. Minneapolis: Fortress, 2006.

Junghans, Helmar. *Martin Luther: Exploring His Life and Times, 1484–1546.* CD-ROM. Minneapolis: Fortress, 1998.

Kittelson, James M. *Luther the Reformer: The Story of the Man and His Career.* Minneapolis: Fortress, 2003.

Lohse, Bernhard. *Martin Luther: An Introduction to His Life and Work.* Translated by Robert C. Schultz. Philadelphia: Fortress, 1986.

Marty, Martin. *Martin Luther.* Penguin Life. New York: Penguin, 2004.

26

John Calvin

❀

John Calvin wrote voluminously as a commentator. The English version of his Biblical Commentary *consists of forty-five volumes. This is a particularly remarkable achievement in light of the fact that Calvin spent the majority of his energy on pastoral and political concerns. Calvin's writings are a result of his sheer determination to see an intersection between careful scriptural exegesis and the spiritual and practical needs of the people in his care. The following excerpt from his commentary on the book of Matthew offers a particularly intriguing opportunity to see how grace and works take their place in Calvin's understanding of Christian life and ministry.*

. . .

Matthew 25:31–46[1]

31. *Now when the Son of man comes in his glory.* Christ follows out the same doctrine, and what he formerly described under parables, he now explains clearly and without figures. The sum of what is said is, that believers, in order to encourage themselves to a holy and upright conduct, ought to contemplate with the eyes of faith the heavenly life, which, though it is now concealed, will at length be manifested at the last coming of Christ. For, when he declares that, when he will come with the angels, then will he sit on the throne of his glory, he contrasts this last revelation with the disorders and agitations of earthly warfare; as if he had said, that he did not appear for the purpose of immediately setting up his kingdom, and therefore that there was need of hope and patience, lest the disciples might be discouraged by long delay. Hence we infer that this was again added, in order that the disciples, being freed from mistake about immediate and sudden happiness, might keep their minds in warfare till Christ's second coming, and might not give way, or be discouraged, on account of his absence.

This is the reason why he says that he will then assume the title of King; for though he commenced his reign on the earth, and now sits at the right hand of the Father, so as to exercise the supreme government of heaven and earth; yet he has not yet erected before the eyes of men that throne, from which his divine majesty will be far more fully displayed than it now is at the last day; for that, of which we now obtain by faith nothing more than a taste, will then have its full effect. So then Christ now sits on his heavenly throne, as far as it is necessary that he will reign for restraining his enemies and protecting the Church; but then he will appear openly, to establish perfect order in heaven and earth, to crush his enemies under his feet, to assemble his believing people to partake of an everlasting and blessed life, to ascend his judgment-seat; and, in a word, there will be a visible manifestation of the reason why the kingdom was given to him by the Father. He says that he will come in his glory; because, while he dwelt in this world as

1. From *Commentary on a Harmony of the Evangelists, Matthew, Mark and Luke*, Volume 3 (Grand Rapids: Christian Classics Ethereal Library). This text was translated from the Latin by William Pringle. The translation has been modified and modernized here.

a mortal man, he appeared in the despised form of a servant. And he calls it his glory, though he elsewhere ascribes it to his Father, but the meaning is the same; for he means simply the divine glory, which at that time shone in the Father only, for in himself it was concealed.

32. *And all nations will be assembled before him.* He employs large and splendid titles for extolling his kingdom, that the disciples may learn to expect a different kind of happiness from what they had imagined. For they were satisfied with this single consideration, that their nation was delivered from the miseries with which it was then oppressed, so that it would be manifest that God had not in vain established his covenant with Abraham and his posterity. But Christ extends much farther the benefit of the redemption brought by him, for he will be the Judge of the whole world. Again, in order to persuade believers to holiness of life, he assures them that the good and the bad will not share alike; because he will bring with him the reward which is laid up for both. In short, he declares that his kingdom will be fully established, when the righteous will have obtained a crown of glory, and when the wicked will have received the reward which they deserved.

As a shepherd separates the sheep from the goats. When our Lord says that the separation of the sheep from the goats is delayed till that day, he means that the wicked are now mixed with the good and holy, so that they live together in the same flock of God. The comparison appears to be borrowed from Ezekiel 34:18, where the Lord complains of the fierceness of the goats, which attack with their horns the poor sheep, and destroy the pastures, and pollute the water; and where the Lord expressly declares that he will take vengeance. And therefore Christ's discourse amounts to this, that believers ought not to think their condition too hard, if they are now compelled to live with the goats, and even to sustain many serious attacks and annoyances from them; secondly, that they ought to beware of being themselves infected by the contagion of their vices; and, thirdly, to inform them that in a holy and innocent life their labor is not thrown away, for the difference will one day appear.

34. *Come, you blessed of my Father.* We must remember Christ's design; for he bids his disciples rest satisfied now with hope, that they may with patience and tranquility of mind look for the enjoyment of

the heavenly kingdom; and next, he bids them strive earnestly, and not become wearied in the right course. To this latter clause he refers, when he promises the inheritance of the heavens to none but those who by good works aim at the prize of the heavenly calling. But before speaking of the reward of good works, he points out, in passing, that the commencement of salvation flows from a higher source; for by calling them blessed of the Father, he reminds them, that their salvation proceeded from the undeserved favor of God. Among the Hebrews the phrase blessed of God means one who is dear to God, or beloved by God. Besides, this form of expression was not only employed by believers to extol the grace of God towards men, but those who had degenerated from true godliness still held this principle. Enter, thou blessed of God, said Laban to Abraham's servant.[2] We see that nature suggested to them this expression, by which they ascribed to God the praise of all that they possessed. There can be no doubt, therefore, that Christ, in describing the salvation of the godly, begins with the undeserved love of God, by which those who, under the guidance of the Spirit in this life, aim at righteousness, were predestined to life.

To this also relates what he says shortly afterwards, that the kingdom, to the possession of which they will be appointed at the last day, had been prepared for them from the beginning of the world. For though it may be easy to object, that the reward was laid up with a view to their future merits, any person who will candidly examine the words must acknowledge that there is an implied commendation of the grace of God. Nay more, Christ does not simply invite believers to possess the kingdom, as if they had obtained it by their merits, but expressly says that it is bestowed on them as heirs.

Yet we must observe another object which our Lord had in view. For though the life of the godly be nothing else than a sad and wretched banishment, so that the earth scarcely bears them; though they groan under hard poverty, and reproaches, and other afflictions; yet, that they may with fortitude and cheerfulness surmount these obstacles, the Lord declares that a kingdom is elsewhere prepared for them. It is no slight persuasive to patience, when men are fully convinced that they do not run in vain; and therefore, lest our minds should be east,

2. Genesis 24:31.

down by the pride of the ungodly, in which they give themselves unre-
strained indulgences—lest our hope should even be weakened by our
own afflictions, let us always remember the inheritance which awaits
us in heaven; for it depends on no uncertain event, but was prepared
for us by God before we were born,—prepared, I say, for each of the
elect, for the persons here addressed by Christ are the blessed of the
Father.

When it is here said only that the kingdom was prepared from
the beginning of the world, while it is said, in another passage, that it
was prepared before the creation of heaven and of earth, this involves
no inconsistency.[3] For Christ does not here fix the precise time when
the inheritance of eternal life was appointed for the sons of God, but
only reminds us of God's fatherly care, with which he embraced us
before we were born; and confirms the certainty of our hope by this
consideration, that our life can sustain no injury from the commotions
and agitations of the world.

35. *For I was hungry.* If Christ were now speaking of the cause
of our salvation, the Papists could not be blamed for inferring that
we merit eternal life by good works; but as Christ had no other design than to exhort his people to holy and upright conduct, it is im-
proper to conclude from his words what is the value of the merits of
works. With regard to the stress which they lay on the word for, as
if it pointed out the cause, it is a weak argument; for we know that,
when eternal life is promised to the righteous, the word for does not
always denote a cause, but rather the order of procedure. But we have
another reply to offer, which is still clearer; for we do not deny that
a reward is promised to good works, but maintain that it is a reward
of grace, because it depends on adoption. Paul boasts that a crown of
righteousness is laid up for him;[4] but whence did he derive that confidence but because he was a member of Christ, who alone is heir of the
heavenly kingdom? He openly avows that the righteous Judge will give
to him that crown; but whence did he obtain that prize but because by
grace he was adopted, and received that justification of which we are
all destitute? We must therefore hold these two principles, first, that

3. Ephesians 1:4.
4. 2 Timothy 4:8.

believers are called to the possession of the kingdom of heaven, so far as relates to good works, not because they deserved them through the righteousness of works, or because their own minds prompted them to obtain that righteousness, but because God justifies those whom he previously elected.[5] Secondly, although by the guidance of the Spirit they aim at the practice of righteousness, yet as they never fulfill the law of God, no reward is due to them, but the term reward is applied to that which is bestowed by grace.

Christ does not here specify every thing that belongs to a pious and holy life, but only, by way of example, refers to some of the duties of charity, by which we give evidence that we fear God. For though the worship of God is more important than charity towards men, and though, in like manner, faith and supplication are more valuable than alms, yet Christ had good reasons for bringing forward those evidences of true righteousness which are more obvious. If a man were to take no thought about God, and were only to be beneficent towards men, such compassion would be of no avail to him for appeasing God, who had all the while been defrauded of his right. Accordingly, Christ does not make the chief part of righteousness to consist in alms, but, by means of what may be called more evident signs, shows what it is to live a holy and righteous life; as unquestionably believers not only profess with the mouth, but prove by actual performances, that they serve God.

Most improperly, therefore, do fanatics, under the pretext of this passage, withdraw from hearing the word, and from observing the Holy Supper, and from other spiritual exercises; for with equal plausibility might they set aside faith, and bearing the cross, and prayer, and chastity. But nothing was farther from the design of Christ than to confine to a portion of the second table of the Law that rule of life which is contained in the two tables. The monks and other noisy talkers had as little reason to imagine that there are only six works of mercy, because Christ does not mention any more; as if it were not obvious, even to children, that he commends . . . all the duties of charity. For to comfort mourners, to relieve those who are unjustly oppressed, to aid simple-minded men by advice, to deliver wretched

5. Romans 8:30.

persons from the jaws of wolves, are deeds of mercy not less worthy of commendation than to clothe the naked or to feed the hungry.

But while Christ, in recommending to us the exercise of charity, does not exclude those duties which belong to the worship of God, he reminds his disciples that it will be an authentic evidence of a holy life, if they practice charity, agreeably to those words of the prophet, I choose mercy, and not sacrifice,[6] the import of which is, that hypocrites, while they are avaricious, and cruel, and deceitful, and extortioners, and haughty, still counterfeit holiness by an imposing array of ceremonies. Hence also we infer, that if we desire to have our life approved by the Supreme Judge, we must not go astray after our own inventions, but must rather consider what it is that He chiefly requires from us. For all who depart from his commandments, though they toil and wear themselves out in works of their own contrivance, will hear it said to them at the last day, Who has required those things at your hands?[7]

37. *Then will the righteous answer him.* Christ represents the righteous as doubting—what they know well—his willingness to form a just estimate of what is done to men. But as this was not so deeply impressed on their minds as it ought to have been, he holds out to them this lively representation. For how comes it that we are so slow and reluctant to acts of beneficence, but because that promise is not truly engraven on our hearts, that God will one day repay with usury what we bestow on the poor? The admiration which Christ here expresses is intended to instruct us to rise above the apprehension of our flesh, whenever afflicted brethren ask our confidence and aid, that the aspect of a despised man may not hinder us from treating him with kindness.

40. *Verily I tell you.* As Christ has just now told us, by a figure, that our senses do not yet comprehend how highly he values deeds of charity, so now he openly declares, that he will reckon as done to himself whatever we have bestowed on his people. We must be prodigiously sluggish, if compassion be not drawn from our bowels by this statement, that Christ is either neglected or honored in the person of

6. Hosea 6:6.
7. Isaiah 1:12.

those who need our assistance. So then, whenever we are reluctant to assist the poor, let us place before our eyes the Son of God, to whom it would be base sacrilege to refuse any thing. By these words he likewise shows, that he acknowledges those acts of kindness which have been performed gratuitously, and without any expectation of a reward. And certainly, when he enjoins us to do good to the hungry and naked, to strangers and prisoners, from whom nothing can be expected in return, we must look to him, who freely lays himself under obligation to us, and allows us to place to his account what might otherwise appear to have been lost.

So far as you have done it to one of the least of my brethren. Believers only are expressly recommended to our notice; not that he bids us altogether despise others, but because the more nearly a man approaches to God, he ought to be the more highly esteemed by us; for though there is a common tie that binds all the children of Adam, there is a still more sacred union among the children of God. So then, as those, who belong to the household of faith ought to be preferred to strangers, Christ makes special mention of them. And though his design was, to encourage those whose wealth and resources are abundant to relieve the poverty of brethren, yet it affords no ordinary consolation to the poor and distressed, that, though shame and contempt follow them in the eyes of the world, yet the Son of God holds them as dear as his own members. And certainly, by calling them brethren, he confers on them inestimable honor.

41. *Depart from me, you cursed.* He now comes to the reprobate, who are so intoxicated by their fading prosperity, that they imagine they will always be happy. He threatens, therefore, that he will come as their Judge, and that he will make them forget those luxurious enjoyments to which they are now so entirely devoted; not that the coming of Christ will strike them with terror—for they think that they have made a covenant with death,[8] and harden themselves in wicked indifference—but that believers, warned of their dreadful ruin, may not envy their present lot. For as promises are necessary for us, to excite and encourage us to holiness of life, so threatenings are likewise necessary to restrain us by anxiety and fear. We are therefore taught

8. Isaiah 28:15.

how desirable it is to be united to the Son of God; because everlasting destruction and the torment of the flesh await all those whom he will drive from his presence at the last day. He will then order the wicked to depart from him, because many hypocrites are now mixed with the righteous, as if they were closely allied to Christ . . . .

44. *Then will they also answer him.* The same kind of striking delineation which Christ had formerly employed is now repeated, in order to inform the reprobate, that their vain excuses, by which they now deceive themselves, will be of no avail to them at the last day. For whence comes the great cruelty of their pride towards the poor, but because they think that they will not be punished for despising them? To destroy this self-complacency, our Lord gives them warning, that they will one day feel—but when it will be too late—what they do not now deign to consider, that those who are now so greatly despised are not less esteemed by Christ than his own members.

Reading Questions

1. Who are "the least of these" in this passage?

2. How does grace operate? Does attentiveness to "the least of these" create merit by which the sheep are ushered into their eternal reward?

3. Reflect on the relationship between Calvinist theology and Calvin's comments on this passage. In particular, what does Calvin have to say about spiritual complacency?

4. How does Calvin interact with the "Papists" here?

5. Describe the relationship between divine "election" and salvation based on the reading above.

6. What are the pastoral concerns evident in Calvin's treatment of this text?

For Further Reading

Barth, Karl. *The Theology of John Calvin.* Translated by Geoffrey W. Bromiley. Grand Rapids: Eerdmans, 1995.

Cottret, Bernard. *Calvin: A Biography.* Translated by M. Wallace McDonald. Grand Rapids: Eerdmans, 2000.

Flaming, Darlene K. "Calvin as Commentator on the Gospels." In *Calvin and the Bible,* edited by Donald K. McKim, 131–63. Cambridge: Cambridge University Press, 2006.

McKim, Donald K., editor. *The Cambridge Companion to John Calvin.* Cambridge Companions to Religion. Cambridge: Cambridge University Press, 2004.

Parker, T. H. L. *Calvin: An Introduction to His Thought.* Louisville: Westminster John Knox, 1995.

Steinmetz, David C. *Calvin in Context.* New York: Oxford University Press, 1995.

27

Jonathan Edwards

Jonathan Edwards (1703–1758) was an eighteenth-century American colonist whose work as a theologian and preacher deeply impacted both early American spirituality and global theology. Edwards preached a sermon entitled "Sinners in the Hands of an Angry God" in which he likened our plight as sinners to a spider being dangled above a flame. The sermon had such a profound affect on the congregation that people ran screaming in terror out of the church. Edwards is still considered an important apologist for the theology of John Calvin, and is famous for his attacks on Arminianism and powerful sermons about divine grace and divine wrath.

. . .

An Exhortation to the Duty of Charity to the Poor, Section 3[1]

We are professors of Christianity; we pretend to be the followers of Jesus, and to make the gospel our rule. We have the Bible in our houses. Let us not behave ourselves in this particular, as if we had never see the Bible, as if we were ignorant of Christianity, and knew not what kind of religion it is. What will it signify to pretend to be Christians, and at the same time to live in the neglect of those rules of Christianity which are mainly insisted on in it? But there are several things which I would here propose to your consideration.

I. Consider that what you have is not your own; i.e. you have only a subordinate right. Your goods are only lent to you of God, to be improved by you in such ways as he directs. You yourselves are not your own. "Ye are not your own, for ye are bought with a price; your body and your spirit are God's."[2] And if you yourselves are not your own, so then neither are your possessions your own. Many of you have by covenant given up yourselves and all you have to God. You have disowned and renounced any right in yourselves or in anything that you have, and have given to God all the absolute right. And if you be true Christians, you have done it from the heart.

Your money and your goods are not your own. They are only committed to you as stewards, to be used for him who committed them to you. "Use hospitality one to another, as good stewards of the manifold grace of God."[3] A steward has no business with his master's goods, to use them any otherwise than for the benefit of his master and his family, or according to his master's direction. He hath no business to use them, as if he were the proprietor of them. He hath nothing to do with them, only as he is to use them for his master. He is to give everyone of his master's family their portion of meat in due season.

---

1. From *The Works of Jonathan Edwards* (Edinburgh: The Banner or Truth Trust, 1834). This is a small portion of a long sermon that was originally preached in January of 1732. The sermons of Jonathan Edwards have been released into the public domain.

2. 1 Corinthians 6:20.

3. 1 Peter 4:9, 10.

But if instead of that, he hoards up his master's goods for himself, and withholds them from those of the household, so that some of the family are pinched for want of food and clothing. He is therein guilty of robbing his master and embezzling his substance. And would any householder endure such a steward? If he discovered him in such a practice, would he not take his goods out of his hands, and commit them to the care of some other steward, who should give everyone of his family his portion of meat in due season? Remember that all of us must give account of our stewardship, and how we have disposed of those goods which our Master has put into our hands. And if when our Master comes to reckon with us, it be found that we have denied some of his family their proper provision, while we have hoarded up for ourselves, as if we had been the proprietors of our Master's goods, what account shall we give of this?

II. God tells us, that he shall look upon what is done in charity to our neighbors in want, as done unto him; and what is denied unto them, as denied unto him. "He that hath pity on the poor lendeth to the Lord."[4] God hath been pleased to make our needy neighbors his receivers. He in his infinite mercy hath so interested himself in their case, that he looks upon what is given in charity to them, as given to himself. And when we deny them what their circumstances require of us, he looks upon it that we therein rob him of his right.

Christ teaches us, that we are to look upon our fellow Christians in this case as himself, and that our giving or withholding from them, shall be taken, as if we so behaved ourselves towards him; see Matthew 25:40. There Christ says to the righteous on his right hand, who had supplied the wants of the needy, "In that ye have done it to one of the least of these my brethren, ye have done it unto me."[5] In like manner he says to the wicked who had not shown mercy to the poor, "Inasmuch as ye did it not unto one of the least of these, ye did it not to me."[6] —Now what stronger enforcement of this duty can be conceived, or is possible, than this, that Jesus Christ looks upon our kind and bounti-

4. Proverbs 19:17.
5. Matthew 25:40.
6. Matthew 25:45.

ful, or unkind and uncharitable, treatment of our needy neighbors, as such a treatment of himself?

If Christ himself were upon earth, a dwelt among us in a frail body, as he once did, and were in calamitous and needy circumstances, should we not be willing to supply him? Should we be apt to excuse ourselves from helping him? Should we not be willing to supply him so, that he might live free from distressing poverty? And if we did otherwise, should we not bring great guilt upon ourselves? And might not our conduct justly be very highly resented by God? Christ was once here in a frail body, stood in need of the charity, and was maintained by it. "And certain women which had been healed of evil spirits and infirmities, Mary called Magdalen, out of whom went seven devils, and Joanna the wife of Chuza, Herod's steward, and Susanna, and many others, which ministered unto him of their substance."[7] So he still, in many of his members, needs the charity of others.

III. Consider that there is an absolute necessity of our complying with the difficult duties of religion. To give to the poor in the manner and measure that the gospel prescribes is a difficult duty, i.e. it is very contrary to corrupt nature, to that covetousness and selfishness of which there is so much in the wicked heart of man. Man is naturally governed only by a principle of self-love. And it is a difficult thing to corrupt nature, for men to deny themselves of their present interest, trusting in God to make it up to them hereafter. —But how often hath Christ told us the necessity of doing difficult duties of religion, if we will be his disciples; that we must sell all, take up our cross daily, deny ourselves, renounce our worldly profits and interests, etc. And if this duty seem hard and difficult to you, let not that be an objection with you against doing it. For you have taken up quite a wrong notion of things if you expect to go to heaven without performing difficult duties; if you expect any other than to find the way to life a narrow way.

IV. The Scripture teaches us that this very particular duty is necessary, Particularly, First, the Scripture teaches that God will deal with us as we deal with our fellow creatures in this particular, and that with what measure we mete to others in this respect, God will measure to us again. This the Scripture asserts both ways. It asserts that if we

7. Luke 8:2–3.

be of a merciful spirit, God will be merciful to us. "Blessed are the merciful, for they shall obtain mercy."[8] "With the merciful thou wilt show thyself merciful."[9] On the other hand it tells us, that if we be not merciful, God will not be merciful to us; and that all our pretenses to faith and a work of conversion will not avail us, to obtain mercy, unless we be merciful to them that are in want. "For he shall have judgment without mercy, that hath showed no mercy. What doth it profit, my brethren, though a man say he hath faith, and have not works? Can faith save him? If a brother or sister be naked, and destitute of daily food; and one of you say unto them, Depart in peace, be you warmed, and filled; notwithstanding ye give them not those things which are needful to the body; what doth it profit?"[10]

Second, this very thing is often mentioned in Scripture as an essential part of the character of a godly man. "The righteous showeth mercy, and giveth."[11] And again, "He is ever merciful, and lendeth."[12] "A good man showeth favour, and lendeth."[13] "He hath dispersed, and given to the poor."[14] So "He that honoureth God, hath mercy on the poor."[15] Again, a righteous man and a merciful man are used as synonymous terms: "The righteous perisheth, and merciful men are taken away," etc.[16]

It is mentioned in the New Testament as a thing so essential, that the contrary cannot consist with a sincere love to God. "But whoso hath this world's goods, and seeth his brother have need, and shutteth up his bowels of compassion from him, how dwelleth the love of God in him? My little children, let us not love in word, neither in tongue, but in deed and in truth. And hereby we know that we are of the truth,

---

8. Matthew 5:7.
9. Psalm 18:25.
10. James 2:13–16.
11. Psalm 37:21.
12. Psalm 37:26.
13. Psalm 112:5.
14. Psalm 112:9.
15. Proverbs 14:31.
16. Proverbs 21:26; Isaiah 57:1.

and shall assure our hearts before him."[17] So the apostle Paul, when he writes to the Corinthians, and proposes their contributing for the supply of the poor saints, tells them what he doth it for: a trial of their sincerity, "I speak to prove the sincerity of your love."[18]

Third, Christ teaches that judgment will be past at the great day according to men's works in this respect. This is taught us by Christ in the most particular account of the proceedings of that day, that we have in the whole Bible.[19] It is evident that Christ thus represented the proceedings and determinations of this great day, as turning upon this one point, on purpose, and on design to lead us into this notion, and to fix it in us, that a charitable spirit and practice towards our brethren is necessary to salvation.

V. Consider what abundant encouragement the Word of God gives, that you shall be no losers by your charity and bounty to them who are in want. As there is scarce any duty prescribed in the Word of God, which is so much insisted on as this; so there is scarce any to which there are so many promises of reward made. This virtue especially hath the promises of this life and that which is to come. If we believe the Scriptures, when a man charitably gives to his neighbor in want, the giver has the greatest advantage by it, even greater than the receiver. "I have showed you all things, how that so laboring ye ought to support the weak, and to remember the words of the Lord Jesus, how he said, It is more blessed to give than to receive."[20] He that gives bountifully is a happier man than he that receives bountifully. "He that hath mercy on the poor, happy is he."[21]

Many persons are ready to look upon what is bestowed for charitable uses as lost. But we ought not to look upon it as lost, because it benefits those whom we ought to love as ourselves. And not only so, but it is not lost to us, if we give any credit to the Scriptures. See the advice that Solomon gives in Ecclesiastes, "Cast thy bread upon the

17. 1 John 3:17–19.
18. See 2 Corinthians 8:8.
19. See Matthew 25:34, etc.
20. Acts 20:35.
21. Proverbs 14:21.

waters, for thou shalt find it after many days."[22] By casting our bread upon the waters, Solomon means giving it to the poor, as appears by the next words, "Give a portion to seven, and also to eight." Waters are sometimes put for people and multitudes.

What strange advice would this seem to many, to cast their bread upon the waters, which would seem to them like throwing it away! What more direct method to lose our bread, than to go and throw it into the sea? But the wise man tells us, No, it is not lost; you shall find it again after many days. It is not sunk, but you commit it to Providence. You commit it to the winds and waves. However it will come about to you, and you shall find it again after many days. Though it should be many days first, yet you shall find it at last, at a time when you most need it. He that giveth to the poor lendeth to the Lord. And God is not one of those who will not pay again what is lent to him. If you lend anything to God, you commit it into faithful hands. "He that hath pity on the poor lendeth to the Lord, and that which he hath given will he pay him again."[23] God will not only pay you again, but he will pay you with great increase. "Give, and it shall be given you," that is, in "good measure, pressed down, and shaken together, and running over."[24]

Men do not account that lost, that is let out to use. but what is bestowed in charity is lent to the Lord, and he repays with great increase. "The liberal deviseth liberal things, and by liberal things shall he stand."[25] Here I would particularly observe: First, that if you give with a spirit of true charity, you shall be rewarded in what is infinitely more valuable than what you give, even eternal riches in heaven. "Whosoever shall give to drink unto one of these little ones, a cup of cold water only, in the name of a disciple; verily I say unto you, he shall in no wise lose his reward."[26]

Giving to our needy brethren is in Scripture called laying up treasure in heaven, in bags that wax not old. "Sell what ye have and

22. Ecclesiastes 11:1.
23. Proverbs 19:17.
24. Luke 6:38.
25. Isaiah 32:8.
26. Matthew 10:42.

give alms, provide for yourselves bags that wax not old, a treasure in the heavens that fails not, where no thief approaches, nor moth corrupts."[27] Men, when they have laid up their money in their chests, do not suppose that they have thrown it away. But, on the contrary, that it is laid up safe. Much less is treasure thrown away, when it is laid up in heaven. What is laid up there is much safer than what is laid up in chests or cabinets.

You cannot lay up treasure on earth, but that it is liable to be stolen, or otherwise to fail. But there no thief approaches nor moth corrupts. It is committed to God's care, and he will keep it safely for you. And when you die, you shall receive it with infinite increase. Instead of a part of your earthly substance thus bestowed, you shall receive heavenly riches, on which you may live in the greatest fullness, honor, and happiness, to all eternity; and shall never be in want of anything. After feeding with some of your bread those who cannot recompense you, you shall be rewarded at the resurrection, and eat bread in the kingdom of God. "When you make a feast, call the poor, the maimed, the lame, and the blind: and thou shalt be blessed; for they cannot recompense you: for you shall be recompensed at the resurrection of the just. And when one of them that sat at meat with him, heard these things, he said unto him, Blessed is he that shall eat bread in the kingdom of God."[28]

Second, if you give to the needy though but in the exercise of moral virtue, you will be in the way greatly to gain by it in your temporal interest. They who give in the exercise of a gracious charity, are in the way to be gainers both here and hereafter; and those that give in the exercise of a moral bounty and liberality, have many temporal promises made to them. We learn by the Word of God, that they are in the way to be prospered in their outward affairs. Ordinarily such do not lose by it, but such a blessing attends their concerns, that they are paid doubly for it. "There is that scatters, and yet increases; there is that withholds more than is meet, but it tends to poverty. The liberal soul

27. Luke 12:33.
28. Luke 14:13–16.

shall be made fat: and he that waters, shall be watered also himself."[29] And "He that gives to the poor, shall not lack."[30]

When men give to the needy, they do as it were sow seed for a crop. When men sow their seed, they seem to throw it away. Yet they do not look upon it as thrown away because, though they expect not the same again, yet they expect much more as the fruit of it. And if it be not certain that they shall have a crop, yet they are willing to run the venture of it; for that is the ordinary way wherein men obtain increase. So it is when persons give to the poor. Though the promises of gaining thereby, in our outward circumstances, perhaps are not absolute; yet it is as much the ordinary consequence of it, as increase is of sowing seed. Giving to the poor is in this respect compared to sowing seed, "In the morning sow thy seed, and in the evening withhold not your hand: for thou knows not whether shall prosper, either this or that, or whether they both shall be alike good."[31] By withholding the hand, the wise man means not giving to the poor.[32] It intimates, that giving to the poor is as likely a way to obtain prosperity and increase, as sowing seed in a field.

The husbandman doth not look upon his seed as lost, but is glad that he has opportunity to sow it. It grieves him not that he has land to be sown, but he rejoices in it. For the like reason we should not be grieved that we find needy people to bestow our charity upon. For this is as much an opportunity to obtain increase as the other.

Some may think this is strange doctrine; and it is to be feared, that not many will so far believe it as to give to the poor with as much cheerfulness as they sow their ground. However, it is the very doctrine of the Word of God, "But this I say, He who sows sparingly, shall reap also sparingly: and he who sows bountifully, shall reap also bountifully. Every man according as he purposes in his heart, so let him give; not grudgingly, or of necessity: for God loves a cheerful giver. And God is

---

29. Proverbs 11:24, 25.
30. Proverbs 28:27.
31. Ecclesiastes 11:6.
32. Ecclesiastes 11:1–2.

able to make all grace abound towards you; that ye always having all sufficiency in all things, may abound to every good work."[33]

Reading Questions

1. What is the character of human nature as described by Edwards? Can you discern his understanding of original sin from this sermon excerpt?

2. Who are "the least of these" in Edwards's understanding?

3. Edwards provides some unique motivations for heeding the imperative to care for the poor. Discuss his rationale.

4. How does the church function in the world, based on this sermon?

5. In this sermon do you see any sign of the "angry God" he mentions elsewhere?

For Further Reading

Marsden, George. *Jonathan Edwards: A Life*. New Haven: Yale University Press, 2003.

McClymond, Michael J. *Encounters with God: An Approach to the Theology of Jonathan Edwards*. Religion in America Series. New York: Oxford University Press, 1998.

Tracy, Patricia J. *Jonathan Edwards, Pastor: Religion and Society in Eighteenth-Century Northampton*. American Century Series. Reprinted, Eugene, OR: Wipf & Stock, 2006.

33. 2 Corinthians 9:6–8.

28

John Wesley

John Wesley (1703–1791) was an Anglican minister and renowned preacher who had a profound influence on eighteenth-century England. Wesley taught an optimistic message about the capacity of divine love and grace to transform human lives and human communities. In his trademark doctrine of "Christian Perfection" he claimed that through scriptural meditation, Holy Communion, accountability, prayer, and other "means of grace" God can transform a person's heart into a state of perfect love. Wesley and his followers, including his musically talented brother Charles, were meticulous about their lifestyle and morality. They would meet regularly for Eucharist, accountability, and self-examination; their patterned behavior earned them the initially derogatory title "Methodists." Though Wesley believed that his teachings and ecclesial practices were compatible with the Anglican Church, the "Methodist" movement gained in momentum and led to a proliferation of modern Protestant movements and denominations.

The sermon that follows reveals the concern for the poor that pervaded Wesley's evangelical impact on England. Reluctant to preach in the open air at first, Wesley found great success preaching to the working class on the streets. The importance of Christian concern for the poor, sick, and imprisoned permeates his writings, so this passage is particularly appropriate for Wesley's theology.

. . .

Sermon 98, On Visiting the Sick[1]

"I was sick, and you visited me." Matthew 25:36

1. It is generally supposed, that the means of grace and the ordinances of God are equivalent terms. We commonly mean by that expression, those that are usually termed, works of piety; viz., hearing and reading the Scripture, receiving the Lord's Supper, public and private prayer, and fasting. And it is certain these are the ordinary channels which convey the grace of God to the souls of men. But are they the only means of grace? Are there no other means than these, whereby God is pleased, frequently, yes, ordinarily, to convey his grace to them that either love or fear him? Surely there are works of mercy, as well as works of piety, which are real means of grace. They are more especially such to those that perform them with a single eye. And those that neglect them, do not receive the grace which otherwise they might. Yes, and they lose, by a continued neglect, the grace which they had received. Is it not hence that many who were once strong in faith are now weak and feeble-minded? And yet they are not sensible whence that weakness comes, as they neglect none of the ordinances of God. But they might see whence it comes, were they seriously to consider St. Paul's account of all true believers: "We are his workmanship, created anew in Christ Jesus unto good works, which God hath before prepared, that we might walk therein."[2]

2. The walking herein is essentially necessary, as to the continuance of that faith whereby we are already saved grace, so to the attainment of everlasting salvation. Of this cannot doubt, if we seriously consider that these are the very words of the great Judge himself: "Come, you blessed children of my Father, inherit the kingdom prepared for you from the foundation of the world. For I was hungry, and you gave me meat: Thirsty, and you gave me drink: I was a stranger, and you took me in: Naked, and you clothed me: I was sick, and you visited

---

1. From John Wesley, *Sermons on Several Occasions* (Grand Rapids: Christian Classics Ethereal Library, 1872 edition).

2. Ephesians 2:10.

me: I was in prison, and you came unto me."[3] "Verily, I say unto you, Inasmuch as you have done it to the least of these my brethren, you have done it unto me."[4] If this does not convince you that the continuance in works of mercy is necessary to salvation, consider what the Judge of all says to those on the left hand: "Depart, you cursed, into everlasting fire, prepared for the devil and his angels: For I was hungry, and you gave me no meat: Thirsty, and you gave me no drink: I was a stranger, and you took me not in: Naked, and you clothed me not: Sick and in prison, and you visited me not. Inasmuch as you have not done it unto one of the least of these neither have you done it unto me."[5] You see, were it for this alone, they must "depart" from God "into everlasting punishment."

3. Is it not strange, that this important truth should be so little understood, or, at least, should so little influence the practice of them that fear God? Suppose this representation be true, suppose the Judge of all the earth speaks right, those, and those only, that feed the hungry, give drink to the thirsty, clothe the naked, relieve the stranger, visit those that are in prison, according to their power and opportunity, shall "inherit the everlasting kingdom." And those that do not shall "depart into everlasting fire, prepared for the devil and his angels."

4. I purpose, at present, to confine my discourse to one article of these, —visiting the sick: A plain duty, which all that are in health may practice in a higher or lower degree; and which, nevertheless, is almost universally neglected, even by those that profess to love God. And touching this I would inquire, I. What is implied in visiting the sick? II. How is it to be performed? —And, III. By whom?

I. First, I would inquire, what is the nature of this duty? What is implied in "visiting the sick?"

1. By the sick, I do not mean only those that keep their bed, or that are sick in the strictest sense. Rather I would include all such as are in a state of affliction, whether of mind or body; and that whether they are good or bad, whether they fear God or not.

3. Matthew 25:34–36.
4. Matthew 25:40.
5. Matthew 25:41–46.

2. "But is there need of visiting them in person? May we not relieve them at a distance? Does it not answer the same purpose if we send them help as if we carry it ourselves?" Many are so circumstanced that they cannot attend the sick in person; and where this is the real case it is undoubtedly sufficient for them to send help, being the only expedient they can use. But this is not properly visiting the sick; it is another thing. The word which we render visit, in its literal acceptation, means to look upon. And this, you well know, cannot be done unless you are present with them. To send them assistance is, therefore, entirely a different thing from visiting them. The former, then, ought to be done, but the latter not left undone.

"But I send a physician to those that are sick; and he can do them more good than I can." He can, in one respect; he can do them more good with regard to their bodily health. But he cannot do them more good with regard to their souls, which are of infinitely greater importance. And if he could, this would not excuse you: His going would not fulfill your duty. Neither would it do the same good to you, unless you saw them with your own eyes. If you do not, you lose a means of grace; you lose an excellent means of increasing your thankfulness to God, who saves you from this pain and sickness, and continues your health and strength; as well as of increasing your sympathy with the afflicted, your benevolence, and all social affections.

3. One great reason why the rich, in general, have so little sympathy for the poor, is, because they so seldom visit them. Hence it is, that, according to the common observation, one part of the world does not know what the other suffers. Many of them do not know, because they do not care to know: they keep out of the way of knowing it; and then plead their voluntary ignorance an excuse for their hardness of heart. "Indeed, Sir," said person of large substance, "I am a very compassionate man. But, to tell you the truth, I do not know anybody in the world that is in want." How did this come to pass? Why, he took good care to keep out of their way; and if he fell upon any of them unawares "he passed over on the other side."

4. How contrary to this is both the spirit and behavior of even people of the highest rank in a neighboring nation! In Paris, ladies of the first quality, yes, Princesses of the blood, of the Royal Family, con-

stantly visit the sick, particularly the patients in the Grand Hospital. And they not only take care to relieve their wants, (if they need anything more than is provided for them,) but attend on their sick beds, dress their sores, and perform the meanest offices for them. Here is a pattern for the English, poor or rich, mean or honorable! For many years we have abundantly copied after the follies of the French; let us for once copy after their wisdom and virtue, worthy the imitation of the whole Christian world. Let not the gentlewomen, or even the countesses in England, be ashamed to imitate those Princesses of the blood! Here is a fashion that does honor to human nature. It began in France; but God forbid it should end there!"

5. And if your delicacy will not permit you to imitate those truly honorable ladies, by abasing yourselves in the manner which they do, by performing the lowest offices for the sick, you may, however, without humbling yourselves so far, supply them with whatever they want. And you may administer help of a more excellent kind, by supplying their spiritual wants; instructing them (if they need such instruction) in the first principles of religion; endeavoring to show them the dangerous state they are in, under the wrath and curse of God, through sin; and pointing them to the "Lamb of God, who takes away the sins of the world."[6] Beside this general instruction, you might have abundant opportunities of comforting those that are in pain of body, distress of mind; you might find opportunities of strengthening the feeble-minded, quickening those that are faint and weary; and of building up those that have believed, and encouraging them to "go on to perfection."[7] But these things you must do in your own person; you see they cannot be done by proxy. Or suppose you could give the same relief to the sick by another, you could not reap the same advantage to yourself; you could not gain that increase in lowliness, in patience, in tenderness of spirit, in sympathy with the afflicted, which you might have gained, if you had assisted them in person. Neither would you receive the same recompense in the resurrection of the just, when "every man shall receive his own reward, according to his own labor."[8]

6. John 1:29.

7. Hebrews 6:1.

8. 1 Corinthians 3:8.

II. 1. I proceed to inquire, in the Second place, how are we to visit them? In what manner may this labor of love be most effectually performed? How may we do this most to the glory of God, and the benefit of our neighbor? But before ever you enter upon the work, you should be deeply convinced that you are by means sufficient for it; you have neither sufficient grace, nor sufficient understanding, to perform it in the most excellent manner. And this will convince you of the necessity of applying to the Strong for strength; and of flying to the Father of Lights, the Giver of every good gift, for wisdom; ever remembering, "There is a Spirit in man that gives wisdom; and the inspiration of the Holy One that gives understanding."[9] Whenever, therefore, you are about to enter upon the work, seek his help by earnest prayer. Cry to him for the whole spirit of humility, lest pride steal into your heart, if you ascribe anything to yourself, while you strive to save others you destroy your own soul. Before and through the work, from the beginning to the end, let your heart wait upon him for a continual supply of meekness and gentleness, of patience and longsuffering, that you may never be angry or discouraged at whatever treatment, rough or smooth, kind or unkind, you may meet with. Be not moved with the deep ignorance of some, the dullness, the amazing stupidity of others; marvel not at their peevishness or stubbornness, at their non-improvement after all the pains that you have taken; yes, at some of them turning back to perdition, and being worse than they were before. Still your record is with the Lord, and your reward with the Most High.

2. As to the particular method of treating the sick, you need not tie yourself down to any, but may continually vary your manner of proceeding as various circumstances may require. But it may not be amiss, usually, to begin with inquiring into their outward condition. You may ask whether they have the necessaries of life; whether they have sufficient food and raiment; if the weather be cold, whether they have fuel; whether they have needful attendance; whether they have proper advice, with regard to their bodily disorder; especially if it be of a dangerous kind. In several of these respects you may be able to give them some assistance yourself; and you may move those that are more

9. Job 32:8.

able than you, to supply your lack of service. You might properly say in your own case, "To beg I am ashamed"; but never be ashamed to beg for the poor; yes, in this case, be an importunate beggar; do not easily take a denial. Use all the address, all the understanding, all the influence you have; at the same time trusting in Him that has the hearts of all men in his hands.

3. You will then easily discern, whether there is any good office which you can do for them with your own hands. Indeed, most of the things which are needful to be done, those about them can do better than you. But in some you may have more skill, or more experience, than them; and if you have, let not delicacy or honor stand in your way. Remember his word, "Inasmuch as you have done it unto the least of these, you have done it unto me";[10] and think nothing too mean to do for Him. Rejoice to be abased for his sake!

4. These little labors of love will pave your way to things greater importance. Having shown that you have a regard for their bodies, you may proceed to inquire concerning their souls. And here you have a large field before you; you have scope for exercising all the talents which God has given you. May you not begin with asking, "Have you ever considered, that God governs the world;—that his providence is over all, and over you in particular?—Does any thing then befall you without his knowledge—or without his designing it for your good? He knows all you suffer; he knows all your pains; he sees all your wants. He sees not only your affliction in general, but every particular circumstance of it. Is he not looking down from heaven, and disposing all these things for your profit? You may then inquire whether he is acquainted with the general principles of religion. And afterwards, lovingly and gently examine, whether his life has been agreeable thereto: whether he has been an outward, barefaced sinner, or has had a form of religion. See next, whether he knows anything of the power; of worshipping God "in spirit and in truth."[11] If he does not, endeavor to explain to him, "without holiness no man shall see the Lord";[12] and

10. Matthew 25:40.
11. John 4:23.
12. Hebrew 12:14.

"except a man be born again, he cannot see the kingdom of God."[13] When he begins to understand the nature of holiness, and the necessity of the new birth, then you may press upon him "repentance toward God, and faith in our Lord Jesus Christ" . . .

6. Together with the more important lessons, which you endeavor to teach all the poor whom you visit, it would be a deed of charity to teach them two things more, which they are generally little acquainted with—industry and cleanliness. It was said by a pious man, "Cleanliness is next to godliness." Indeed the want of it is a scandal to all religion; causing the way of truth to be evil spoken of. And without industry, we are neither fit for this world, nor for the world to come. With regard to both, "whatsoever thy hand findeth to do, do it with thy might."[14]

III. 1. The Third point to be considered is, by whom is this duty to be performed? The answer is ready: By all that desire to "inherit the kingdom" of their Father, which was "prepared forth from the foundation of the world." For thus saith the Lord, "Come, you blessed; —inherit the kingdom;—For I was sick, and you visited me."[15] And to those on the left hand, "Depart, you cursed;—for I was sick, and you visited me not."[16] Does not this plainly imply, that as all who do this are "blessed", and shall "inherit the kingdom"; so all who do it not are "cursed," and shall "depart into everlasting fire?

2. All, therefore, who desire to escape everlasting fire, and to inherit the everlasting kingdom, are equally concerned, according to their power, to practice this important duty. It is equally incumbent on young and old, rich and poor, men and women, according to their ability. None are so young, if they desire to save their own souls, as to be excused from assisting their neighbors. None are so poor, (unless they want the necessaries of life,) but they are called to do something, more or less, at whatever time they can spare, for the relief and comfort of their afflicted fellow-sufferers.

13. John 3:3.
14. Ecclesiastes 9:10.
15. Matthew 25:34.
16. Matthew 25:41.

3. But those "who are rich in this world,"[17] who have more than the conveniences of life, are peculiarly called of God to this blessed work, and pointed out to it by his gracious Providence. As you are not under a necessity of working for your bread, you have your time at your own disposal! You may, therefore, allot some part of it every day for this labor of love. If it be practicable, it is far best to have a fixed hour; (for any time, we say, is no time) and not to employ that time in any other business, without urgent necessity. You have likewise a peculiar advantage over many, by your station in life. Being superior in rank to them, you have the more influence on that very account. Your inferiors, of course, look up to you with a kind of reverence. And the condescension which you show in visiting them, gives them a prejudice in your favor, which inclines them to hear you with attention, and willingly receive what you say. Improve this prejudice to the uttermost for the benefit of their souls, as well as their bodies. While you are as eyes to the blind, and feet to the lame, a husband to the widow, and a father to the fatherless, see that you still keep a higher end in view, even the saving of souls from death, and that you labor to make all you say and do subservient to that great end.

4. "But have the poor themselves any part or lot in this matter? Are they any way concerned in visiting the sick? What can they give to others, who have hardly the conveniences, or perhaps necessaries, of life for themselves?" If they have not, yet they need not be wholly excluded from the blessing which attends the practice of this duty. Even those may remember that excellent rule: "Let our conveniences give way to our neighbor's necessities; and our necessities give way to our neighbor's extremities." And few are so poor, as not to be able sometimes to give "two mites";[18] but if they are not, if they have no money to give, may they not give what is of more value? Yes, of more value than thousands of gold and silver. If you speak "in the name of Jesus Christ of Nazareth," may not the words you speak be health to the soul, and marrow to the bones? Can you give them nothing? Nay, in administering to them the grace of God, you give them more than all this world is worth. Go on, go on, thou poor disciple of a poor

17. 1 Timothy 6:17.
18. Mark 12:42.

Master! Do as he did in the days of his flesh! Whenever thou hast an opportunity, go about doing good, and healing all that are oppressed of the devil; encouraging them shake off his chains, and fly immediately to Him: Who sets the prisoners free, and breaks; The iron bondage from their necks. Above all, give them your prayers. Pray with them; pray for them; and who knows but you may save their souls alive?

5. You that are old, whose feet are ready to stumble upon the dark mountains, may not you do a little more good before you go hence and are no more seen? Remember: 'Tis time to live, if you grow old; Of little life the best to make; And manage wisely the last stake! As you have lived many years, it may be hoped you have attained such knowledge as may be of use to others. You have certainly more knowledge of men, which is commonly learned by dear-bought experience. With what strength you have left, employ the few moments you have to spare, in ministering to those who are weaker than yourselves. Your grey hairs will not fail to give you authority, and add weight to what you speak. You may frequently urge, to increase their attention: Believe me, youth; for I am read in cares; And groan beneath the weight of more than threescore years. You have frequently been a sufferer yourself; perhaps you are so still. So much the more give them all the assistance you can, both with regard to their souls and bodies, before they and you go to the place whence you will not return.

6. On the other hand, you that are young have several advantages that are almost peculiar to yourselves. You have generally a flow of spirits, and a liveliness of temper, which, by the grace of God, make you willing to undertake, and capable of performing, many good works, at which others would be discouraged. And you have your health and strength of body, whereby you are eminently qualified to assist the sick and those that have no strength. You are able to take up and carry the crosses, which may be expected to lie in the way. Employ then your whole vigor of body and mind in ministering to your afflicted brethren. And bless God that you have them to employ in so honorable a service; like those heavenly "servants of his that do his pleasure," by continually ministering to the heirs of salvation.

7. "But may not women, as well as men, bear a part in this honorable service?" Undoubtedly they may; nay, they ought; it is meet,

right, and their bounden duty. Herein there is no difference; "there is neither male nor female in Christ Jesus. Indeed it has long passed for a maxim with many, that "women are only to be seen, not heard." And accordingly many of them are brought up in such a manner as if they were only designed for agreeable playthings! But is this doing honor to the sex? or is it a real kindness to them? No; it is the deepest unkindness; it is horrid cruelty; it is mere Turkish barbarity. And I know not how any woman of sense and spirit can submit to it. Let all you that have it in your power assert the right which the God of nature has given you. Yield not to that vile bondage any longer. You, as well as men, are rational creatures. You, like them, were made in the image of God; you are equally candidates for immortality; you too are called of God, as you have time, to "do good unto all men."[19] Be "not disobedient to the heavenly calling." Whenever you have opportunity, do all the good you can, particularly to your poor, sick neighbor. And every one of you likewise "shall receive your own reward, according to your own labor."[20]

8. It is well known, that, in the primitive Church, there were women particularly appointed for this work. Indeed there was one or more such in every Christian congregation under heaven. They were then termed Deaconesses, that is, servants; servants of the Church, and of its great Master. Such was Phebe, (mentioned by St. Paul, Romans 16:1) "a Deaconess of the Church of Cenchrea." It is true, most of these were women in years, and well experienced in the work of God. But were the young wholly excluded from that service? No: Neither need they be, provided they know in whom they have believed; and show that they are holy of heart, by being holy in all manner of conversation. Such a Deaconess, if she answered her picture, was Mr. Law's Miranda. Would anyone object to her visiting and relieving the sick and poor, because she was a woman; nay, and a young one too? Do any of you that are young desire to tread in her steps? Have you a pleasing form, an agreeable address? So much the better, if you are wholly devoted to God. He will use these, if your eye be single, to make your words strike the deeper. And while you minister to others, how many

19. Galatians 6:10.
20. 1 Corinthians 3:8.

blessings may redound into your own bosom! Hereby your natural levity may be destroyed; your fondness for trifles cured; your wrong tempers corrected; your evil habits weakened, until they are rooted out; and you will be prepared to adorn the doctrine of God our Savior in every future scene of life. Only be very wary, if you visit or converse with those of the other sex, lest your affections be entangled, on one side or the other, and so you find a curse instead of a blessing.

9. Seeing then this is a duty to which we are called, rich and poor, young and old, male and female, (and it would be well parents would train up their children herein, as well as in saying their prayers and going to church,) let the time past suffice that almost all of us have neglected it, as by general consent. O what need has every one of us to say, "Lord, forgive me my sins of omission!" Well, in the name of God, let us now from this day set about it with general consent. And I pray, let it never go out of your mind that this is a duty which you cannot perform by proxy; unless in one only case,—unless you are disabled by your own pain or weakness. In that only case, it suffices to send the relief which you would otherwise give. Begin, my dear brethren, begin now; else the impression which you now feel will wear off; and, possibly, it may never return! What then will be the consequence? Instead of hearing that word, "Come, you blessed!—For I was sick, and you visited me";[21] you must hear that awful sentence, "Depart, you cursed!—For I was sick, and you visited me not!"[22]

21. Matthew 25:34.
22. Matthew 25:41.

Reading Questions

1. What do the poor and the sick have to do with the "means of grace"?

2. Is it sufficient, according to Wesley, to give generously to good causes? Must we actually go to prisons? To the poor?

3. Besides alleviating the immediate needs of those who suffer (loneliness, hunger, etc.), what does Wesley think the Christian can offer people in need?

4. What does Wesley mean by the phrase: "Rejoice to be abased for his sake"?

5. What sort of lifestyle is Wesley advocating? What sort of spirituality produces this kind of lifestyle?

For Further Reading

Burnett, Daniel L. *In the Shadow of Aldersgate: An Introduction to the Heritage and Faith of the Wesleyan Tradition.* Eugene, OR: Cascade Books, 2005.

Collins, Kenneth J. *John Wesley: A Theological Journey.* Nashville: Abingdon, 2003.

Oden, Thomas C. *John Wesley's Scriptural Christianity.* Grand Rapids: Zondervan, 1994.

Stone, Ronald H. *John Wesley's Life and Ethics.* Nashville: Abingdon, 2001.

29

George Whitefield

※

It is difficult for the modern reader to understand the impact that George Whitefield (1714–1770) had on the American colonies or on early Methodism. His booming voice, entertaining style, and compelling preaching made him a popular draw in England, where he showed compassion and concern for the impoverished and neglected working class. Whitefield joined the religious revival initiated by John and Charles Wesley, eventually convincing John to preach in the open air when crowds grew too large or local churches would not admit them. Whitefield and John Wesley would eventually differ over theological and practical issues, but they should be seen in tandem as the two pivotal figures in the founding of Methodism. Whitefield's greatest fame came in a remarkable preaching tour of the colonies, where at one point in time an astounding 80% of the American settlers had heard him preach in person. He was the first media sensation on the continent, deftly using newsprint and word-of-mouth advertisement to assemble crowds numbering in the thousands. Whitefield did not disappoint; Benjamin Franklin marveled at his ability to effectively address enormous audiences after hearing him at a revival in Philadelphia.

Most preachers of this era read their sermons from handwritten manuscripts and notes. Whitefield was known for bucking this trend, departing from his notes and preaching extemporaneously. This makes the manuscript below a shadow of his actual sermon, in which it is likely that he adjusted his message, eliciting additional emotion in his listeners. In this way, Whitefield greatly influenced the way sermons are delivered and should be considered a founder of modern Evangelicalism.

. . .

Selected Sermons of George Whitefield:
The Almost Christian[1]

Acts 26:28—"Almost thou persuadest me to be a Christian."

The chapter, out of which the text is taken, contains an admirable account which the great St. Paul gave of his wonderful conversion from Judaism to Christianity, when he was called to make his defense before Festus a Gentile governor, and king Agrippa. Our blessed Lord had long since foretold, that when the Son of man should be lifted up, "his disciples should be brought before kings and rulers, for his name's sake, for a testimony unto them." And very good was the design of infinite wisdom in thus ordaining it; for Christianity being, from the beginning, a doctrine of the Cross, the princes and rulers of the earth thought themselves too high to be instructed by such mean teachers, or too happy to be disturbed b such unwelcome truths; and therefore would have always continued strangers to Jesus Christ, and him crucified, had not the apostles, by being arraigned before them, gained opportunities of preaching to them "Jesus and the resurrection." St. Paul knew full well that this was the main reason, why his blessed Master permitted his enemies at this time to arraign him at a public bar; and therefore, in compliance with the divine will, thinks it not sufficient, barely to make his defense, but endeavors at the same time to convert his judges. And this he did with such demonstration of the spirit, and of power, that Festus, unwilling to be convinced by the strongest evidence, cries out with a loud voice, "Paul, much earning doth make thee mad." To which the brave apostle (like a true follower of the holy Jesus) meekly replies, I am not mad, most noble Festus, but speak forth the words of truth and soberness." But in all probability, seeing king Agrippa more affected with his discourse, and observing in him an inclination to know the truth, he applies himself more particularly to him. "The king knoweth of these things; before whom also I speak freely; for I am persuaded that none of these things are hidden from him." And then, that if possible he might complete his wished-for conversion, he with an inimitable strain of oratory, addresses himself

---

1. George Whitefield, *Selected Sermons of George Whitefield* (Bellingham, WA: Logos Research Systems Incorporated), public domain.

still more closely, "King Agrippa, believest thou the prophets? I know that thou believest them." At which the passions of the king began to work so strongly, that he was obliged in open court, to own himself affected by the prisoner's preaching, and ingenuously to cry out, "Paul, almost thou persuadest me to be a Christian."

Which words, taken with the context, afford us a lively representation of the different reception, which the doctrine of Christ's ministers, who come in the power and spirit of St. Paul, meets with now-a-days in the minds of men. For notwithstanding they, like this great apostle, "speak forth the words of truth and soberness"; and with such energy and power, that all their adversaries cannot justly gainsay or resist; yet, too many, with the noble Festus before-mentioned, being like him, either too proud to be taught, or too sensual, too careless, or too worldly-minded to live up to the doctrine, in order to excuse themselves, cry out, that "much learning, much study, or, what is more unaccountable, much piety, hath made them mad." And though, blessed be God! All do not thus disbelieve our report; yet amongst those who gladly receive the word, and confess that we speak the words of truth and soberness, there are so few, who arrive at any higher degree of piety than that of Agrippa, or are any farther persuaded than to be almost Christians, that I cannot but think it highly necessary to warn my dear hearers of the danger of such a state. And therefore, from the words of the text, shall endeavor to show these three things:

First, What is meant by an almost-Christian.

Secondly, What are the chief reasons, why so many are no more than almost Christians.

Thirdly, I shall consider the ineffectualness, danger, absurdity, and uneasiness which attends those who are but almost Christians; and then conclude with a general exhortation, to set all upon striving not only be almost, but altogether Christians.

I. And, First, I am to consider what is meant by an almost Christians.

An almost Christian, if we consider him in respect to his duty to God, is one that halts between two opinions; that wavers between Christ and the world; that would reconcile God and Mammon, light and darkness, Christ and Belial. It is true, he has an inclination to religion, but then he is very cautious how he goes too far in it: his false heart is always crying out, Spare thyself, do thyself no harm. He prays indeed, that "God's will may be done on earth, as it is in heaven." But notwithstanding, he is very partial in his obedience, and fondly hopes that God will not be extreme to mark every thing that he willfully does amiss; though an inspired apostle has told him, that "he who offends in one point is guilty of all." But chiefly, he is one that depends much on outward ordinances, and on that account looks upon himself as righteous, and despises others; though at the same time he is as great a stranger to the divine life as any other person whatsoever. In short, he is fond of the form, but never experiences the power of godliness in his heart. He goes on year after year, attending on the means of grace, but then, like Pharaoh's lean kine [cow?], he is never the better, but rather the worse for them.

If you consider him in respect to his neighbor, he is one that is strictly just to all; but then this does not proceed from any love to God or regard to man, but only through a principle of self-love: because he knows dishonesty will spoil his reputation, and consequently hinder his thriving in the world.

He is one that depends much upon being negatively good, and contents himself with the consciousness of having done no one any harm; though he reads in the gospel, that "the unprofitable servant was cast into outer darkness," and the barren fig-tree was cursed and dried up from the roots, not for bearing bad, but no fruit.

He is no enemy to charitable contributions in public, if not too frequently recommended: but then he is unacquainted with the kind offices of visiting the sick and imprisoned, clothing the naked, and relieving the hungry in a private manner. He thinks that these things belong only to the clergy, though his own false heart tells him, that nothing but pride keeps him from exercising these acts of humility; and that Jesus Christ, in the 25th chapter of St. Matthew, condemns persons to everlasting punishment, not merely for being fornicators, drunkards, or extortioners, but for neglecting these charitable offices, "When the Son of man shall come in his glory, he shall set the sheep on his right-hand, and the goats on his left. And then shall he say unto them on his left hand, depart from me, ye cursed, into everlasting fire prepared for the devil and his angels: for I was an hungered, and ye gave me no meat; I was thirsty, and ye gave me no drink; I was a stranger, and ye took me not in; naked, and ye clothed me not; sick and in prison, and ye visited me not. Then shall they also say, Lord, when saw we thee an hungered, or a-thirst, or a stranger, or naked, or sick, or in prison, and did not minister unto thee? Then shall he answer them, Verily I say unto you, inasmuch as ye have not done it unto one of the least of these my brethren, ye did it not unto me: and these shall go away into everlasting punishment unto me: and these shall go away into everlasting punishment." I thought proper to give you this whole passage of scripture at large, because our Savior lays such a particular stress upon it; and yet it is so little regarded, that were we to judge by the practice of Christians, one should be tempted to think there were no such verses in the Bible.

But to proceed in the character of an Almost Christian: If we consider him in respect of himself; as we said he was strictly honest to his neighbor, so he is likewise strictly sober in himself: but then both his honesty and sobriety proceed from the same principle of a false self-love. It is true, he runs not into the same excess of riot with other men; but then it is not out of obedience to the laws of God, but either because his constitution will not away with intemperance; or rather because he is cautious of forfeiting his reputation, or unfitting himself for temporal business. But though he is so prudent as to avoid intemperance and excess, for the reasons before-mentioned; yet he always goes to the extremity of what is lawful. It is true, he is no drunkard; but then he has no Christian self-denial. He cannot think our Savior to be so austere a Master, as to deny us to indulge ourselves in some particulars: and so by this means he is destitute of a sense of true religion, as much as if he lived in debauchery, or any other crime whatever. As to settling his principles as well as practice, he is guided more by the world, than by the word of God: for his part, he cannot think the way to heaven so narrow as some would make it; and therefore considers not so much what scripture requires, as what such and such a good man does, or what will best suit his own corrupt inclinations. Upon this account, he is not only very cautious himself,

but likewise very careful of young converts, whose faces are set heav-
enward; and therefore is always acting the devil's part, and bidding
them spare themselves, though they are doing no more than what the
scripture strictly requires them to do: The consequence of which is,
that "he suffers not himself to enter into the kingdom of God, and
those that are entering in he hinders."

Thus lives the almost Christian: not that I can say, I have fully
described him to you; but from these outlines and sketches of his character, if your consciences have done their proper office, and made a
particular application of what has been said to your own hearts, I cannot but fear that some of you may observe some features in his picture,
odious as it is, to near resembling your own; and therefore I cannot
but hope, that you will join with the apostle in the words immediately
following the text, and wish yourselves "to be not only almost, but
altogether Christians."

II. I proceed to the second general thing proposed; to consider
the reasons why so many are no more than almost Christians.

1. And the first reason I shall mention is, because so many set out
with false notions of religion; though they live in a Christian country,
yet they know not what Christianity is. This perhaps may be esteemed
a hard saying, but experience sadly evinces the truth of it; for some
place religion in being of this or that communion; more in morality;
most in a round of duties, and a model of performances; and few, very
few acknowledge it to be, what it really is, a thorough inward change
of nature, a divine life, a vital participation of Jesus Christ, an union
of the soul with God; which the apostle expresses by saying, "He that
is joined to the Lord is one spirit." Hence it happens, that so many,
even of the most knowing professors, when you come to converse with
them concerning the essence, the life, the soul of religion, I mean our
new birth in Jesus Christ, confess themselves quite ignorant of the
matter, and cry out with Nicodemus, "How can this thing be?" And
no wonder then, that so many are only almost Christians, when so
many know not what Christianity is: no marvel, that so many take up
with the form, when they are quite strangers to the power of godliness;
or content themselves with the shadow, when they know so little about

the substance of it. And this is one cause why so many are almost, and so few are altogether Christians.

2. A second reason that may be assigned why so many are no more than almost Christians, is a servile fear of man: multitudes there are and have been, who, though awakened to a sense of the divine life, and have tasted and felt the powers of the world to come; yet out of a base sinful fear of being counted singular, or contemned by men, have suffered all those good impressions to wear off. It is true, they have some esteem for Jesus Christ; but then, like Nicodemus, they would come to him only by night: they are willing to serve him; but then they would do it secretly, for fear of the Jews: they have a mind to see Jesus, but then they cannot come to him because of the press, and for fear of being laughed at, and ridiculed by those with whom they used to sit at meat. But well did our Savior prophesy of such persons, "How can ye love me, who receive honor one of another?" Alas! have they never read, that "the friendship of this world is enmity with God"; and that our Lord himself has threatened, "Whosoever shall be ashamed of me or of my words, in this wicked and adulterous generation, of him shall the Son of man be ashamed, when he cometh in the glory of his Father and of his holy angels?" No wonder that so many are no more than almost Christians, since so many "love the praise of men more than the honor which cometh of God."

3. A third reason why so many are no more than almost Christians, is a reigning love of money. This was the pitiable case of that forward young man in the gospel, who came running to our blessed Lord, and kneeling before him, inquired "what he must do to inherit eternal life"; to whom our blessed Master replied, "Thou knowest the commandments, Do not kill, Do not commit adultery, Do not steal:" To which the young man replied, "All these have I kept from my youth." But when our Lord proceeded to tell him, "Yet lackest thou one thing; Go sell all that thou hast, and give to the poor; he was grieved at that saying, and went away sorrowful, for he had great possessions!" Poor youth! He had a good mind to be a Christian, and to inherit eternal life, but thought it too dear, if it could be purchased at no less an expense than of his estate! And thus many, both young and old, now-a-days, come running to worship our blessed Lord in public, and kneel before

him in private, and inquire at his gospel, what they must do to inherit eternal life: but when they find they must renounce the self-enjoyment of riches, and forsake all in affection to follow him, they cry, "The Lord pardon us in this thing! We pray thee, have us excused."

But is heaven so small a trifle in men's esteem, as not to be worth a little gilded earth? Is eternal life so mean a purchase, as not to deserve the temporary renunciation of a few transitory riches? Surely it is. But however inconsistent such a behavior may be, this inordinate love of money is too evidently the common and fatal cause, why so many are no more than almost Christians.

4. Nor is the love of pleasure a less uncommon, or a less fatal cause why so many are no more than almost Christians. Thousands and ten thousands there are, who despise riches, and would willingly be true disciples of Jesus Christ, if parting with their money would make them so; but when they are told that our blessed Lord has said, "Whosoever will come after him must deny himself"; like the pitiable young man before-mentioned, "they go away sorrowful"" for they have too great a love for sensual pleasures. They will perhaps send for the ministers of Christ, as Herod did for John, and hear them gladly: but touch them in their Herodias, tell them they must part with such or such a darling pleasure; and with wicked Ahab they cry out, "Hast thou found us, O our enemy?" Tell them of the necessity of mortification and self-denial, and it is as difficult for them to hear, as if you was to bid them "cut off a right-hand, or pluck out a right-eye." They cannot think our blessed Lord requires so much at their hands, though an inspired apostle has commanded us to "mortify our members which are upon earth." And who himself, even after he had converted thousands, and was very near arrived to the end of his race, yet professed that it was his daily practice to "keep under his body, and bring it into subjection, lest after he had preached to others, he himself should be a cast-away!"

But some men would be wiser than this great apostle, and chalk out to us what they falsely imagine an easier way to happiness. They would flatter us, we may go to heaven without offering violence to our sensual appetites; and enter into the strait gate without striving against our carnal inclinations. And this is another reason why so many are only almost, and not altogether Christians.

5. The fifth and last reason I shall assign why so many are only almost Christians, is a fickleness and instability of temper. It has been, no doubt, a misfortune that many a minister and sincere Christian has met with, to weep and wail over numbers of promising converts, who seemingly began in the Spirit, but after a while fell away, and basely ended in the flesh; and this not for want of right notions in religion, nor out of a servile fear of man, nor from the love of money, or of sensual pleasure, but through an instability and fickleness of temper. They looked upon religion merely for novelty, as something which pleased them for a while; but after their curiosity was satisfied, they laid it aside again: like the young man that came to see Jesus with a linen cloth about his naked body, they have followed him for a season, but when temptations came to take hold on them, for want of a little more resolution, they have been stripped of all their good intentions, and fled away naked. They at first, like a tree planted by the water-side, grew up and flourished for a while; but having no root in themselves, no inward principle of holiness and piety, like Jonah's gourd, they were soon dried up and withered. Their good intentions are too like the violent motions of the animal spirits of a body newly beheaded, which, though impetuous, are not lasting. In short, they set out well in their journey to heaven, but finding the way either narrower or longer than they expected, through an unsteadiness of temper, they have made an eternal halt, and so "returned like the dog to his vomit, or like the sow that was washed to her wallowing in the more!"

But I tremble to pronounce the fate of such unstable professors, who having put their hands to the plough, for want of a little more resolution, shamefully look back. How shall I repeat to them that dreadful threatening, "If any man draw back, my soul shall have no pleasure in him:" And again, "It is impossible (that is, exceeding difficult at least) for those that have been once enlightened, and have tasted of the heavenly gift, and the powers of the world to come, if they should fall away, to be renewed again unto repentance." But notwithstanding the gospel is so severe against apostates, yet many that begun well, through a fickleness of temper, (O that none of us here present may ever be such) have been by this means of the number of those that turn back unto perdition. And this is the fifth, and the last reason I shall give, why so many are only almost, and not altogether Christians.

III. Proceed we now to the general thing proposed, namely, to consider the folly of being no more than an almost Christian.

1. And the First proof I shall give of the folly of such a proceeding is, that it is ineffectual to salvation. It is true, such men are almost good; but almost to hit the mark, is really to miss it. God requires us "to love him with all our hearts, with all our souls, and with all our strength." He loves us too well to admit any rival; because, so far as our hearts are empty of God, so far must they be unhappy. The devil, indeed, like the false mother that came before Solomon, would have our hearts divided, as she would have had the child; but God, like the true mother, will have all or none. "My Son, give me thy heart," thy whole heart, is the general call to all: and if this be not done, we never can expect the divine mercy.

Persons may play the hypocrite; but God at the great day will strike them dead, (as he did Ananias and Sapphira by the mouth of his servant Peter) for pretending to offer him all their hearts, when they keep back from him the greatest part. They may perhaps impose upon their fellow- creatures for a while; but he that enabled Elijah to cry out, "Come in thou wife of Jeroboam," when she came disguised to inquire about he sick son, will also discover them through their most artful dissimulations; and if their hearts are not wholly with him, appoint them their portion with hypocrites and unbelievers.

2. But, Secondly, What renders an half-way-piety more inexcusable is, that it is not only insufficient to our own salvation, but also very prejudicial to that of others. An almost Christian is one of the most hurtful creatures in the world; he is a wolf in sheep's clothing: he is one of those false prophets, our blessed Lord bids us beware of in his sermon on the mount, who would persuade men, that the way to heaven is broader than it really is; and thereby, as it was observed before, "enter not into the kingdom of God themselves, and those that are entering in they hinder." These, these are the men that turn the world into a luke-warm Laodicean spirit; that hang out false lights, and so shipwreck unthinking benighted souls in their voyage to the haven of eternity. These are they who are greater enemies to the cross

of Christ, than infidels themselves: for of an unbeliever every one will be aware; but an almost Christian, through his subtle hypocrisy, draws away many after him; and therefore must expect to receive the greater damnation.

3. But, Thirdly, As it is most prejudicial to ourselves and hurtful to others, so it is the greatest instance of ingratitude we can express towards our Lord and Master Jesus Christ. For did he come down from heaven, and shed his precious blood, to purchase these hearts of ours, and shall we only give him half of them? O how can we say we love him, when our hearts are not wholly with him? How can we call him our Savior, when we will not endeavor sincerely to approve ourselves to him, and so let him see the travail of his soul, and be satisfied!

Had any of us purchased a slave at a most expensive rate, and who was before involved in the utmost miseries and torments, and so must have continued for ever, had we shut up our bowels of compassion from him; and was this slave afterwards to grow rebellious, or deny giving us but half his service; how, how should we exclaim against his base ingratitude! And yet this base ungrateful slave thou art, O man, who acknowledgest thyself to be redeemed from infinite unavoidable misery and punishment by the death of Jesus Christ, and yet wilt not give thyself wholly to him. But shall we deal with God our Maker in a manner we would not be dealt with by a man like ourselves? God forbid! No. Suffer me, therefore.

To add a word or two of exhortation to you, to excite you to be not only almost, but altogether Christians. O let us scorn all base and treacherous treatment of our King and Savior, of our God and Creator. Let us not take some pains all our lives to go to haven, and yet plunge ourselves into hell as last. Let us give to God our whole hearts, and no longer halt between two opinions: if the world be God, let us serve that; if pleasure be a God, let us serve that; but if the Lord he be God, let us, O let us serve him alone. Alas! why, why should we stand out any longer? Why should we be so in love with slavery, as not wholly to renounce the world, the flesh, and the devil, which, like so many spiritual chains, bind down our souls, and hinder them from flying up to God. Alas! what are we afraid of? Is not God able to reward our entire obedience? If he is, as the almost Christian's lame way of serving him, seems to grant, why then will we not serve him entirely? For the same reason we do so much, why do we not do more? Or do you think that being only half religious will make you happy, but that going farther, will render you miserable and uneasy? Alas! this, my brethren, is delusion all over: for what is it but this half piety, this wavering between God and the world, that makes so many, that are seemingly well disposed, such utter strangers to the comforts of religion? They choose just so much of religion as will disturb them in their lusts, and follow their lusts so far as to deprive themselves of the comforts of religion. Whereas on the contrary, would they sincerely leave all in affection, and give their hearts wholly to God, they would then (and they cannot till then) experience the unspeakable pleasure of having a mind at unity with itself, and enjoy such a peace of God, which even in this life passes all understanding, and which they were entire strangers to before. It is true, it we will devote ourselves entirely to God, we must meet with contempt; but then it is because contempt is necessary to heal our pride. We must renounce some sensual pleasures, but then it is because those unfit us for spiritual ones, which are infinitely better. We must renounce the love of the world; but then it is that we may be filled with the love of God: and when that has once enlarged our hearts, we shall, like Jacob when he served for his beloved Rachel, think nothing too difficult to undergo, no hardships too tedious to endure, because of the love we shall then have for our dear Redeemer. Thus easy, thus delightful will be the ways of God even in this life: but when once we throw off these bodies, and our souls are filled with all the fullness of God, O! what heart can conceive, what tongue can express, with what unspeakable joy and consolation shall we then look back on our past sincere and hearty services. Think you then, my dear hearers, we shall repent we had done too much; or rather think you not, we shall be ashamed that we did no more; and blush we were so backward to give up all to God; when he intended hereafter to give us himself?

Let me therefore, to conclude, exhort you, my brethren, to have always before you the unspeakable happiness of enjoying God. And think withal, that every degree of holiness you neglect, every act of piety you omit, is a jewel taken out of your crown, a degree of blessedness lost in the vision of God. O! do but always think and act thus, and you will no longer be laboring to compound matters between God and the world; but, on the contrary, be daily endeavoring to give up yourselves more and more unto him; you will be always watching, always praying, always aspiring after farther degrees of purity and love, and consequently always preparing yourselves for a fuller sight and enjoyment of that God, in whose presence there is fullness of joy, and at whose right-hand there are pleasures for ever more. Amen! Amen!

Reading Questions

1. According to Whitefield, what are some of the characteristics of an "almost Christian"? Are these symptoms of the eighteenth century, or are they familiar in Christianity today?

2. Whitefield lays heavy stress on "the least of these" parable, reading it in full to stress the fact that Christians often neglect the importance of this passage. Why does Whitefield think it is neglected?

3. Slavery was one area of disagreement between Wesley and Whitefield. Whitefield owned slaves and was a supporter of slavery in the American colonies, helping entrench racial divides that continue to exert pressure in the United States. He uses an illustration in the sermon above from slavery. Evaluate and critique the connection he makes between "almost Christians" and ungrateful slaves.

4. Evaluate Whitefield's use of "the least of these" parable in light of his defense of slavery. Does his ownership of slaves make the preacher of this sermon an "almost Christian"? Worse?

For Further Reading

Lambert, Frank. *Pedlar in Divinity: George Whitefield and the Transatlantic Revivals, 1737–1770*. Princeton: Princeton University Press, 1994.

Pollock, John. *George Whitefield and the Great Awakening*. Garden City, NY: Doubleday, 1972.

Stout, Harry S. *The Divine Dramatist: George Whitefield and the Rise of Modern Evangelicalism*. Library of Religious Biography. Grand Rapids: Eerdmans, 1991.

Select Bibliography

1. Reference Works

Bornstein, Daniel E., editor. *Medieval Christianity.* A People's History of Christianity 4. Minneapolis: Fortress, 2007.

Burrus, Virginia, editor. *Late Ancient Christianity.* A People's History of Christianity 2. Minneapolis: Fortress, 2005.

Di Berardino, Angelo, editor. *Encyclopedia of the Early Church.* Translated by Adrian Walford. Foreword by W. H. C. Frend. 2 vols. New York: Oxford University Press, 1992.

Dowley, Tim. *Introduction to the History of Christianity: First Century to the Present Day, with CD-ROM.* Rev. ed. Minneapolis: Fortress, 2006.

Cross, F. L., and E. A. Livingstone, editors. *The Oxford Dictionary of the Christian Church.* 3d ed. Oxford: Oxford University Press, 1997.

Eliade, Mircea, editor. *Encyclopedia of Religion.* 16 vols. New York: Macmillan, 1987.

Ferguson, Everett, editor. *Encyclopedia of Early Christianity.* 2d ed. New York: Garland, 1997.

Frend, W. H. C. *The Early Church: From Beginnings to 461.* 3d ed. London: SCM, 1991.

Horsley, Richard A., editor. *Christian Origins.* A People's History of Christianity 1. Minneapolis: Fortress, 2005.

Irvin, Dale T., and Scott W. Sunquist, editors. *History of the World Christian Movement.* Vol. 1: *Earliest Christianity to 1453.* Minneapolis: Fortress, 2001.

Krueger, Derek, editor. *Byzantine Christianity.* A People's History of Christianity 3. Minneapolis: Fortress, 2006.

Matheson, Peter, editor. *Reformation Christianity.* A People's History of Christianity 5. Minneapolis: Fortress, 2006.

New Catholic Encyclopedia. 2d ed. 15 vols. Detroit: Gale, in association with Catholic University of America, 2003.

Porterfield, Amanda, editor. *Modern Christianity to 1900.* A People's History of Christianity 6. Minneapolis: Fortress, 2007.

2. Readers

Bettenson, Henry, and Mark Maunder, editors. *Documents of the Christian Church.* 3d ed. Oxford: Oxford University Press, 1999.

Bowden, Henry Warner, and P. C. Kemeny, editors. *American Church History: A Reader.* Nashville: Abingdon, 1998.

Collins, Kenneth J. *Exploring Christian Spirituality: An Ecumenical Reader.* Grand Rapids: Baker, 2000.

Ehrman, Bart D. *After the New Testament: A Reader in Early Christianity.* New York: Oxford University Press, 1999.

————, and Andrew S. Jacobs, editors. *Christianity in Late Antiquity, 300–450 C. E.: A Reader.* New York: Oxford University Press, 2004.

Gaca, Kathy, and L. L. Welborn, editors. *Early Patristic Readings of Romans.* New York: T. & T. Clark, 2005.

Janz, Dennis. *Reformation Reader: Primary Texts with Introductions.* Minneapolis: Fortress, 1999.

Johnson, William Stacy, and John H. Keith, editors. *Reformed Reader: A Sourcebook in Christian Theology.* Vol. 1: *Classical Beginnings, 1519–1799.* Louisville: Westminster John Knox, 1993.

Kidd, B. J., editor. *Documents Illustrative of the Continental Reformation.* 2 vols. 1911. Reprinted, Eugene, OR: Wipf & Stock, 2004.

Lund, Eric. *Documents from the History of Lutheranism.* Minneapolis: Fortress, 2002.

Mason, Steve, and Tom Robinson, editors. *Early Christian Reader: Christian Texts from the First and Second Centuries in Contemporary English Translations including the New Revised Standard Version of the New Testament.* Peabody, MA: Hendrickson, 2004.

McGrath, Alister E. *The Christian Theology Reader.* Malden, MA: Blackwell, 2001

Ruth, Lester, editor. *Early Methodist Life and Spirituality: A Reader.* Nashville: Kingswood, 2005.

Stevenson, J., and W. H. C. Frend, editors. *Creeds, Councils and Controversies: Documents Illustrating the History of the Church AD 337–461.* Rev. ed. London: SPCK, 1989.

Stroup, George W., editor. *Reformed Reader: A Sourcebook in Christian Theology.* Vol. 2: *Contemporary Trajectories, 1799 to Present.* Louisville: Westminster John Knox, 1993.

3. Monographs

Bainton, Roland. *The Age of the Reformation.* Princeton: Van Nostrand, 1956.

———. *Christendom: A Short History of Christianity and Its Impact on World Civilization.* 2 vols. New York: Harper & Row, 1966.

———. *Early and Medieval Christianity.* Boston: Beacon. 1962.

———. *The Reformation of the Sixteenth Century.* Boston: Beacon, 1952.

———. *Women of the Reformation, from Spain to Scandinavia.* Minneapolis: Augsburg, 1977.

———. *Women of the Reformation in France and England.* Minneapolis: Augsburg, 1973.

———. *Women of the Reformation in Germany and Italy.* Minneapolis: Augsburg, 1971.

Brown, Peter. *Body and Society: Men, Women, and Sexual Renunciation in Early Christianity.* New York: Columbia University Press, 1988.

———. *Late Antiquity.* Cambridge: Belknap, 1998.

Chadwick, Henry. *The Church in Ancient Society: From Galilee to Gregory the Great.* Oxford History of the Christian Church. Oxford: Oxford University Press, 2001.

———. *Early Christian Thought and the Classical Tradition: Studies in Justin, Clement, and Origen.* Oxford: Oxford University Press, 1966.

———. *East and West: The Making of a Rift in the Church—From Apostolic Times until the Council of Florence.* Oxford History of the Christian Church. Oxford: Oxford University Press, 2003.

Chadwick, Owen. *The Early Reformation on the Continent.* Oxford History of the Christian Church. Oxford: Oxford University Press, 2001.

Handy, Robert T. *A History of the Churches in the United States and Canada.* Oxford History of the Christian Church. Oxford: Oxford University Press, 1977.

Latourette, Kenneth Scott. *A History of Christianity.* 2 vols. Rev. ed. New York: Harper & Row, 1975

Miles, Margaret R. *Fullness of Life: Historical Foundations for a New Asceticism.* 1981. Reprinted, Eugene, OR: Wipf & Stock, 2006.

———. *Practicing Christianity: Critical Perspectives for an Embodied Spirituality.* 1988. Reprinted, Eugene, OR: Wipf & Stock, 2006.

Rupp, Gordon. *Religion in England, 1688–1791.* Oxford History of the Christian Church. Oxford: Clarendon, 1986.